Fears Flutterby

Fears Flutterby

By
rm Lamatt

Outskirts Press, Inc.
Denver, Colorado

Fears Flutterby

Outskirts Press
http://www.outskirtspress.com

ISBN-10: 1-59800-019-5
ISBN-13: 978-1-59800-019-1

Acknowledgments

Thank you Charlie. You inspired me and helped me believe I could do it. You pushed beyond the call of duty, and kept me writing when all I wanted was to put it back in a drawer.

This book is dedicated to Valerie, a friend and confidant who passed away suddenly.

My humble thanks go to the support groups and places I worked. They invited me into their lives to listen and see more than I had ever known.

Thanks to family and friends who said keep going. You know who you are.

Most of all thank you Mom, for the breath of life.

Author's Note

This story is based on my experiences over a period of time. Names have been changed, characters combined, and events compressed. Certain episodes are imaginative re-creation, and those episodes are not intended to portray actual events. rmLamatt@aol.com/ Box 137, Geneva, FL. 32732

For Carol

THOUGHTS

TILL DEATH do you part? These are the words I had heard more than forty years ago standing in front of a Catholic Priest. I had said, "I do" to that question, and now at sixty-two wonder what they meant. Do they mean when the heart stops beating or do they mean when the brain stops sending signals?

These thoughts have been near, but the words so far from my brain. I have kept them hidden or unknown to my own self, stuffed in the back of my mind where others couldn't know of them. Now that they have finally come forward, I'm constantly in front of the computer getting them down on paper.

Needing a break I came outside to sit on the porch, in a rickety old yellow web chair a friend had given me when I moved here in 2001. Under the balcony the squirrels are playing, running from tree to tree and mockingbirds mocking, flitting back and forth from limb to limb. The butterflies intrigue me the most, when they come to the second floor to say hello.

Today I feel like a vine that has climbed out of the dirt to show itself to the sun for the first time. I've been in the same clothes for days – beige ragged tee shirt, black silk shorts and tan moccasins. I disconnect myself from the computer screen once in awhile to eat and drink. Food shopping happens possibly once a week, if I'm up to it, otherwise it's a slice of bread out of the freezer, toasted with peanut butter and a glass of milk or a bowl of my favorite cereal. Not such a great diet this past year and a half. I'm eating less but still have put on weight from sitting and no exercise. I'm sure my fingers have lost weight from everyday typing, sometimes ten and twelve hours a day. The book is almost done, maybe a few corrections here and there.

My condo overlooks the ninth green of the golf course, which gives me more reflection to write than I've ever had. I've lived here just over three years and don't know a soul, except to say hello to the next door neighbors who arrive in fall and leave in spring. Snowbirds they're called, and I'm sure they probably think I'm a hermit or someone who's a little loony, staying inside all day when there are tennis courts, a pool and a golf course right below me. Maybe one day I'll join in the fun but not just yet. I've got this quest to finish and finding the little black books has helped me further the story.

Sometimes I feel old – older than the folks who live here, who are seventy, eighty and more. Me? I'm in my early sixties, but feel older when the words won't come and I fight to remember.

Sipping a glass of ice water and lemon I watch the golfers come off the green from their day of fun. They're checking scorecards and getting ready to go home and start dinner. I loved this time of day years ago playing golf – late afternoon sun making shadows so long you couldn't see the holes on the greens. This course is small and quaint, similar to another I lived on once before.

I remember the days of golf when it was a passion, and sometimes the only thing in my life. But what the heck, I never thought there was anything wrong with that. It kept me sane and out in the world of nature, which I loved. The winds of time have changed now, for illness is attacking my body. Funny, these bodies don't last long. You'd think God would have given us a body like Abraham, who lived three hundred years or more. Golf did bring me God though, if that's possible. Green grass, trees, birds, squirrels, butterflies – all living energies of God, were the feelings I had while walking the course.

I once knew golf like the back of my hand. I could make the ball go right or left, stop or roll. Yes, I knew it like the back of my hand, but my hand has changed over the twenty years. Now it shows wrinkles, blue lines and brown dots. My life is being lived like my beginning days of golf, when I didn't know which way the ball would go when the club struck it. I thought life got easier when you aged. But it gets more difficult each year. At least this last year and a half have been productive.

I'm feeling my mortality and thinking I don't know where I'll be next year. My lease was signed for another year in November of 2003 and it's almost the middle of the next year. It's sliding by too fast and the book *has* to be done by the end of the year. The money or my health must not run out before then.

When the paramedics were called last summer I thought for sure it was the end. I was angry because I still hadn't finished the story. I had started it when I was sixteen, when my life changed so drastically, then again at age forty-one, when I found out who I really

3

was. And now I've found the little black books that
have led me further. I know now, I can't put it away
again.

Sitting, staring at the tree outside I close my eyes
and wonder about the words – Till death do you part.

FEAR

SOON SHE was asleep and it is Tuesday morning December 1958. In Joanna's bedroom is a small dressing table with an oval mirror attached to the back; a crocheted skirt made by her mom wraps around the table, with cheap perfumes on the glass top. There's a three-drawer chest containing her underwear, socks, gloves, and other items. In the tiny closet are three dresses, two skirts, a couple of blouses and a pair of jeans, which she had boiled to shrink, as her friends had done. In one corner is a flowered fabric chair that her mom covered, along with a crocheted bedspread, which covers the blue wool blanket she's under. A white robe hangs on a hook inside the closet door, with another set of flannel pajamas.

"Mom. How can I be so sick? I've been healthy all of my sixteen years."

"Joanna, you know the Asian flu is sweeping the country. You have a fever of 104. The doctor says to try the usual, gargle with salt water and drink tea with lemon and honey. If you don't get better, we'll call him again."

Joanna wiped the brown mucus pouring out of her nose. Her mom gave her a sip of brandy and said, "this will be good for your head and chest congestion."

5

Her mom walked to the doorway and began talking with Joanna's brother, Paul. They seemed to be in a long, dark tunnel. Their words were garbled and their bodies had shadowy outlines around them. It was like being in a dream with her eyes partially open.

She looked at the photo of her grandmother, Joanna Lamatt, who she was named after in nineteen forty-two. Then, stared at the picture of St. Theresa, holding a bouquet of roses. She clutched her rosary beads and murmured, "Please, dear Lord don't let me die," then fell back to sleep.

***

The next day Paul, who worked in a pharmacy while attending college, brought home a bottle of big red pills, which made her feel better. She was able to get out of bed but only to go to the hallway bathroom.

Her father and mother worked, and her younger brother, Marc, was also studying to become a pharmacist, so Joanna was home alone. Still weak, she slept off and on or listened to the radio. In a news broadcast, she learned that thousands were dying of the flu, which clearly had come to visit her.

A few days later, before her mother, Maria, left for work, she asked Joanna how she felt, uneasy at leaving her sick daughter home alone. But she had no choice – the family depended on her salary to cover household expenses. Her husband, Vincent, reinvested his salary into company stock. Maria never told her children how much she loved them, but *she* knew how much she did. She gave all of herself to her sons and daughter, but found it hard to express her feelings. She only hoped they knew.

"Would you like oatmeal or a poached egg on toast

this morning?" she asked.

"Neither, Mom, my stomach is still upset. Maybe tea with honey and a slice of toast with jelly."

"Well, I'll make oatmeal too and you can leave what you can't finish."

A few minutes later she was back with a tray of oatmeal, toast and hot tea with honey and lemon.

"Thanks, Mom. I think I'm feeling better this morning, other than my stomach."

Kissing Joanna on the forehead and saying good-bye, Maria cautioned, "now make sure you rest. I don't want you out of bed unless you need to go to the bathroom. I'll see you when I get home for lunch."

"Okay, Mom, I'll see you later."

This scene was essentially repeated every morning, lunchtime, and dinner until Joanna felt strong enough to sit at the dinner table and watch TV in the living room. The pills Paul had brought home had helped, and she was beginning to feel like a real person again

***

Three weeks later, Joanna's mom had the day off and asked her to go to the store for a box of number nine-spaghetti. The distance to the store was less than a mile and Joanna was eager to get out of the house. It was great to be outside and breathe the air, but her head still felt stuffed and she had trouble hearing. The street was empty of cars and no one was outside in their front yards. She noticed the cracks in the street where puddles had formed, after a short rain and thought of when she was younger and would skip flat rocks across the water. With woods bordering each side of the road, she could always spot snakes crawling across or birds flying. She loved her childhood because of the friendly wildlife.

As she turned the corner to the main road, she came upon the auto body shop, where her boyfriend's brother worked. She spotted him with a drill in hand ready to attack someone's car. They were a year apart in age but he wanted to quit school and work on cars instead.

"Hi Keith, are you working hard?"

Keith looked up startled. "Well, hi there, what are you doing home from school?"

"I've been sick and finally got out today for the first time. Have you heard from Ed?"

"Yeah, Mom got a letter from him last week. He's in Europe and said he'll be home in a few weeks on leave. Well, I'd love to chat with you but I better get back to work before they fire me. Hope you feel better."

"Thanks Keith, take it easy and stay out of trouble."

A little further on she was passing the butcher shop and wanted to stop and get a chunk of bologna, as she did when she was a little girl and her mom would send her for soup bones. The butcher would give her a large chunk of bologna to snack on, for her walk back home. Up a few stores from him was the candy store, where she stopped after elementary school, for a chocolate egg cream and a pretzel, getting all for seven cents. She had happy memories of growing up in the small town Elmont. She had even taken the bus to New York City on this main road.

The A&P grocery was the last store on the block, just before Belmont Racetrack, where as a child she peeked through the fence to watch the horses. Across the street was the movie house where she spent her Saturday afternoons for a quarter, now the price was a dollar fifty.

Her legs were feeling slightly tired, but it was good to be outside again. Opening the door to the grocery store she felt a little strange. She searched the aisles finding the spaghetti, then looked for number nine. The numbers were blurred and she had trouble focusing. She finally found the right box and while reaching up, she felt her heart pound hard in her chest.

What was that? she wondered.

Then it came again, and once more. Fearful, she hurried to the check out counter where two women were in front of her on line.

I wish the clerk would hurry up, she thought. What happens if I pass out, right here? Am I having a heart attack? As her heart pounded. These thoughts crowded her mind while standing there and sweat dripped down her neck and onto her chest. Even her forehead became drenched with perspiration. Then she began to feel dizzy.

The chime of the register bell brought her back to reality.

"Is that it Miss?"

Staring at him dazed, she answered, "Uh – Yes that's it."

She paid him, sticking the change in the pocket of her jeans and ran out of the store. Feeling as if she couldn't breathe, she raced home, this time not taking notice of the stores or people along the way.

All she could think was, I want to be home safe.

She ran past Keith not saying a word. Rounding the corner to her street she could see the house in the distance. It looked so far away.

The hammering kept up in her chest – she was back in bed ill again, with thoughts of dying. She ran faster, and once inside gave her mother the spaghetti and change, then headed straight to the bathroom.

Looking in the mirror she saw a red face with glassy eyes and felt her heart pounding now in her head, as if it were going to explode. Bending over the sink, she ran cold water over the back of her head and face, then cupped her hands to drink from it.

The thought of death wouldn't let go.

She went to the kitchen for a glass of ice water, thinking it might help. Her mom wanted to chat but Joanna was in another place within her mind, and didn't want to upset Maria by telling her she felt ill again.

The phone rang and broke the insanity.

She ran for it, knowing she could avoid talking to her mother.

"Hello?"

"Hi Joanna, how're you doing? I saw you run past the house awhile ago and wondered why you didn't stop?" It was Sally, a friend from up the block, whom she hadn't seen since she became ill.

Quickly thinking, "Mom wanted me home in a hurry. I had to get her some things, for dinner."

They chatted awhile and Joanna described her illness, but never mentioned the fear of death.

"Do you think you're going to school tomorrow?" Sally asked.

"Yeah, I think so. I'll stop by on my way to the bus stop."

Joanna had known Sally since second grade and when they were old enough, they started walking to school together.

"Okay, I'll see ya in the morning then. Good-bye."

"Bye, Sally."

Hanging up the phone, she heard her mom, "your father's coming home late tonight, so we won't be eating till eight o'clock."

"Okay Mom. I'm going to my room to study."

Once in her room she noticed, since the phone call, she had felt better and was looking forward to going back to Sewanhaka High, with her friends. The thought of death had left her and she'd calmed down. She went to sleep that night looking forward to the morning.

***

The next morning on her way to Sally's house, Joanna felt good. She had had a good night's rest and wasn't thinking of the day before. As they approached the bus stop they saw the bus pull away.

"Hey … Wait … Stop," they yelled as they ran trying to catch it.

Finally the bus driver saw them and stopped. Joanna noticed when she stopped running her legs felt weak and she was out of breath.

When the bus stopped in front of the school, they heard someone yelling through a bullhorn.

"Anyone who's been out sick, please wait on line over there, to get a pass." The person pointed to a long line that snaked around the school. It looked as though more than half the students had been ill.

While waiting in line, everyone spoke of how awful their sickness was. Some said they threw up and had bad headaches, while others told of how they were not able to get out of bed. But no one spoke of their hearts pounding or a sense of imminent death. Joanna didn't describe what she had felt, and only hoped the feeling would never return.

***

Days later after returning to the classroom, Joanna began to have the same feelings and became confused, since she couldn't find a reason for the fear and panic. She was a strong well-rounded kid, loved sports and belonged to the choir, having many friends. When these so called attacks occurred, she wanted to run out of class. She constantly checked the hands on the clock looking forward to leaving the room. At times, she *did* run out or go to the teacher saying she wasn't feeling well. The teacher sent her to the nurse and then called home.

When her brother, Marc, answered, they'd tell him to come pick Joanna up. Borrowing the neighbor's car he'd come to her rescue. Joanna was happy to see his face, but once in the car he'd ask, "what's the matter with you now?"

"I don't feel good." That would be the whole conversation. Him mad, because he had to pick his little sister up during his study time, and her feeling embarrassed and uneasy because she felt sick but didn't know why. Once back home, Joanna felt safe and the feeling of dying would leave.

After months of this, it began to happen everywhere. If an attack struck while Joanna was in a store – she'd run outside. If she were walking home – she'd break into a run to get there. In church, she'd almost pass out from fright and would leave. It seemed no matter where she was, the fear was with her. It had become a part of her, keeping her from living a normal teenage life. Her friends and family never sensed any of this and Joanna was unwilling to appear weak in their eyes. She was too embarrassed to tell anyone and didn't know whether it was a serious illness or not, but for her

igh school was spent running
iick, encapsulated in fear.

home saying, "If Joanna is
going to graduate."

to go to school?" her mom

iorning."

)d?"

a reason she'd say, "I think
I have cramps," or she'd
and Maria would let her

d too many burdens as it
them by telling her of the
cure for them in her own

* * *

When Ed came home on leave that year he picked
her up to go bowling for her birthday. Joanna had
turned eighteen and in three months, she'd be out of
school. The two had been dating for almost two years
now. Ed was older by four years and she had known
him most of her life. He lived five houses up the block
and had spent most of his younger years with Marc, his
friend and classmate.

On the way to bowling Ed spoke of his trip overseas
and how sick he had gotten crossing the ocean to the
Mediterranean. Joanna spoke of what courses she was
taking in school and the friends they had in common.
While driving they listened to the top hits on the radio
and Joanna sang along. Ed didn't have an ear for music
but Joanna thought he was good looking in his uniform
even though he couldn't sing.

13

While bowling Joanna began to have one of her attacks. It was a bad one and her hands began to shake holding the ball. Her balance was off when she approached the alley to release the ball. She walked back slowly weaving and told Ed, "I'd like to go home."

"Why, what's the matter?"

"I don't know. I feel odd. My heart feels like it's skipping beats and pounding." There, she told someone what was happening to her.

She wasn't comfortable telling him of her weakness, and she knew she needed help. She felt like she was going to pass out, as it had happened in recent months.

"Do you want to go to the doctor?" he asked.

She was centered on what was going on within her body, but finally said, "I'm afraid of what he's going to find. I don't want Mom or Dad to know."

"I won't tell them. C'mon, let me take you to the doctor. You don't look well." Ed had a convincing tone.

Joanna felt a little more at ease knowing that she'd finally told someone how she felt. Driving to the neighborhood doctor she told Ed of the flu and the feeling of death she had experienced.

"It's probably nothing. When I was onboard ship with high waves, I got sick a number of times and the doctor gave me pills to stop it. Maybe there's a pill for what you're experiencing."

He was older and wiser and maybe the doctor *could* give her a pill. With this thought, she started to feel better. After all, the big red pills had cured her of the flu, so maybe another pill would get rid of the pounding in her chest and all that went with it.

The doctor's fee was five dollars, which she borrowed from Ed, and the doctor said the feelings were from her nerves and to take the tranquilizers he gave her. From then on when she had one of her attacks all she had to do was take a pill.

***

Joanna did graduate that year, and was glad she wouldn't have to be running out of classrooms any more. She found a job doing bookkeeping for a bank in town, and she and Ed continued to date after he got out of the service. She liked the work, but the fears persisted, and she tried her best to maneuver around them.

***

Joanna's father often said, "Your mother married when she was sixteen. What are *you* waiting for?"

So with her father's words she thought getting married would make the fears leave. Especially being Ed was the only other person who knew of them, it just might work. So two years later, at age twenty, she married Ed. She really wanted to go to New York City and become a businesswoman, but that was totally out of the question with her fears. Before the flu, she had taken the bus and subway with Sally to Rockafeller Plaza and Central Park to ice skate or to see a movie on Forty-second Street.

How her life had changed since the flu! Panic was the primary factor in the way she lived her life. Fear ruled – Panic and fear followed her everywhere.

***

Married life proved enjoyable for Joanna in the small one bedroom, one bath, upper floor apartment, of

15

a private house. She enjoyed cooking and doing household chores and Ed was rarely home. He worked during the day and attended classes at night, studying first for a bachelor's degree, then on for his master's. They were rarely together, except when he came home from school at eleven o'clock at night. Sometimes they'd walk around the corner to a hamburger joint and get ice-cream. Afterwards it was home to bed, to prepare for another day.

A year went by and Joanna became pregnant. She quit work and stayed at home the last few months of her pregnancy, happy to be starting a family. Subconsciously, she thought this would dispel the panic attacks, but instead, they rebounded in force. She consulted a priest, who sent her to a psychiatrist, and she told him of her terror of dying. He prescribed tranquilizers and said the feelings could be hormone-related, because of pregnancy.

***

In 1964 Matthew was born. Joanna thought surely the fears would leave her, but in the following months they became even stronger. At night, while Ed was in school and Matthew was sleeping, they would overwhelm her. She'd pick up Matthew from his crib, go into the living room, and hold him on her chest, wanting to feel the warmth of another living soul. This child, whom she had brought into the world, was easy to care for, and, as he grew, he became her little friend. Ed was seldom home except on weekends, and sometimes worked even then, so Joanna was alone with her little friend, and the fears. Her partnership with Ed worked well, but she felt a void she didn't understand.

***

It's 1965, and Joanna and her family have moved from the one-bedroom apartment into a small ranch house, with three bedrooms and a large fenced backyard, where they can play. They play badminton with the neighbors, who come over with their children for barbecues, to swim in the new pool, and spend the summer playing with their children.

Joanna, Maria and Matthew rescue a dog, named Tender from the pound, and adopt a black-and-white cat named Plinky, that appeared one morning on their doorstep.

Ed is teaching nights at a small college to earn extra money, and with a colleague he has started his own business. They are on a tight budget, but Joanna has faith that he will make the business grow. He's asked her if she will do some work at home for him, and this makes her feel a part of him and the business. She has also taken a small job stuffing and mailing envelopes for a mail order house. This brings in a little money for extra items and treats, like going to the movies. She has become a volunteer at a nursing home because of the need to get out of the house and to help people who are ill.

The work at the nursing home turns out to be enjoyable. Once a week, at a sing along, she serves coffee and cake and dances with the men. The smiles on their faces bring her out of herself and this is a blessing. Her life is changing for the better.

She has also started attending night school, trying to follow her dream of going to college, while her mom comes to baby-sit. Maria stays overnight on most occasions, and when Ed is home to stay with Matthew, Maria joins Joanna on the trip to the nursing home to volunteer her help.

***

Joanna's mom is fifty-nine years old and separated from her dad, who moved to Florida. She is on her own for the first time since the age of sixteen, when she married Vincent. Their separation was triggered by Joanna's dad's excessive drinking, which made him combative, and Maria had absorbed too much abuse from him during Joanna's growing-up years.

Joanna has never forgotten one particular incident that occurred when she was fourteen. Vincent had drunk far too much wine, and argued with Maria both during and after dinner. Out of disgust, she took the bottle of wine and poured its remaining contents down the drain, which enraged Vincent. He started to strangle Maria and threatened to kill her. Donna, Joanna's future sister-in-law, was present and she advised Joanna to call the police, while Donna tried to intercede and stop the fight.

Joanna picked up the phone and asked the operator for the police, sobbing, "My Father is trying to kill my Mother."

At first, the operator couldn't understand her, so she repeated the sentence, again hearing her own words as off in a distance. This was not a common occurrence in the household and very painful for Joanna to watch. This behavior happened across the street or in another house, but not in theirs. Feeling as though hours passed, the police soon knocked on the door and Joanna let them in. Still yelling, Vincent was pushed back by the police officer and told to stay away from Maria. Upset Joanna left the room and went outside. Donna soon joined her on the stoop, while the police spoke to Maria and Vincent. They stayed until Vincent went to bed. One of the officers told Maria, "I can't do anything unless you press charges against him."

***

Many years after that incident, Joanna received a call from one of her mother's neighbors, whom she had known since childhood. "Your mom is outside sitting on the milk box. I think you should come and get her."

Joanna dressed Matthew and drove to see what had happened. Sure enough, her mom was sitting outside on the milk box in the dead of winter. Vincent had locked her out of the house after an awful fight. She never saw her father that day, and didn't wish to. Vincent called the next day and asked if Maria was there. Joanna told him, "yes"

"Well, she can come home now," he said.

Joanna blanketed the phone with her hand, "Mom, do you want to go home?"

Maria looked at Joanna with tears and fear in her eyes, which Joanna understood, and she made her mother's mind up for her.

"Dad, I don't think Mom's coming home just yet."

"Well, I cooked dinner and she can come home," almost in a pleading voice.

"Okay Dad, we'll see. I'll talk to you in a few days, bye."

Maira breathed a sigh of relief as the two sat with cups of coffee in front of them and Joanna said, "Mom, you know you can stay here. I'd love to have you, and you know Ed would agree, and the kids think you're the greatest cook."

"Oh, is that the only reason you want me to stay, because I can cook?" She was laughing and Joanna knew the air had become lighter in the room.

"Mom, stay as long as you want."

So it was settled, Maria would stay.

Maria stayed with Ed and Joanna then went to each of her son's homes for visits. Marc helped her find a lawyer, who arranged a legal separation from Vincent and she was a much happier person after that, no longer living in an abusive situation.

FIRST FLIGHT

NOW that Maria is living with them, Joanna and Ed have decided to take a mini-vacation to Florida. They've made reservations at a large golf resort and are looking forward to playing golf and enjoying warmer weather. This will be Joanna's first airplane trip. Scared but excited, she feels calm knowing Ed will be with her. Boarding the plane, she turns to Ed, "This is wider than our house." The attendant laughs and Ed pushes her forward to their seats.

Once seated, she's nervous but looking forward to the takeoff. Airplanes have always excited her. Growing up, her house was in the flight path of Kennedy International Airport and while dating, Ed parked his convertible in a spot near the airport's runway. With the top down, they'd sit on the back of the seats and watch jets soar over their heads. The roar of the engines as they passed over sent vibrations through her body.

As their plane took off, she felt a rush of adrenaline and looked out at the ground moving by faster and faster. Lifting, the plane tilted upward and she felt her body pushed back against the seat. Her ears began to ache and pop and Ed told her to open her mouth as a cure or chew gum. Feeling the plane bank was the most magnificent experience of her sheltered life. Joanna wanted to learn to fly, thinking it must be great to guide this big machine off the ground and soar through the air. The flight attendant brought martinis for them – after all, they were celebrating their first flight together. Ed had flown many times before, during his three-year stay in the military. Joanna had traveled no farther than upstate New York to visit relatives with her mom, taking trains and buses.

"Let go of the armrest," Ed said.

"What?" then looking down at her hands griping the arms of the seat. "I can't. I'm too nervous."

"You're flying a white knuckle flight. Look at your knuckles, they're white."

After seeing she was holding on for dear life, she then tried to relax.

Ed fell asleep after his fourth martini and Joanna was drinking soda feeling more relaxed. Looking out the window at cotton clouds, she let her imagination run wild. It's beautiful, she thought, like heaven. She imagined herself bouncing from cloud to cloud without wings and grinned. She'd never make it as an angel. Ed was snoring by now and she couldn't share the fantasy with him. An hour into the flight, the plane started jumping, which frightened her. The pilot came on the public-address system and warned of clear-air turbulence and ordered the attendants to sit down. Clear-air turbulence, what was that? She wondered.

An attendant passed by and she grabbed his jacket. "Is it supposed to be like this?" she asked in a shaky voice.

"It's just a little turbulence, make sure your seat belt is fastened."

Apparently he didn't notice she hadn't taken it off yet. Less than ten minutes later with Ed still asleep the pilot came back on. "Folks, I'm sorry but I've radioed ahead and there is clear air turbulence for the rest of the trip, so sit back and relax."

"Relax? What's he crazy? How can anyone relax? It's like a carnival ride or driving down a road full of potholes," she mumbled, seeing the lady in front of her turn around shaking her head in agreement.

She woke Ed a few times in hopes of sharing her fear with him and he slurred, "Go to sleep, we'll be there in no time."

Two and a half-hours later they landed safely in Miami and she wanted to kiss the ground. They rented a car and drove to the resort. It was beautiful, brass railings leading to the main entrance and bellhops and workers riding around in golf carts helping people with their luggage. They signed in and a young man in a cart took their luggage and drove them to their cottage. Joanna and Ed unpacked quickly ridding themselves of the winter clothes on their backs and changed to golf wear. They hoped to get in nine holes before dinner.

Joanna liked hitting the ball, but never intended to be a golfer. The sport was slow and boring, and she had a family to care for and household chores. But more importantly she had her fears to deal with, which had already filled her life with distraction. Nevertheless, she remembered fantasizing about what it would be like to be free, still playing sports as she did as a child.

The warm sun felt wonderful on her back as they played the course. The balmy weather penetrated every part her body and she could relax after the scary experience on the plane. They had eagerly anticipated this trip, since Ed and she were rarely together because of his school and work. After play they showered and dined in one of the restaurants on the grounds.

Up early the next day they paired up with a couple from Long Island. Ed talked of how he had played mostly public courses and the couple described a private club they played at, on the North Shore of Long Island. One person mentioned was Catherine Benbrock. She was a golfer in her thirties who was written up in local newspapers to be the next Babe. Ed knew of Catherine when he had caddied in his teens at private clubs and Joanna had read about her in the local papers.

***

At the same time in Stony Brook, Long Island Catherine was getting ready to go to work at her parents' business. After showering and dressing, the last she needed to do was comb her dark brown hair.

Looking in the mirror she thought, I'm just under six feet tall, strong, with a slim body and I can hit a golf ball over two hundred and fifty yards. Life sure has changed since Dad died and Mom got sick. I could have been a pro, traveled the tour with my friends, but no, I had to do the right thing and come home to help the family.

Catherine was in her fifth year of playing the amateur golf circuit from New York to Florida when her mother fell across the street from the family business. Catherine had just spoken to her on the phone the night before and everything was fine then the next moment she was hurrying to New York Hospital to be at the bedside of her mother who had had a stroke. How her life had changed in six months; her mother unable to communicate and paralyzed on one side, and her father taken with cancer.

While making the last finger sweeps at her hair, in the distance Catherine could hear Anne rattling dishes downstairs, getting breakfast ready. Thank God her mom had said yes to Anne moving in with them. What help she'd been for Catherine and her mother. She never would have been able to care for her alone and work too. Anne took her to speech therapy, fed and bathed her during the day while Catherine was at work. Taking one final look at herself, she headed downstairs thinking how lucky she was to have Anne around.

Catherine kissed her mother, who was seated by the kitchen window in the sunlight and said good morning, to Anne. She then stuck a piece of toast in her mouth and took a few bites, downing it with a cup of coffee and headed for the front door. She hated the everyday morning scene. It hurt to see her mother in an almost vegetated state.

***

Maria wanted to live on her own and not be a burden to any of her children, even though they had told her what a great baby-sitter she was. So when Joanna and Ed returned home from vacation, she and Maria looked at a one-bedroom apartment within walking distance to the bus stop and nearby stores, since Maria didn't drive. Finding a suitable one, Maria signed a five-year lease and proceeded to furnish it with a convertible couch, for the grandchildren to spend the nights. Maria was depressed at times in her new life but on the whole, she was happy meeting new neighbors, widows and divorcees, in the same situation.

***

Joanna's therapist has helped her deal with her

fears, and she enjoys being in high school again, taking evening college-preparatory courses. Happily, she's found she can stay in the same classrooms she ran out of years ago. She had always wished to attend college as her brothers did and at last, she took algebra and biology, the two subjects required for admission into college. Now, she enjoyed going to school, listening and learning, preparing for a normal productive life. She was still young enough to become something.

A year later, she registered for night classes at a junior college located half an hour's drive from her home in Syosset. This was another new experience, and she loved it, taking English literature and creative writing. She had wanted to be a writer and had written at age fourteen a short story, entitled 'The Day the Russians Bombed Us.' This was an era when the fear of a war with Russia prompted teachers to direct children to hide under their desks whenever the bell signaled an air raid drill. Joanna wondered how that could protect them from a bomb attack, but she did as told and then wrote of it. Having seen newsreels depicting war at the movies, she was convinced that no wooden desk was going to stop a bomb.

Later, during the Vietnam War, she wrote another short story about the nursing home where she volunteered. She described the elderly rising to their feet from wheelchairs and with proud hearts singing, 'God Bless America', while some Americans stomped on or burned their national flags. A huge chasm separated the rebellious young and the patriotic old. Her little piece was published in the local newspaper after she proudly granted permission to the editor. It thrilled her that others were going to read her description of matters about which she had such strong convictions.

***

Although life was going well for Ed, Matthew, and Joanna, she felt that Matthew needed a brother or sister. She didn't want him growing up being an only child. He was a handsome child and fun to be around.

One day she dropped Matthew off at her mom's apartment while she went to serve the elderly residents coffee and join them in singing and dancing. While stopped at a red light, something happened. Joanna felt she had been transported from a real place to a fantasy world. Not able to concentrate on the now, she gave herself over to distant daydreaming. When the light turned green, she felt paralyzed, not sure of where she was or which way to go. Nothing seemed familiar, although she had been there many times before.

Joanna's fears raised their ugly heads once again and she became panic-stricken.

Her heart pounded, and her mind stopped in place. She began to shake and sweat profusely, gripping the steering wheel tighter and gasping for breath.

She needed to escape and quickly made a U-turn and headed straight to her mom's apartment. Once there, she knocked on the door, impatient for Maria to answer. She could hear Matthew playing inside, and just wanted to put him in the car and speed back to the little ranch house, away from the feelings.

Maria answered the door surprised to see Joanna, "What are you doing back so soon?"

"I'm not feeling well."

"Come in and sit down and I'll make some tea."

"No, not now Mom, I want to go home. C'mon

27

Matthew, let's get dressed."

Matthew whined, "Oh Mom, I don't want to go. I'm having fun with Nanna."

"We need to go now. So please get dressed," Joanna, feeling she was losing control.

Quickly helping Matthew on with his coat, pulling his hat on over his ears, while her mom kept saying, "Stay." She kissed her mother on the cheek and headed down the apartment hall steps with Matthew in her arms.

She couldn't leave fast enough. Once in the car, headed home, she began to calm down, and that inner turbulence gradually subsided. But in the back of her brain she knew it was back. She was in a deep dark hole, frantically trying to climb up the sides, but the dirt kept falling away, preventing her from going forward. Her short reprieve from fear was over.

A NEW WAY

BECAUSE OF Joanna's weakness, she feels sorry for anyone who is around her. Ed is the only one who still knows of it and now again, he's told her she needs help.

Her fears are still latent, and show themselves in unfamiliar ways and patterns. She has become a recluse and even though the neighbors are friendly, she stays inside when Matthew goes off to preschool for half a day. Afraid to leave the house alone, she waits for Ed to come home from work to food shop. Again, she is having a hard time adjusting to life.

Taking Ed's suggestion she finds a psychiatrist within a mile of her home. Dr. Spinner puts her on anti-anxiety and antidepressant drugs. She sees him at night once a week while Ed waits in the car with Matthew.

Joanna has become someone she doesn't know at all any more. She doesn't even recognize the fear because the drugs are making her sleep both day and night. Ed tells her that her personality has changed, but she can't remember what her personality was.

***

A year passes and Matthew is in Kindergarten full time and Joanna is by herself all day. There is a chill in the air, the fall skies are cloudy, and the leaves are falling. She hates this time of year, not being in the sun in the pool with Matthew on her shoulders as she goes underwater and he screams out in laughter. In the days of summer she was less depressed as she sat outside and tanned, while reading a book, making sure Matthew wasn't alone in the pool. Matthew learned to swim right away, jumping off the platform holding his nose first then holding his legs and yelling out, "Cannonball." He could tread water sometimes for ten minutes as he yelled, "Mom, time me – time me now Mom, please?" Joanna would time him, amazed at how long he could stay afloat, and figured it was because of his large flat feet. She wasn't a good swimmer, even though her dad had been a lifeguard in his younger days at Coney Island. She could swim to save her life and with the new pool she'd learned different strokes, but still couldn't float on her back. Matthew even beat her at dead-man's float, she'd be out of the water long before his face was even up. They played ring around the rosy underwater looking at each other grinning. Yes, the summer was easier to live the normal way.

***

She lies on the bed after Ed and Matthew leave for school and work and stares out the window, till she finally falls asleep and is out of the world of aloneness. Once awake the heavy cloud still lies above her. She doesn't even want to go to the kitchen for ice cream to lift her spirits. She's gotten so deep in the hole that she doesn't know if she will make it halfway up this time.

She doesn't want to live anymore and gets the bottles of pills. Filling a glass with water in the kitchen, she takes a handful of green and purple pills. While walking through the dining room she thinks, 'No, I don't want this,' and runs to the bathroom. Holding her head over the toilet, sticking her finger down her throat, she throws up not only the pills but this morning's breakfast. Looking in the mirror she cries out.

"God, why can't I get better? I don't want to live like this." And then finds comfort back in bed.

***

Weeks go by with the same pattern but this morning she's wakened with terrors. It seems her mind is where *it* wants to be. She can't focus on anything except the fear of being alone and wishes she hadn't been born rather than to live like this. Ed has come out of the bedroom to eat breakfast before leaving for work. Matthew is asleep and doesn't have to be in school till nine and it's only five-thirty. Ed and Joanna eat, but neither of them speak. She is in a vicious cycle of death and aloneness within her mind. She is absorbed only with fear. When Ed gets up to leave, she clutches his arm, pleading.

"Please don't leave me!"

"What the heck are you talking about, I have to go to work."

Again she pleads, "Please – please don't leave. I'm afraid to be alone – please don't go," crying hysterically and out of control.

Ed tries reassuring her, "Can't you visit one of the neighbors or friends, then you won't be alone."

She hears him but only thinks of what is going on inside her head, and it's pure terror. Ed picks up the phone, "Hello doctor Spinner. We've got a problem here. Joanna won't let me leave for work." after a pause, "Okay we'll meet you there."

She walks into the living room, when Ed calls, "Joanna, we're meeting Doctor Spinner at the hospital.

31

Marcy is coming over to watch Matthew. I can't go on like this anymore." Marcy was the neighbor next door, which Joanna had become friendly with, but not friendly enough.

Joanna knew he was annoyed by his tone and didn't argue, hoping only that she would be helped at the hospital.

At the hospital the doctor leads Joanna into a room.

"Sit down and tell me what's going on?"

"I can't be alone. I'm afraid, and I don't know what I'm doing anymore. I even tried to kill myself a few weeks ago." then describes the morning's terror.

Sitting on top the desk with his legs crossed, he looks at her, studying her.

"Maybe it's time to try Electroshock Therapy. Possibly this will help you."

"Are you serious? Are you talking about shocking my brain?"

"Yes, it's been helpful for some people with the same phobias you have."

"No way – I can't do that. Thank you very much, but no. I need to leave now. Thank you – good-bye."

Joanna gets up and leaves the room. Seeing Ed in the outer waiting room, she says, "Let's go home."

In the car, she tells Ed to drop her off at the house and go to work. She thinks, maybe the doctor was putting her to a test, or maybe not, but she knows she doesn't want anything done to her brain.

Ed dropped her off in front of the house and she watched him pull away, no longer having the feeling of terror she woke with. Once in side, Marcy had Matthew eating breakfast. Joanna thanked her, saying it was just a bad migraine she had woken with this morning.

Marcy is okay with this explanation and leaves. Joanna gets Matthew ready for the school bus then walks with him to the bus stop as he runs ahead to meet his friends.

Waving good-bye to Matthew she headed home. Going through such an attack brought on total exhaustion and she crashed on the couch. She knew she never wanted to go through an ordeal like that again, and needed to find another way to rid herself of the panic attacks, depression and phobia of being alone. She then fell asleep.

***

When she woke and thought more of what had gone on that morning, she let her 'fingers do the walking' and found a psychologist nearby, who specialized in relaxation and desensitization therapy. She had never gone this route before but was willing to try anything so she dialed the number and luckily they had an opening a night Ed wouldn't be in school. She dialed Ed at work and left a message of her appointment on his answering machine.

Three evenings later Ed and Matthew dropped Joanna off at the doctor's office. She was nervous but hopeful. In the waiting room the woman behind the desk gave her papers to fill out for insurance, new patient information and for what her problems were. The pages were full of questions: Do you have panic attacks? Do you have phobias? Are you depressed most of the time? Are you nervous? Do you have sweats and fast heartbeat?

Joanna felt she was reading her life on the paper sitting on her lap. A good feeling came over her as she brought the filled out papers back to the receptionist, thinking this might be the right doctor, finally. Sitting waiting, she thumbed through magazines looking at the pictures, but unable to concentrate on words.

A few minutes later a man came through the inner doorway - average height, thin, with blonde curly hair and a short goatee.

"Hello, Mrs. Shaker?" reaching out his hand.

"Yes."

"I'm Doctor Josh. Nice to meet you."

"Hello," was all Joanna could say, still feeling a bit nervous.

"I see you've finished the paperwork. So let's get started."

He led her down the hallway to another room and asked her to sit in the reclining chair. She had no idea what to expect. Was this a new kind of therapy? When they shook hands she felt a warmth to his hand and a feeling of confidence in him came over her. The office was the size of a large closet that held two chairs and a small table next to him.

"Do you know how desensitization works?"

"No," moving her head side to side at the same time.

"It's similar to hypnosis but not fully."

"Hypnosis? Oh, I don't know about that. You won't be able to hypnotize me," she announced, in a negative tone.

"Well, it's fairly new and we've had great success with your type problem, but you'll need to do some homework on your own."

Joanna felt this definitely was a new way of attacking her fears. She had never been asked these questions before. It was always about her father or mother and past history.

"I'm willing to do anything to get rid of these demons of fear."

He smiled, and said "they're demons that you have made, therefore you are the only one who can get rid of them."

This approach *was* different from the other doctors.

Doctor Josh asked her to sit back and put her feet up with her hands on the arms of the chair, not touching any part of her body. He asked her to close her eyes, but she preferred to have them open. He said she would need to focus on a spot in the room and stare at it without moving. She then was asked to breathe in through her nose and blow slowly out through her mouth. He told her to make a fist, focus on the tension in her fist and hold it while he counted from one to ten. Then he said to release it, as he counted from ten to one, breathing out slowly. "Feel the difference, make your mind sense the difference," he said. He started with one arm and then each limb, including the face and back, until the whole body was tensed, then relaxed.

Joanna's body felt noticeably different.

"Now, picture a place in your mind where you are safe," he said in a soft voice.

Joanna searched her mind, at first not coming up with anything, then a picture of grass and wild flowers, leading down to a rowboat with a large shade tree overhanging it, entered her mind. She could see a blanket in the bottom of the boat. Telling him her mind's picture, he said, "now climb inside the boat and lie down, because you're tired."

She saw herself lying in the boat with the blanket covering her, looking up at the sky and then she closed her eyes as the boat drifted out onto the pond. Joanna felt a peace within she had never felt before, except maybe as a child, sitting in a tree she had just climbed to daydream.

The doctor reinforced how relaxed she was and how wonderful her whole body and mind felt. She heard his words but they were off in the distance.

"I'm going to count back slowly from ten to one. At the count of ten move your fingers, then your hands on eight, by six, stretch your arms, and at four stretch your legs, then at three stretch your whole body. Open your eyes on the count of two, and at one you will be fully awake."

Her eyes opened wide, feeling refreshed, at the count of one.

"Wow, I've never had a feeling like this before. I feel so relaxed. I've never smoked pot but this must be what it's like. Is that what it feels like?" she asked.

Doctor Josh smiled and said with a grin, as if he had but didn't want to say, "I don't know, I've never smoked it either. What did it feel like, physically?"

Joanna thought a moment and said, "I felt like I was oil, slowly being poured over the chair, oozing down all over it."

"Good, you have been hypnotized."

"Hypnotized? No – I don't believe it. Really? But I was awake the whole time and I knew what was happening. I could hear you talking all the time. It wasn't like on TV where the person falls asleep."

"It's not like TV. It's self-hypnosis. You did it yourself."

"I did it myself? That's fantastic! Everyone should go through this."

Joanna marveled in amazement, still feeling the calmness within her, without a fear or care in the world.

"Thank you, Doctor. You're a Godsend."

"No, not really. You have a lot of work to do this week. I want you do the same exercise with this tape I made while I was talking to you. Do the exercise at least ten times a day and make an appointment for next week with the receptionist."

"I really don't know how to thank you. I feel great. Thank you so much – good-bye," shaking doctor Josh's hand, in appreciation for what he'd done for her.

When she got downstairs Ed and Matthew were waiting in the car. Opening the door Ed stated, "It's about time."

His words put a damper on what she had learned with Doctor Josh in the large closet, and had the feeling Ed would think it a hoax, especially if she told him she was hypnotized. Since he was the one paying for the visits with insurance, she only told some of the truth.

***

At home she practiced self-hypnosis and desensitizing the body.

After six visits instead of the years again of psychoanalysis, she had learned how to relax every muscle in her body through self-hypnosis. A professional taught her, that if the body is relaxed, it can't go into a fear mode, with all the physical symptoms associated with it. She learned the past is the past, and the future we have no control over. We have control *only* over the present, so she begins a new thought pattern. It's hard to change a mind that has been thinking only fear since the age of sixteen. She prays constantly whenever driving alone in the car and, without fail, before falling asleep each night, asking God to rid her of destructive thoughts and to strengthen her so she can live a normal life.

In books about faith and love, Joanna reads that fear is the opposite of love, and where there is love, fear cannot exist. She reads the words, but finds it difficult to embrace them. The doctor said there would be homework and he was right, but she didn't know how much of herself she would need to change.

HOPE

ONE NIGHT in 1971 Marc telephoned with the news of their dad's passing in Florida. Vincent hadn't been expected to live more than six months, when Joanna had seen him less than a year earlier at Paul's home at a family reunion. Her dad had looked well, though he called her Maria by mistake and she assumed the cancer had spread to his brain.

It was the same night Ed and Joanna had decided to adopt a child. Joanna spoke to many agencies about adopting a black child but Ed wouldn't hear of it. She felt there were too many children who needed homes and she wasn't particular about how a child looked. She had been to the doctor and was told she'd have a hard time getting pregnant again, and the first time was just a stroke of luck.

She finally convinced Ed to adopt a Korean child and contacted an agency. They went through interviews, including psychiatric evaluation of Joanna, because of the therapy she'd received for so many years. The legalities took two years, and finally on the eleventh of April in 1973, they headed to the airport to pick up their daughter. She was flying in on the seven-forty-five night flight from Korea.

Ed and Joanna had chosen the name Hope for their daughter, for they felt she was going to bring hope into their lives. They stopped at Ed's parents for dinner, on the way to the airport. Everyone was excited about this new child coming into the family.

"Just think," Joanna said, "how great that we're getting a baby that's almost two years old. Her birthday is April 17, just six days from today."

"I always wanted a granddaughter to spoil, now I'll have my own China doll," said Ed's father.

At five-thirty, Ed announced, "Well, we better get going. We should be there early and then we'll stop back later." And they left to get Hope.

On the way to the airport Matthew asked, "Can Hope play chess and checkers with me?"

Looking over the seat at her son, who was excited and happy. "Matthew, she's only two years old. I doubt it, but maybe you can teach her." He seemed satisfied with the answer. "She's coming from another country, remember? So she'll look and speak differently than you." Even though Joanna had shown pictures to Matthew, she wanted to prepare him for that night.

When the three arrived at the airport, they took seats and waited for the plane's arrival. An announcement came over the PA system that the flight had landed. The Shaker family and other waiting parents jumped from their seats and headed to the large window, peering out at the plane in anticipation. Over fifty children were arriving for adoption. A speaker asked the adoptive parents to stand in a separate area until their names were called. As names were called, people went to the desk to receive their child or children.

"Shaker, please report to the desk," sounded over the loudspeaker and Joanna, Ed and Matthew went to the desk.

"I'm Mrs. Shaker and this is my husband, Ed, and our son, Matthew."

"Congratulations, you have a girl. Please sign here," said the attendant, as she handed them the papers for Hope.

Introducing them to their daughter, the attendant handed Hope to Joanna and told them they were free to leave. Hope wore a salmon colored dress, which complimented her beautiful black shiny hair. On her feet were rubber shoes shaped like tiny canoes, with oriental designs imprinted on them. Excited and happy, Joanna fought back tears and tried to control her emotions. To hold a new child in her arms again was a joy she couldn't describe. Matthew was seven now and she hadn't held him in a long time, but this came natural to her once again.

Hope didn't cry, but looked sad. She had flown over twenty-one hours and didn't understand what was happening to her.

"Here, let me hold her," Ed said. While he carried her, Joanna held Matthew's hand and the four of them headed out of the terminal to the car, without labor pains.

Once in the car the three looked at Hope and Joanna knew they had a full family and someone for Matthew to grow up with. Seated in the back seat Matthew took Hope's hand, talking to her as if she were his age, even though he didn't get any response. Tired, she fell asleep within minutes. With the plane an hour late and everyone tired, they headed for Ed's parents' house.

Taking an hour to get there, Hope woke when Joanna picked her up. They piled out of the car to see Hope's new grandparents and to use the bathroom, not knowing if this new child was potty trained.

Ed's parents were overjoyed to meet Hope, but after a few minutes of excitement, Joanna took Hope upstairs to see if she needed to use the bathroom. She had brought diapers just in case, although she had noticed Hope didn't have one on when she arrived. Joanna sat on the toilet first showing this little girl in pink what to do. The little girl stood in front of her staring, while in sign language Joanna tried to explain what she was doing. Then Joanna put Hope on the toilet and to her delight, she *was* potty trained.

"This is a great way to have kids – get them when they're potty trained," Joanna remarked, walking down the stairs with Hope in her arms.

After forty-five minutes, they were on the road again for their last stop – home. Hope and Matthew fell asleep in the backseat and Ed and Joanna talked.

"I am so happy, Ed. She's so beautiful."

"Yeah, she is cute, isn't she?"

"I think Matthew likes her already. This is a good thing we've done for him and us," were Joanna's last words. She sat and stared out the window at the blackness along the highway and could hear nothing but quiet in the car, except maybe the sound of two small children breathing in the back seat.

Once home they had cookies and milk and Matthew went to his bedroom, while Joanna put Hope in her own room between Matthew's and the master bedroom.

"Welcome home, Hope," and she kissed her new daughter on the cheek, as she laid her down, pulling the sides up on the bed. "Sweet dreams, good-night."

She looked so tiny, lying there staring up at Joanna with large black olive eyes. A night-light was left on and the door slightly ajar, as Joanna left the room. After a few minutes Hope began crying and Joanna didn't know what the problem was, for she had gone to the bathroom and had had milk. After an hour of crying off and on, and Joanna going back and forth to check on her, she went to Matthew's room with Hope in her arms.

"I want you to sleep with Hope," waking him.

"Oh, Mom, do I have to?"

"Yes, I think she'll feel better if you're with her."

Back to Hope's room and Joanna pulled the mattress onto the floor. When Matthew saw this he changed his tune, "Gee, Mom, this is like camping. I'm going to like this, even if Hope doesn't."

Bending down kissing both of them good night, Joanna receded to the master bedroom where Ed lay snoring. Above the snore she could hear two children making sounds and Matthew trying to play the older-brother role saying, "It's all right Hope. Go to sleep, I'll be here with you. Don't be scared."

Before falling asleep Joanna knew it was going to be a learning experience for all of them until Hope got used to her new surroundings.

***

The next day Joanna let Matthew stay home from school because of getting to bed so late, besides it would be good for both children. For dinner Joanna made spaghetti and meatballs for three, and a dish, Kimshi, for Hope, which the orphanage said she was used to. During dinner, Hope kept reaching for

Matthew's plate of spaghetti and eating it. So Joanna made a small dish for Hope, who proceeded to eat the whole bowl. From that day on, she ate only American food.

The day after Matthew went to school, Ed went to work and Hope and Joanna stayed home – just the two of them. Joanna loved holding Hope, but found that when she tried to put her down, she cried. It was nice to have a child so small to hold again, but after three days of this, Joanna's hip began to hurt, plus, she was unable to get anything done in the house. She set Hope down on the floor, "If you want to follow me, you can, but I can't hold you any more." Hope cried briefly, then was up following Joanna through the house, wherever she went. She was so tiny, Joanna sat her on the front of the carpet sweeper and pushed her around the house.

***

Hope was fun to have around and was a child who played well by herself or with Matthew, when he came home from school. Matthew was happy to have someone to play with, but Joanna noticed a jealousy developing in him, after the novelty of Hope had worn off. Joanna made a special point of spending time with Matthew, after all, he had been her little friend for seven years before his new sister came along.

Hope spoke one word, 'Umma' which meant Momma in Korean. She began to pick up English words quickly and was speaking sentences after a few months. Both Joanna's family and Ed's treated her just like any of the other kids. Her nine cousins made her feel a part of the group. Either the American food she was eating or the change in living conditions, caused

Hope to sprout up by the weeks. She was a happy child, always laughing or smiling, which seemed interesting, considering she had come from an orphanage. Joanna thought she would have had a hard time adjusting, but Hope proved that theory wrong.

***

On a night when Joanna's family was visiting Maria, her mother called her into the kitchen.

"Sit down, I have something to tell you."

Joanna figured it was bad news, and the breast cancer from years ago had returned.

"What's the matter, Mom? Are you ill?"

Maria smiled, "No, why do you ask?"

Joanna told of her concern for her health and her mother laughed.

"Joanna Marie, you always think the worst. I just wanted to tell you that your brother Marc has introduced me to a gentleman and he wants to take me to a New Year's Eve dance." Her mom always called her Joanna Marie when she was serious.

"That's great, Mom. What's his name?"

"John, and he seems like a very nice man."

"Do you think I should let you go?" said Joanna smiling.

She was relieved it wasn't bad health again, and that her mom was going to enjoy herself. Never in a million years had she thought her mother would ever see any other man except her father. Because of the unhappiness he had caused her, Joanna thought for sure, Maria would never go out with a man again.

Maria looked relieved that Joanna had said 'great' to her secret, for she had been a little apprehensive bringing it up.

"What do you plan on wearing?"

"I thought I'd get a new dress."

"A new dress? With all the clothes you have?" Joanna said, rolling her eyes.

"Well, something new *would* be nice."

"We can go to the mall and find a new outfit. But you have to promise me something."

"And what's that?" asked her mother.

"That you'll be home at a decent hour."

"My, my, the tables surely have turned. Now you're the one who wants *me* home at an early hour?"

***

Maria's friend, John, quickly became part of the family. He'd bring Maria to Joanna's house and baby-sit while Ed and she went to a movie. Joanna loved him from the first day she'd met him, mainly because he was good to her mother and treated her with the respect she deserved. When he walked into the house, he sat at the piano and happiness flowed out of every corner. John worked with Paul and Marc at the drugstore as a deliveryman and when he played Santa Claus at the store, all the grandchildren and neighborhood loved him.

Less than a year later, Joanna was maid of honor for her mother and Paul walked her down the aisle. It was a church wedding, with a reception following and a photographer to record it all. Maria made a beautiful bride and never stopped smiling. Happiness showed all over her face as she danced with her children and grandchildren and Maria and Joanna danced 'The Twist' and she found her mom to be a better dancer than she.

ALIVE AGAIN

THE VISITS to Dr. Josh have been over for years, and Joanna feels she is going backward once again. A change has occurred in her but she doesn't know if it's for the good or bad. These days she's wondering a lot about how she's living her life.

Her thoughts are – 'I love my children and my family and friends but I'm in love with no one. There isn't anyone to whom I've given my true self. Have I ever been in love with anyone? Till death do you part. Does this mean until your husband dies, or does it mean, when the love isn't there any more?' She repeats the same prayer every night, "Dear Lord, I love you above everything and everyone. Please take the fears away and let me rest in Your Love."

Ed has been a good man to put up with her fears all these years. He must love her very much, and she feels guilty about not being able to reciprocate that affection. His drinking has become excessive, and she feels to blame. Their marriage was one of convenience and has never been a happy one, although it appears that way on the surface. She accepted Ed's proposal to escape her controlling father and thought it would rid her of the fears. She feels something is missing in her life. There is no reason to live, and no hopes of the future, even though she does her relaxation exercises every day. Some days are hard to keep going.

At thirty-five, she realizes her life has been spent mostly in hell, tormented with fear and turmoil within herself every day. She does want to change her way of thinking and has tried many times but it's much easier said than done.

***

In the spring of 1975 they move into the house of their dreams. A four-bedroom, four-bath, colonial structure built of clapboard, painted yellow with black shutters, a black front door, and a brass knocker. It has a central hall with the living room on one side and dining room on the other. The kitchen has a breakfast nook and is in the back of the house, with the family room, a separate laundry room and a food pantry. The property has several wooded acres with nearby horse stables. A split rail fence marks the borders on two sides. There's a stoop and a red brick walkway that goes up to the front door and around to the side alcove door. It's truly the house of their dreams. She loves *it*. Ed and Joanna had admired the house many times – and other attractive homes in upscale neighborhoods, while taking their Sunday drives, beginning when she was sixteen years old and he was twenty. They had said that someday they were going to own a house like that. Now, many years later, they did.

Will it lessen her problems? She thinks it will surely help, and her fears will again subside.

***

One week after the move Joanna, Maria, and Hope were sitting on the back stoop waiting for the rugs to dry, after being steam cleaned, when a woman came through the back woods.

"Hi. Welcome to the neighborhood. I'm Rosie, your back-door neighbor."

"It's nice to meet you. I'm Joanna and this is my mother, Maria, and my daughter, Hope."

"I'm glad you moved in. The house has been empty for a long time. Where did you move from?"

"Syosset. Do you know where it is?" Joanna answered.

"Sure, My husband has family there. I go into Nassau County all the time with him."

"Really? This is out in the sticks compared to the other house. It had become a small city where we lived. It's more country like here."

"Do you play golf?" Rosie asked.

"No, not really, only a few times a year with my husband, Ed. Does your husband play?"

"Yeah, we belong to a club not far from here, in Stony Brook,"

"That's nice, do you have any children? Hope, you've met and my son, Matthew, is in school."

Hope kept passing between them making sure they knew she was still there, while Maria tried to keep her busy skipping rope and counting how many times she jumped.

"Yes, my two girls think your son is handsome. They go to the same school."

"Interesting, Matthew hasn't said a word about meeting your girls. I guess he's bashful. It's a new school and he's eleven. I guess he's at that age."

"Well, I better get going. I just wanted to stop by to say hello before I pick up the younger one and take her to ballet class, so I'll see you later, maybe. Maybe someday we can play golf, if you'd like."

"Yes, that would be nice, thanks. It was good meeting you, Rosie."

Rosie said good-bye to Hope and Maria and vanished back into the woods.

"She seems nice," Maria said.

Joanna pushed the hair back from her eyes. The late day heat made her perspire more than usual. "Yes, she does. Okay, let's go see if the rugs are dried and get dinner started. How about we barbecue chicken for tonight."

"Yeah, Mom, with home fries too?" asked Hope.

"Sure anything you want," taking Hope's hand. "Mom, you make the home fries, and I'll do the chicken and salad," answered Joanna.

***

The first year was spent decorating and fixing the house to their tastes. Like most large properties, it needed lots of work. On the weekends, Ed and Joanna planted shrubs and trees, especially on the side without a fence, as a natural barrier to the street, which ran parallel to the yard. They chose pine trees, and interspersed flowering forsythia to add color. They had sketched it all on paper first then, following the plan; they hired a carpenter to build a raised deck off the back door. Around the deck, Joanna planted roses of many varieties and colors. On one side she made a rock garden and in the middle planted a red dwarf cut-leaf maple tree four feet high, with lemongrass clumps throughout, dispersed with yellow daffodils to match the color of the house. The overall look was a small Chinese garden.

In the summer months, they kept busy working

together. Even Hope joined in, riding high atop a heap of dirt in the wheelbarrow with whoever was pushing it. Maria and John were there, serving meals and fetching drinks and giving moral support. Joanna, her mom and the kids planted a victory garden of tomatoes, various kinds of squash, peppers, string beans, and other vegetables. It brought memories of Joanna's childhood working on a farm at nine years old, picking bushels of string beans for twenty-five cents, then helped her dad tend the garden that fed them all winter long, while her mom did the canning. Marc and Joanna took their red wagon full of tomatoes, selling them door to door. Some kids sold lemonade, they sold tomatoes. One old lady, whom everyone was afraid of, including Marc, gave Joanna a nickel tip, which she never forgot. The work on their new home brought back childhood memories, and she loved sharing it now, with her children.

***

Soon Ed's business improved and the house was furnished to their liking. Ed and Joanna decided to join the golf club where Rosie and her husband, Jeff, belonged. Ed could use his membership to entertain clients when they were in town. He took a family membership so they all could play golf and have fun together.

In the summer months after work, Rosie and Jeff invited Joanna and Ed and the kids for family cookouts and swim parties. Putting on their father's boxer shorts the children enjoyed the underwear swim races. Rosie and Joanna on opposite ends of the pool yelling, "C'mon you can do better than that. Jan's in the lead, no wait – now it's Matthew and a close third is Hope, but she seems to be losing her drawers," and laughter filled the air.

Joanna and Rosie became close friends and Jeff and Ed had deep conversations about business and the world's situation. For the first time Joanna confided in someone else of her fears and Rosie questioned one day, "Why can't you drive? I don't understand."

"I just can't drive far distances alone. A fear comes over me and I begin to panic."

"Have you gone to anyone for help?"

"Yes, a number of doctors. I'm a lot better than I used to be. At one time I'd perspire and shake so bad I couldn't hold the steering wheel straight. You wouldn't believe I'm the same person."

"You'll get rid of those fears, you wait and see. I'll have you in so many golf matches you won't be able to think of anything else." Rosie said convincingly.

***

Rosie becomes a good friend trying hard to understand the fears and Joanna is relaxed talking to her about them. They drive together in the mornings to play golf, after the children have left for school. Joanna is comfortable if someone's in the car with her but rarely drives alone, except to go to the stores a few blocks away. When she drives alone she plays loud music as a distraction, sings, or listens to relaxation tapes to keep her fears at bay.

Slowly, like an infant, she evolves into a human being that feels other emotions besides fear and panic. She loves walking the golf course, being outside, surrounded by nature, making her feel nearer to God. Until now, she's only existed, rather than lived. Now strolling the course, she thinks pleasant thoughts, noticing the birds and flowers, not terrifying ones of fast heartbeats and dying. The fresh air clears her mind and she even daydreams.

Joanna and Rosie spend the spring, summer and fall months playing golf, sometimes with other women who are just as enthusiastic about the game as they are. They play partners in tournaments and even travel to other clubs for team matches.

DENIAL OF DEATH

ST. ANDREWS golf club dates back to the 1800's and has three hundred club members. It's not a luxurious club, but its members are reasonably well off. For Joanna, it's the challenging golf course she likes.

She's played in the ladies league for a few years now and has fun with all the women she meets. She's in a regular foursome twice a week, and on two other days Rosie and she play as a twosome for nickels and dimes. On Sundays she plays with Ed in the husband and wife tournaments and Saturdays are for shopping, cleaning and doing yard work.

One day, while walking toward the side door of the clubhouse, Joanna looked towards the eighteenth hole and saw two figures pulling golf carts approaching the green. One of them had a long, beautiful stride, and Joanna found herself mesmerized by the slowness and waltz of the woman's gait, as though she were walking to background music. Joanna felt drawn to her but didn't understand why. She liked watching players with different golf swings on TV or while playing other opponents, but she found she couldn't take her eyes off this person.

Finally, pulling herself together she asked Rosie, "Who are the two women coming up eighteen?"

"Oh, that's Catherine and Anne. They've been here for years, probably the best golfers at the club."

Joanna thinks, *Catherine, the gal in the newspaper.* "Did you ever play with them?" she asks.

"Yeah, a few years ago I joined them in a tournament. Anne's handicap is a one and Catherine is a three. Just watching them swing a club helped me with my game."

"Oh, is that why you beat me all the time?" Joanna smiled.

"Really? Oh, I just love taking your nickels and dimes. If you ever get a chance to play with them, don't pass it up. They're great to play with and nice gals on top of it. I heard they once took the black caddies out for a round, just to see what the members would say."

"No kidding...good for them. I like them already. Boy, that must have created a big stir." Joanna opened the door of the clubhouse to head for the ladies locker room and they stopped chatting, not knowing who would be sitting at the table in the locker room listening.

"So you think we can improve these handicaps today?" Rosie asked, who was a fourteen and Joanna a sixteen, both trying desperately to improve.

* * *

Joanna met Catherine and Anne on a warm spring day in 1981, when they were running a charity tournament at the club. Rosie and Joanna, and several other women, were competing in it. As they walked up to the sign-in table, Catherine was standing dressed in a pair of flowered paisley pants with a pale blue shirt. Anne was seated, wearing solid beige pants and a dark

55

brown shirt.

Rosie spoke first. "Hi Catherine, Hi Anne. I want you to meet my friend, Joanna. She's my partner today." After greeting one another Catherine turned to Joanna.

"Hello Joanna, it's nice to meet you. We're glad you could join us today. This is Anne."

Joanna reached for Catherine's outstretched hand to shake and thought, 'she has a strong grip, and is so tall and thin. She looks just like her pictures in the papers.' There is magnetism to her voice and her stature. Joanna was struck in awe, then finally found words.

"I'm happy to meet you Catherine. I've heard a lot about the both of you." Then she reached down to shake Anne's hand, who was seated. She could feel the bones in her hand; she was frail and thin not like Catherine. Joanna had heard Anne *was* ill, and felt moved to say a silent prayer as she touched her, 'Dear Lord, please heal this woman.' This was something she didn't normally do, except to pray for herself and family.

In a weak voice Anne spoke. "I'm glad you both could make it today. You'll find tees, pencils and scorecards over there," pointing to the end of the table.

They headed for the first tee where they were joined by another twosome. Joanna didn't see Catherine or Anne again for the rest of the day. Prizes were awarded after lunch and Joanna and Rosie left with glass bowls for their efforts in finishing third.

***

One of the club members told Joanna that Anne lived with Catherine and had helped take care of Catherine's mother until she recently passed away, also that Anne suffered from advanced lung cancer and was undergoing chemotherapy and radiation treatments. Occasionally Joanna saw Catherine driving a brown car on her way home from golf. She was always headed in the opposite direction, and, although Joanna saw Catherine, Catherine never noticed Joanna. Joanna hoped Catherine would look in her direction so she could wave, but she never did. Catherine was visiting Anne at the hospital, on these drives.

***

Something about Catherine fascinated Joanna, but she didn't know what. Her heart went out to Catherine and on impulse she phoned one day.

"Hello Catherine. It's Joanna from the club. I was wondering if you'd like to play a round of golf?"

Not knowing what else to say after asking her, she fell silent and Catherine spoke.

"No thank you," in a firm voice.

"I hope Anne is doing better and maybe we can play another time. How are you?" Joanna was nervous but wanted to talk with her awhile.

"I'm fine. Thank you for calling," she responded and Joanna could hear a dull tone to her voice and possibly even tears, as she hung up without saying good-bye.

She wanted to get to know Catherine more deeply or perhaps she felt she already *did* know her.

***

Weeks turned into months, and one day, coming up the eighteenth hole, Rosie and Joanna spotted the flag flying at half-mast.

"Uh oh ... I wonder who we lost now? I bet it's Anne," said Rosie.

There were many elderly members at the club so the flag flew at half-mast lots of times. But something inside, made Joanna think it might be Anne this time. When they walked into the clubhouse, they were told that Anne had passed away during the night. Joanna was sorry to hear this and several women were sitting crying and talking of her. She thought, what a well-loved person she must have been, to have so many people care so deeply for her. She was sorry she hadn't gotten to know her well.

***

The next day Joanna answered the phone with Rosie on the other end. They lived next door but still spoke on the phone a few times during the day when they didn't see each other at golf. Ed and Jeff just didn't understand this. "You just saw Rosie today, why the heck do you have to call her tonight?" Ed would say.

"It's a woman thing," Jeff would say.

The men just didn't understand why women needed to talk so often on the phone.

"Joanna, they're having a viewing for Anne tonight at the funeral parlor. Would you like to go with me? I sure would appreciate it."

"I'd rather not. I really didn't know Anne well, and I'm not crazy about deaths."

"Please Joanna. I really don't want to go alone."

Joanna of course could readily understand that feeling. So that evening Joanna drove around the corner to pick up Rosie, and they set out for something she hated.

"I may not go inside Rosie. I hate these things."

"It shouldn't be that bad. I just want to pay my

58

respects and then we'll leave, I promise."

When they got there it was crowded and they recognized members from the club.

Anne's was not an open casket, so Joanna felt a little more at ease. They went to the casket and knelt, to say a prayer – which is customary at a Christian wake. Joanna felt more than uneasy in the presence of death, which she had feared for many years. It brought back memories of her uncle's death. When she was a child her mother had brought her to the funeral and was told to kneel at the casket. The casket was open and all she could remember was looking at a dead person and it had been all she could do not to run in the opposite direction, but her mother held her hand tightly as everyone wept.

After Joanna and Rosie took seats, the priest came out and said a few words. He spoke of Anne and Catherine – how devoted they were to each another and that was the way life should be lived. He said he'd never met two people who had given so much of themselves to others. Joanna listened and thought how nice he was speaking of two women. Afterward, everyone gave their condolences.

As Joanna walked over to Catherine, who was standing alongside the closed casket, she saw a tall stately woman, one who looked sure of herself and knew exactly where she was going in life and where she had been.

***

Catherine dressed in a dark blue skirt-suit this morning, and has greeted people all day, as she did when working. Now in 1981, less than a year after her mothers' death, Catherine stood alongside Anne's casket, who was healthy less than six months ago when they were playing golf, laughing and joking around with another twosome.

They traveled from club to club playing in tournaments, and now at age fifty-five she was standing next to the one she loved and admired, who was only sixty years old. Anne became ill so fast – one day they were playing golf and the next day she was ill with the flu. It left her with a cough that needed chest x-rays and within weeks they said she had cancer throughout her whole body. Catherine asked herself, "how did this happening so fast? What went wrong? Where did the time go? Twenty some years of happiness and sorrow but mostly happiness – so short a period of time."

***

Joanna looked at Catherine and didn't see a tear in her eyes but she felt the tears all through Catherine's body. She shook her hand and kissed her on the cheek saying,

"Now you don't have to worry, she's in a place out of pain."

"Thank you … thank you for coming," was all Joanna heard.

Rosie also took her hand and Joanna heard the same words again.

"Thank you for coming."

Walking out of the funeral parlor Joanna remembered the first time she'd seen them coming up the eighteenth hole and then playing in the tournament they ran to raise money for cancer research.

Later that night Joanna lay in bed thinking about the words – thank you for coming, which she had heard a few hours prior. At Joanna's suggestion to Rosie, they had stopped for an ice-cream sundae after the wake, to rid herself of the feeling of death she had just experienced. Now she was tossing and turning thinking how she hated the word death, and being near it. Punching the pillow a few times and trying to settle down to sleep, she realized what she felt for Catherine she had never felt for another before. Seeing Catherine next to her friend's casket and hearing the words the priest spoke, made her think differently on the subject of death before drifting off to sleep – maybe she had finally come to grips with the denial, all in one night.

***

During 1982, Joanna didn't see Catherine on the golf course often. She didn't play in the golf matches and Joanna played in what had been Catherine's number-one position on the team. Rosie was number two, followed by three other women. They did poorly, finishing fourth at the end of five matches, instead of their usual second place. But they vowed to do better next year and surprise everyone by winning. The last day of play was a team party at the home of one of the team members. Catherine came and stayed a short while and Joanna was happy to see her, even though not a word was said between them.

***

Joanna's attacks of panic had lessened and she was able to drive fifteen minutes to the golf course alone. Of course, she still prayed and listened to loud music, to divert her mind from the fear of being alone in the car.

Late one afternoon, Joanna had taken Hope to play a couple of holes, when she saw Catherine on the practice putting green. Catherine approached them and introduced herself to Hope. Joanna was honored that Catherine had made this jester and felt proud to be in the company of a great golfer and person. Riding in the golf cart, Joanna explained to Hope, who Catherine was in the golf community. Hope seemed interested, but mainly she just wanted to hit the little white ball. Joanna passed her old set of clubs to Hope but they were too long for her to handle, even so her game showed promise.

COMPETITION

EVERY YEAR, except during the war years, the Ladies Club Championship was played the end of September. The two women left after playing at least five matches against others, then played thirty-six holes, to determine who was the best woman golfer in the club.

On Tuesday in 1983 Joanna dressed in red bermuda shorts, a white shirt and red socks, and a brand new pair of white golf shoes. Walking the course, she had developed a large blister on the back of her foot. After eighteen holes of play she was down in the match, minus three, and knew she would lose at the rate she was going, or might not even be able to finish the next eighteen holes.

She had finished going over her scorecard after the first eighteen, making sure it was correct, then gave her shoes to the locker room attendant.

"Hi Jane, sorry I picked up so much mud out there. Do you think you can clean theses?' handing the shoes over to the attendant.

"Mine also," said Rosie.

Joanna showed Jane the large blister that now was bleeding.

"Oh stop complaining." Rosie chimed in. "Just

because I'm beating you. I'm winning today. My game is on and nothing is going to stop it."

Jane whispered to Joanna, "Wait a minute, I have something for you," and she opened a closet door and was gone.

After a few seconds she came out with a pair of dark blue and white spectator golf shoes. "Here, wear these for the next eighteen."

"They're beautiful, but I can't do that. They probably wouldn't fit my feet. No one has feet as big as mine. Who do they belong to?"

"They're size 10, your size, and I'm sure the person who brought them in, would want you to have them."

Sure enough they were a size 10, which few, if any, of the gals wore at the club.

Joanna looked at Jane and saw that she wasn't going to get any more information as to where they came from. "Okay, I'll try them on, thanks Jane." They fit like a glove as if they were made for her.

***

While Rosie and Joanna were having lunch, some of the members came to their table saying they would be out to watch them and wished them luck on the next eighteen holes. Two hours later after eating and a short rest they were back on the first tee for another eighteen. Joanna and Rosie shook hands, wished each other luck, and started the duel once again. Joanna had on the blue and white shoes Jane had given her and they felt good. Jane had put lamb's wool padding in the heel for cushion and Joanna said a prayer that they would last the holes left she had yet to go. She had to win back three holes she had lost and more, to win the match.

The first hole, she was on the green in three and

sank the putt for par, to win the hole. The second hole a par five, she put a long straight drive down the middle and proceeded to get on the green and in the hole, for her par. Rosie sank her putt for a bogey six. Now Joanna was losing by only one. The third hole she put her ball to the right, up on a hill in the trees and thought she was going to lose, but Rosie went out of bounds and Joanna won that hole. Now they were tied, and it was just like starting all over.

They stopped at the halfway house, went to the rest room and got a drink. When they came out a crowd had gathered. Before, the only person with them was the rules person and a few friends that had started the morning walk with them, now there were at least twenty-five faces. Joanna's shoes felt great and she had a fresh timing in her step that was light and bouncy, which kept pushing her forward. She felt she had everything in hand and *could* win the match.

Nearing the end people were applauding and Joanna knew she and her partner would fight to the end to win. It was all about sportsmanship. On the eighteenth hole, tied once more, Joanna and Rosie, both nervous and exhausted, stopped in the clubhouse to use the bathroom.

"God, Rosie do you believe the amount of people out there watching us?"

"It's really something this time. Everyone's out there, even the gals that don't play anymore."

"I don't know about you but I'm a nervous wreck. Would you please win the next hole so we can end this?"

"Sure, I'd love to, if you'd let me." Rosie said grinning.

They wished it were just the two of them on the course, and not all the other eyes watching them. They walked to the first tee for the third time and shook hands, wishing each other luck once more.

They had walked thirty-six holes of golf and were mentally drained from the pressure. Joanna knew they were both play-to-the-end golfers, as did Rosie, but neither of them said it aloud. They tied after the first hole and the crowd applauded. Joanna won the match on the second hole, with a par five and Rosie with a bogey six. Looking at each other with great respect, they hugged, kissed and Rosie said, "Thank God it's finally over – let's go have a drink." Everyone was clapping and cheering for both of them, saying what a great match. They said it reminded them of Anne's and Catherine's matches' years ago. Joanna heard what they were saying, but it went in one ear and out the other. She was tired and shocked and didn't realize she'd even won.

In the locker room, while taking showers, Rosie yelled, "Hey girl, do you realize we played thirty-eight holes today?"

"Wow, we really did, didn't we? I think we would have died out there if one of us didn't win. The skin finally fell off my blister and it hurts bad."

"Oh, Joanna, knock it off. You should of fell in a ditch." Rosie kidding. "I have to say though, I enjoyed every minute with you."

"Me too Rosie. I have you to thank. Getting me out of the house and the years it took. Remember back when?"

"I'm proud of you Joanna, but you did it on your own. I was there just in case you fell."

"I know that and I love you for it."

Alice, one of the members, came in the locker room. "Okay girls, let's get going, they're waiting for you two upstairs."

"We're coming," Joanna and Rosie both replied.

Rosie, dressed in a green silk blouse with white slacks, and Joanna dressed in a white silk blouse and beige slacks, and a tan long sleeved blazer to cover the hair she hated so much on her arms. She had been teased about it throughout her childhood and adult life. Walking up the carpeted stairs to the main area, they looked at each other saying how great they looked. As they entered the dining room and bar, they saw a packed house with members they hadn't seen for years. The crowd stood up, clapping and shouting, "hoorays and hoorahs." Joanna looked at Rosie and neither of them ever dreamed it would to be like this. This hadn't happened at the club for the years Joanna had been there for the Ladies Club Championship. Rosie and Joanna had brought them together again. With tears in their eyes they walked over to the bar, each wanting to buy the other a drink.

Time came for Joanna to make a speech. She held her champagne glass high toward her friend Rosie, "I can only say, thank you Rosie, for introducing me to the game of golf. I had fun out there today with this great opponent."

Rosie patted her on the head smiling and said, "sit down." And they clinked their glasses together.

Last year's winner awarded Joanna a bouquet of red roses inside a large silver cup. All she said was, "where am I going to put this in my home?" She later found out, she didn't get to take the cup home. It was placed in the trophy case at the club in the upstairs living room. Her name had been inscribed on it while she was taking a shower. There she was along with the other great golfers who went before her. It dated back before the 1920's, and Joanna saw Catherine's and Anne's names on it many times, where they also had gone head-to-head.

If it hadn't been for the shoes that Jane had given her that morning, Joanna would never have been able to last the entire match. She found later, the shoes were Anne's. Catherine had donated them to the club.

CHANCE

BY THE END of fall it had already begun to get cold, with wind-chill factors making it even colder. Golf was played on days above sixty degrees, called bonus days. There was shopping to do for Thanksgiving and Christmas and Joanna and Rosie were busy making pumpkin pies. Having jack-o-lanterns left over from Halloween, Hope and Maria helped peel and cut the pumpkins into pieces to be cooked. There's nothing greater than a homemade pumpkin pie, starting with creamed pumpkin, chiffon pumpkin and plain pies with nutmeg and cinnamon. The smells filled the air between both houses, of warm pumpkin pies.

Hope was usually in the house with her friends or at her girlfriends' down the block. Matthew was dating a girl much younger than he, working nights and coming home at the break of dawn. He had graduated in the summer making up classes he hadn't attended during the school year, because of his own choice. He had gotten in with a group of guys that Joanna was not happy with, and she knew she was losing him but couldn't stop the process. He was fourteen, and then suddenly nineteen – changed overnight into someone she didn't know. She told him she loved him, but she didn't like what he was doing. Ed said Matthew was just sowing his oats and growing up but Joanna didn't think there was any reason to be disrespectful.

While lying in bed one evening, Joanna heard a noise and poked her head out the window to see someone climbing through the living room window, down stairs below her. A car was waiting alongside the road.

"Hey, get out of here," she yelled.

The young man looked up and that's when she recognized one of Matthew's friends. When he heard and saw her he ran to the waiting car and took off. The incident had kept her up all night, while Ed slept. The next day she told Matthew what she'd seen the night before.

"Oh, Ma, they're just fooling around," and he laughed it off.

"Fooling around? That's no way to act, breaking in to someone's home."

"They didn't mean anything by it."

"Maybe not, but you better tell them, if they try it again, I'm calling the cops."

***

Ed and Joanna's marriage was strained, fighting most of the time over Matthew and they were growing more apart. Ed played tennis and racquetball with Marc and other friends while Joanna had found her own friends in golf. Most winter nights Joanna and Hope watched happy families on television and she wondered why hers wasn't like them. The winters were hard being stuck in the house, and Joanna hated them. It was like being behind bars again, in fear. Snowstorms came leaving them stuck without electrical power, meaning no heat or stove to cook on. Thank God for the fireplace, where they spent hours building card houses, or just keeping warm listening to the portable radio. With the power out she unloaded the fridge and cooked on the outside barbecue. She'd meet Rosie and the kids on the hill outside, and go sleigh riding. These small things broke up the winter and the depression that went along with it.

***

Before long the snow was melting, and the crocuses were blossoming under the mailbox. The forsythia was a brilliant yellow along side the house and the purple lilacs were also sprouting.

Starting in March 1984, wearing silks and layers of shirts and sweaters, they started to play golf, like animals let out of a cage. Near one hole on the course was a liquor store where Lori climbed over the fence to buy a bottle of blackberry brandy. Sipping brandy on the back nine kept them from freezing to death. They laughed a lot and just enjoyed being outside in one another's company.

In May they started the team matches and played like women on a mission. Catherine, Joanna, Rosie, Lori, and Val were on the first team. Joanna followed Catherine and loved it, because she got a chance to watch a great golf swing in action. Catherine was doing the driving and with all five going to other clubs. She told stories of golf games with different people and spoke little of Anne and her game. Joanna had seen a scorecard incased in glass hanging on the wall in the woman's locker room with Anne's name, showing when she had shot the lowest score ever played at St. Andrews, by man or woman.

***

Their team took second place this year, which wasn't bad because of the competition being so tough. At the team party celebrating their wins and discussing the individual matches, Joanna got a chance to talk to Catherine about the golf swing. Joanna had become a fanatic about the game, but saw Catherine was a greater fan. They stood in Lori's living room swinging imaginary golf clubs and Joanna watched Catherine's excitement talking about the swing. She couldn't get enough of her instruction.

"I have a golf book that'll stop you from bending your left elbow. You're welcome to borrow it," Catherine offered.

"That'd be great, thanks. I really appreciate the help." Joanna excited over the attention she was being given from this great golfer.

The night went on and soon Joanna knew Catherine was about to leave. She felt a sadness within and wanted the night to go on and on.

Catherine said goodnight to everyone and left. A few seconds later, she stuck her head back inside the door and threw Joanna a back pillow.

"Here, use this when you drive your car. It'll help your aching back."

"Thanks," Joanna just about got out, and Catherine flew out the door.

Joanna wanted to be a golfer like the one she had seen walking in front of her in the matches. She devoted her time to reading anything she could find referring to the golf swing.

***

Joanna, Rosie and Lori were having lunch one day at the halfway house after playing the first nine holes,

72

when Catherine came in for a coke. Joanna noticed her and decided to get a drink out of the fridge.

"Hi Catherine. How are you doing?"

"Good, and you?"

"I have to tell you, I enjoyed our conversation at Lori's house." Joanna shyly said.

Catherine sort of smiled, "Yes, so did I and I meant it. I have a book that can help your swing. I've watched you on the practice tee and you can hit a pretty nice ball."

"Thank you, but I *do* need help. I've read some books on golf but I just can't make the swing sink into my brain. I've taken a few lessons from the pro here but then forget what he's told me and the ball goes left or right. It rarely goes straight."

"The hardest thing in golf is to hit a straight ball. Did you know that?" Catherine revealed.

"No, I didn't. I feel better now that you've told me. Would you like to play a round with me?" Joanna figured the only thing she could say was 'no' like the past phone calls.

Catherine took a little black book out of her pocket and thumbed through the pages. Joanna watched pages fly by, filled with writing. Catherine looked up and said, "How about next Tuesday?"

Joanna stunned, "That would be great. I look forward to it, thank you. Have a good game today and I'll see ya next week," and walked away beaming.

When she returned to the table where Rosie and Lori were seated. Looking at her, Lori said, "Gee, we don't have a little black book with *our* golf dates." Joanna still surprised and excited at Catherine's, 'yes' paid little attention to Rosie's and Lori's jokes about the little black book. All she knew was, she was going to play golf with the woman she had read about years ago in the newspapers.

***

Catherine called the day before the date and as soon as Joanna heard her voice she had a feeling she was going to cancel. "Hi Joanna, it's Catherine. We still on for tomorrow?"

"You bet. In fact, my new clubs just came in the mail. I'm debating about bringing them with me."

"Yes, by all means, bring them. We can play with them and I'll bring my measuring tool to see if they're right for you, as far as swing weight and length."

Joanna had no idea what she was talking about. 'Swing weight – what was that?'

"Okay, I'll bring my regular clubs too, just in case the new ones don't work out. I'm looking forward to it. You said around 1:30, right?"

"Yes, I figure there are less people on the course at that time and we can play two balls."

Two balls? Joanna thought. She had a hard enough time playing one and having it go straight. Two balls meant more trouble – trees or water. "All right, see you tomorrow. Have a good evening."

"Thanks, you too," and Catherine hung up.

Joanna was eager to play but didn't want to make a fool of herself. She was nervous that night and unable to sleep, thinking about what to say or whether to just keep quiet and play the game. She tossed and turned most of the night, waking every few hours looking at the clock. Thank God the date was made for the afternoon, at least she could go back to sleep after Hope went to school.

74

***

After a night of restlessness she did try to fall back to sleep after Hope left for school, but was unable to, anticipating the day.

The two met at the pro shop. Catherine reached out to shake her hand, as in the past, then saw the new clubs.

"Nice set of clubs you have there," Catherine said with some other words Joanna didn't understand at all. Heck, Joanna didn't know the parts of a club like hosel or flange. She only knew you held the club and hit the heck out of the little white ball, like her daughter.

Joanna really got nervous when Catherine said, "Let's play match play."

"Oh … gee, I don't know about that. You'll slaughter me."

"No I won't. I'll give you five strokes on the front side and five on the back. How's that sound?"

"All right. I guess," said Joanna. "That seems fair enough, but I know you're still going to kill me."

***

With five holes behind her Joanna began to relax even though she had spent most of the night awake in anticipation. Joanna learned Catherine had a way about her that made you feel comfortable.

Joanna struggled with her game but Catherine took each shot as it came and hit the ball straight down the middle. Joanna was off to the right or to the left, in woods and water, but with the handicap of five each nine, it seemed to work out. After nine holes they stopped at the halfway house, sat at a picnic table outside having lemonade and peanut butter crackers.

"Tell me about your daughter. Is she interested in

playing golf?"

"Well, it's hard to say. She's at the age where boys are starting to enter the picture. She gets good marks in school and reads all the time. Sometimes she's reading a book while setting the kitchen table. I have to say to her, Hope, put the book away for now before you fall."

"She's a beautiful child, Joanna. I noticed when I saw her with you, the clubs she had were too long for her. I have a set of cut downs, that she's welcome to, if it's okay with you."

Joanna was touched that Catherine had remembered her daughter's name or anything else about her. She felt Catherine was a cut above herself, yet she didn't feel uneasy being with her.

"That's so nice of you Catherine. Yes, they are long for her. I picked them up at the Salvation Army. I'm sure Hope would love to have yours."

While enjoying each other's company a butterfly came close by and Joanna heard Catherine say, "Hello flutterby."

"What did you say?"

"I said hello to the flutterby – the butterfly that came to say hello to us."

Joanna thought about what she had said, "That's an interesting name. Why do you call it that?"

"It's just something I started a long time ago and never stopped. I think they're beautiful creatures."

"I'll have to remember that. I guess I never looked closely at a butterfly."

Almost through the back nine Joanna was sorry the day was coming to an end. She was having far too much fun watching Catherine swing a club while she gave her tips. Joanna watched her every move but didn't make it too obvious and made mental notes.

The last hole, a par five, Joanna hit her ball behind a tree while Catherine was in the middle of the fairway. Catherine hit her third shot just short of the green, on the up slope to the hole. Joanna hit her third shot from behind the tree, onto the green and breathed a sigh of relief.

From the middle of the fairway Catherine yelled, "Great shot." Joanna was happy, she had pulled it off. Catherine put her next shot near the hole, and Joanna putted next to the hole. They both sank their putts for pars, with Catherine winning by four shots.

As they walked back to their cars, "I enjoyed the game and the shot you pulled out of your pocket on the last hole was really something," said Catherine.

"Thanks. I kind of liked it myself but I don't know where it came from, luck I guess. Too bad my whole game isn't like that one shot."

"I think I can help you with some pointers, if you'll let me. I know you picked up some things today," Catherine offered.

As they neared the cars, Joanna again didn't want the moment to end. "Sure, I'd be happy if you'd help me."

"I have to go out of town next week for a few days. Suppose I give you a call when I get back and we can set up another date."

"That'd be great. I look forward to it."

They waved goodbye to each other as Joanna watched Catherine's brown car drive away.

That night she wondered if it were Anne's clubs Catherine had mentioned for Hope. Joanna was curious about this woman. There were so many things she wanted to know. She wanted to know about her whole life, but knew she couldn't ask. She certainly wanted to swing a golf club like her that was for sure.

THE GIFT

JOANNA WAITED every day for Catherine's call, hoping she hadn't forgotten. When it finally came on Thursday late morning, she was overjoyed and it showed in her voice when she answered.

"Well hello. How are you? Did you have a good trip?" Happy, she couldn't get enough sentences in, and felt like a bumbling idiot, not giving Catherine a chance to speak.

"Yes, very nice, thank you. I wondered if you would you like to play golf tomorrow afternoon around one thirty?"

Joanna hesitated not believing the words from the other end of the phone line. She had hoped for this, but it was hard to believe a person of Catherine's caliber of golf would want to join her again. Trying to make the other person on the phone believe she was sure of herself she answered, "Of course, I'd love to. I'm looking forward to watching you swing a club again. I've been practicing in the back yard, pitching into buckets. Hope took pictures, so I can see what I'm doing wrong." After hearing her self again she knew she was rambling.

"That's a good idea. I have a video camera I can bring with me. Then we can break your swing down and see the fine points and the bad. What do you think?" Catherine asked. Joanna hears excitement in her voice.

"Boy, that would be fantastic." She couldn't believe this was happening so fast. Joanna wanted so badly to play like Catherine, to swing a club with the same grace.

***

She slept a little easier this time and didn't awaken like the time before. She looked forward to the afternoon when she woke the next morning.

On Friday at 1:30 p.m. they met once again for a match with the same strokes of five a side. This time Catherine took pictures and when Joanna beat her, Catherine said, "no more five shots a side. Next week you get two for each nine."

"Two?" Joanna complained. "Good god, that's nothing, how about four?" They kidded with each other until it was time to part.

***

Catherine and Joanna began to play golf every week along with Rosie and Lori or whoever was floating around looking for a game. Joanna felt Catherine had taken her under her wing to teach her the finer points of the game, especially when they watched the video at Catherine's condo and she pointed out where Joanna needed help. Catherine worked with Joanna chipping balls on the living room rug or on the grass outside. She knew much more of the game than Joanna – the finesse of a shot and how you didn't have to hit a long ball to play a good game or win a match. The short game around the green was a big part in playing a good round of golf. It was all about placement of the ball for the *next* shot. "Think one and two shots ahead before you hit the ball." Catherine would say.

Days when Hope came home early from school they'd take her out to play. Joanna saw how much patience Catherine had with Hope, and had her using Anne's old clubs.

Ed played golf on the weekends while Matthew slept in from a night on the town Friday night and getting ready for another, on Saturday. Matthew was twenty now, and Hope was thirteen. They seemed to grow up quickly despite their mothers' fears.

As Joanna played golf with Catherine, the fears were there, but didn't have full power over her any more. She began to take an interest in the game of golf *and* Catherine. This seemed to take away all her thoughts of aloneness.

***

One Sunday afternoon Joanna heard the front door knocker and wondered, 'No one ever uses the front door. Who can that be?' Opening the door she saw Catherine standing holding a package in her arms.

"Hi. Am I interrupting anything?"

"No, by no means ... I was just reading the Sunday paper. Come in, I'll make a pot of coffee. My mom and step-dad were here earlier after church, and brought pastries. There's plenty left over."

This was the first time Catherine had been inside Joanna's house. The foyer was plain with slate tile and a colonial chandelier, with a table made in the early 1900's that Joanna had stripped down and varnished. She was proud of it and loved the look of the top, which was held together by wood planks and wood bow ties. And Catherine noticed it right away.

"What beautiful furniture you have. I see you have Williamsburg furniture, also."

"Not really. I guess you could say, old furniture redone to look like Williamsburg. Would you like to see the rest of the house?"

"Yes, I'd like that."

As Joanna took Catherine into the rooms, Catherine told Joanna about her mom and dad visiting her when she was in college in Williamsburg, Virginia and how her mom would buy something on every trip.

Joanna mentioned how it had taken almost a year before Ed and she had gotten the house the way they wanted and how Maria made the curtains.

When seated in the breakfast nook, having coffee and cheese pastry, Catherine gave Joanna the box she had been holding throughout the house tour.

"Here, this is for you. I ordered it last month and it just came. I think you'll like it."

Joanna didn't have a clue what it could be and opened the cardboard package carefully seeing a pillow, curved differently than the one Catherine had thrown back to her at the team party.

"That will fit *your* car seat. It's made especially for bucket seats."

"Thank you very much. That's so thoughtful of you, now I can give you back your own."

At that Hope came flying in, running over to Catherine, giving her a big hug. "Hi, Miss B. What are you doing here? Are we going to play golf?" Hope called Catherine Miss B, because her last name was too hard to pronounce. Catherine liked the name she was given and thought it was cute.

"Calm down Hope. Miss B came by just to drop

something off."

Hope reached across to grab a pastry but her mother caught her hand before it touched anything. "Go wash your hands first and then you can join us."

"Oh, okay, Mom," and went over to the kitchen sink to wash up. "Are you staying for lunch? It's just Mom and me." Hope had more energy than three teenagers put together, but you had to love her excitement. In a few seconds she was back at the table having a cheese pastry and glass of milk.

Catherine and Joanna talked golf, while Hope chewed and listened, butting in once in awhile to offer comments. After ten minutes, she was up and leaving through the side door.

Joanna heard the garage door open and figured Hope was getting her bike to ride to her friends.

"She's really something, that girl of yours. She has a marvelous personality."

"Yes, and growing taller every day. She's almost as tall as I am. She fits into my tops already. I thought Orientals were supposed to be petite. I guess it's the American food she's eating," Joanna said laughingly.

"She a delightful child," Catherine answered, without commenting on the petite part. Catherine herself was six foot tall and Joanna guessed, had never felt petite.

A few minutes later Hope came in with a bunch of cut lilacs from the bush outside. "Here Miss B, I thought you might like these to take home with you."

"Oh, Hope, thank you. They're beautiful. That was sweet of you to do." Catherine put her arm around Hope's waist and Hope learned her head on Catherine's shoulder.

Joanna was delighted that her daughter had taken it on herself to give the gift of flowers to Miss B. Joanna thought she must be raising her daughter right, after all. What had happened to Matthew? Where did she go wrong? She didn't know but prayed it would work itself out some way.

"Well, I've got to get going now. Come outside I want to show you something," and the three headed for the side door to the driveway.

Seeing Ed's car Joanna wondered where he was and guessed he was visiting Jeff.

"Do you like it?" Catherine asked.

"What?" Joanna replied.

"My new car. I picked it up yesterday."

"Oh – that's yours? It's the same as Ed's – same exact color. In fact, I thought he came home while we were inside." Joanna slightly confused but realized it *was* the same exact color. "Yes, I like it and wish you good luck with it."

"Thanks, I'll need it after the last one. It was in the shop more than on the road," laughed Catherine.

Catherine hugged Hope thanking her again for the flowers and made a golf date with Joanna for the coming week. Walking back up the brick walkway, Joanna put her arm around Hope's shoulders, "I'm really proud of you. You made Miss B very happy by giving her the flowers. She doesn't have children around her and I think you made her feel at home. I know it touched her."

Hope looked up at her mom and smiled.

***

Playing golf the next week, Joanna mentioned to Catherine, "Ed and I are going to the dance on Saturday night. Are you going?"

"No, I've been to enough dances at the club. It's not my thing anymore. Hope isn't staying home alone is she?"

"No, Matthew will bring his girl friend over and they'll watch movies together."

"I'd love to take her to my place for the night. If it's all right with you and Ed."

"Are you sure? She'll drive you nuts with questions."

"Honest. I would love it and I promise I'll take good care of her. We could go to a movie then out for dinner, if it's okay." Catherine insisted.

"Oh, I'm sure she'll love that. Listen, can I go too?" Joanna said. "I hate these get-togethers at the club. Ed doesn't dance, so we sit and drink all night."

"Good, so it's settled. I'll pick her up around four and you and Ed can have the whole night to yourselves."

"Okay" replied Joanna, without joy. She would rather go with Catherine and Hope instead of drinking at the club.

When Joanna told Hope, she jumped up and down, clapping her hands, chanting, 'goody, goody.' Catherine honked the horn at four on the dot and while walking to the car, Joanna gave her daughter rules on being someone's houseguest.

Hope kissed her mother goodbye then jumped into the passenger seat, "Hi Miss B," giving her a peck on the cheek.

After all seat belts were on and good-byes were said, Catherine added, "Go, have a good time and don't worry. We'll call you tomorrow."

Joanna waved goodbye seeing a big grin on her daughter's face, and wishing she were with them.

***

Joanna showered and dressed in a blue silk pantsuit and Ed in his conservative pinstripe gray suit. They left the house at five-thirty saying few words except casual talk and made cocktail hour by six. They met Rosie and Jeff at the bar along with the usual other couples, watching the left over golf games on TV. Joanna switched to soda after two drinks, again wishing she were with the girls, then at midnight she drove home with Ed asleep in the passenger seat.

***

Catherine dropped Hope off the next day and Hope raved about the great time she had at Miss B's. "You should see Mom, Miss B has these tiny rabbits made of pussy willows in a picture frame. They're really cute. I asked her if I could have them when she died."

"That's terrible, Hope. Why did you say such a crazy thing?"

"I was just kidding her. Miss B knows that. Look," Hope opened a piece of paper. "She gave me this that says she'll leave them to me."

"Well, I don't really think Miss B is going anywhere just yet. I'm sure she'll be around for a long time to come."

Sure enough, Catherine had written up a Will that said Hope would get the pussy willows and Joanna laughed inside herself.

***

The summer months came and one morning Catherine waited in Joanna's driveway having told her the night before to wear a bathing suit and comfortable clothing – she wouldn't need anything else. She had seen Catherine drive up, and hurried out the door looking forward to the day with her friend. "Where are we going?" she asked buckling her seat belt.

"Not telling – it's a surprise," Catherine said, tilting her head and giving Joanna a wink. "I want to show you something of my life from long ago."

My life from long ago, the words hung on Joanna's mind as they drove. She wondered where this 'something' would be. They stopped at the Stony Brook deli and Catherine asked, "Will you wait here while I pick up lunch?"

"Can I give you a hand?" Joanna offered.

"Nope. Thank you, I told you it's my treat today," and Joanna watched those long strides leave her.

Joanna sat thinking of how she'd come to trust Catherine with her fears. She still had thoughts of them at times, but they didn't stop her from living anymore. In a few minutes Catherine approached the car holding a large brown paper bag and they started on their trip again.

"Is it far?" Joanna asked, when Catherine had pulled away from the curb.

"No. Only a few more miles."

Joanna watched the trees fly by and Catherine pointed to houses where people she knew lived.

They entered a road Joanna had never been before. In front of her on the right side of the street was a row of cottages and on the other side was a small stream. Behind the cottages, was the Long Island Sound.

Catherine pulled into the driveway of a white cottage with black trim and turned off the engine.

"This is it. West Meadow Beach – this is where I

spent the summers with my mom and dad as a child."

"It's adorable." Joanna had no other words for the cottage. It was out of a fairytale book. She could see in her mind's eye Catherine as a child running and playing in the summer months. "Who owns it now?"

"The woman who bought it lives in California with her son. Her children use it maybe once a year. She told me to use it anytime I want. I used to come here after work and on the weekends with my friends."

"I bet you had a great time here."

"Yes, I did … it has some beautiful memories. Come, I'll show you around."

The windows where boarded up around to the back of the cottage that overlooked the Sound.

"We can leave our things here," Catherine said, walking up three steps that led to a black deck floor with a white railing. She had packed a canvas bag with two blue towels and other items. After setting the bags on the floor she said, "Come, take a walk with me and see the beauty."

On the sand was a wood slat path, leading through the dunes to the water.

It was low tide and Joanna could see sandy flats that came to the waters' edge. While walking the flats searching for clams, Catherine talked of her yesteryears.

Pointing to the water to an old wooden floating dock, "That's where I kept my rowboat anchored. When Mom asked me to go to the store I'd take the boat instead of the car. It was shorter and more fun to row than drive. I'd dig for clams, buy corn at the store, then make a pit and cook them in seaweed. Before you knew it the whole block would be here."

"God, that had to be fun."

"Yes, it was. They were the best years of my life. Dad built the dock so the kids on the block could dive off. I'd lie in the sun all day and get as brown as an Indian. When I met Anne in college we'd come for the summer and Mom would join us on the weekends. She was a great friend and came to live with us after Mom had a stroke."

Catherine spoke of her past with happiness and love for her mother. Joanna listened quietly, because she *did* want to know everything about this woman. She had come to like her very much and Catherine had quickly become a part of Joanna's life, yet still she felt she had known her all her life.

An hour later and hungry, they walked back to the cottage retrieving the bag from the deli. Inside were two ham and cheese sandwiches, two bottles of lite beer and napkins. They then walked back down the slat path and sat on a log at the water's edge, eating sandwiches and drinking beer, getting to know each other more. Joanna told Catherine of her fears, which had kept her in the house for so long and the fights with Ed over problems with Matthew and the happiness Hope had brought to her. Golf crept into the conversation and took over most of it. Catherine told Joanna of the golf teachers she had had in college and playing on the Amateur tour from New York to Florida, then having to give it up because of illness in the family.

"I loved playing so much, not to say I don't now. It's just that it was my whole life back then," she said in a sadness Joanna could relate to.

"I'm sorry you had to give it up. I read about you many times in the paper."

"Did you?" said Catherine in surprise.

"Yes, you were suppose to be the next Babe Zaharius. Ed really gave me what little education on golf I had back then. He caddied in his teens at the clubs you played."

"You know I did get a chance to be in the Babe's presence once. She was a great golfer, but better, she was an all around person."

"Catherine, you should play in the Club Championship this year."

"I've thought about it, but with my low handicap, I feel it would be unfair," she replied.

"Well, there is plenty of competition for you and if you keep helping me with my game, who knows, I just might beat you. There's Rosie and Lori and others who have really turned their games around."

After Joanna talked Catherine in to playing the championship they went for a walk down the block. Catherine showed Joanna an Artisian Well, where they filled their empty beer bottles up to drink.

"This is the best water I've ever tasted. I've never drunk from a well before."

"There is only one problem I've found with it. It's loaded with minerals, especially iron so if you drink too much, you'll get stomach cramps," Catherine revealed.

As they walked back to the cottage Joanna checked her watch, "Hope will be home from camp soon and I need to be getting back. I enjoyed today and I want to thank you for sharing your life stories with me. I'm honored that you did."

They loaded everything back in the car and headed towards home.

As they neared Joanna's house she thanked

Catherine again for the surprise day. "I'll never forget it."

Catherine dropped Joanna off at three forty-five that afternoon and Hope walked in the door at four.

***

For the rest of the summer Catherine picked Joanna and Hope up to go to the beach cottage, on the weekends after church. Joanna watched the two of them in the water like fish playing games, swimming underwater and carrying on like two ten year olds. Catherine would throw Hope in the water making large splashes, which upset the people around them and they would say they were sorry, while Joanna on shore gave them the evil eye, as if to say 'will you two knock it off.' They would look at her and smile sheepishly and Joanna sometimes thought she had two kids in the water instead of one.

Not too long after that Matthew was working in the garage on his truck he had picked up for fifty dollars, and had taken the whole engine apart to redo. Catherine walked in the garage and saw him sitting in place of the engine and took a picture. She'd talk carburetors and spark plugs with him as if she knew the engine as well as he did. Catherine had been trying to get Joanna to check the oil and water in her car. Joanna's reply was, "I never open the hood of a car. That's what mechanics are for," and Catherine would just shake her head from side to side.

***

The summer flew by and soon it was September with the championship around the corner. The trees were turning colors and the air had turned cooler. Catherine and Joanna had practiced at night at the lighted golf driving range and Catherine was teaching Joanna all she knew about the game.

This year Joanna lost right off the bat to a woman from Norway. The gal was a good golfer and for some reason, Joanna didn't care she'd lost. Rosie hung in there almost till the end, until she lost to Catherine. So it came down to the Norwegian gal and Catherine. Joanna was asked to be rules person and stay with them all during the match. She did her job and was proud to be a part of making sure there was fair play for the full eighteen holes and then another twelve, when Catherine chipped in the hole and won the match. Everyone yelled their congratulations to Catherine and condolences to the Norwegian gal.

In the clubhouse when it came time for the awards, Catherine had a speech all prepared and written in front of her. "I think I need to hold on to a chair, before I fall down," and Joanna slid one of the barstools over. "I want to thank everyone for coming today and special thanks to the women I played against. You were all great opponents and I've enjoyed every minute with you. It's been a long time since I've played in the Ladies Championship and I want to thank Joanna for convincing me to play." She looked at Joanna who was sitting at the bar, and Joanna could see tears in Catherine's eyes. "As all of you know, I've had a few hard years behind me, and I want to thank all of you for being there for me. All I can say is it's great to be back."

Everyone stood giving Catherine a standing ovation, yelling 'it's good to have you back, champ', and she handed the microphone to Joanna.

Joanna said a few words praising Catherine's game

and gave Catherine the silver cup with a dozen red roses in it. The same one she'd received last year. It was the custom for the previous champion to present the cup and flowers. Catherine thanked Joanna and Joanna gave her a big hug, "It's good to have you back, Champ." She never felt so much compassion for someone and knew how happy she had made Catherine by bringing her back to the ladies championship. Catherine had recovered from the feelings of loss she had been suffering.

***

A few days before Thanksgiving on the golf course, having a bonus day, Joanna asked Catherine, "Would you like to come for Thanksgiving dinner?"

"I'd love to, if you'll let me bring something."

Joanna knew she didn't cook. "There'll be more than enough food but if you want, you can bring a small desert."

When Catherine arrived for dinner she brought homemade cranberry jelly, which surprised Joanna, and she wondered if someone else had made it, but didn't ask. Catherine got to meet Joanna's whole family – her mother and John, Paul and Marc and their wives and children. With Catherine there that day, Joanna felt she had everyone she loved together at one table. John said grace and they enjoyed each other's company and the good food. Marc, Paul and Ed talked golf with Catherine while Matthew asked her car questions. Needless to say Hope sat right at her side, watching every move Catherine made. Afterward, Maria, Hope and Joanna cleared the table and did the dishes, while everyone else went for a walk.

***

After Thanksgiving, Catherine and Joanna spent the days together, taking Maria shopping and out to lunch. Joanna's mom liked Catherine and laughed when Catherine bent down to kiss her on the cheek. To Joanna they looked like Mutt and Jeff since Catherine was six feet tall and Maria was less than five feet. John played the piano while Maria made lunch for them on rainy days and on the warm days they played their favorite game and Catherine beat Joanna every time, with even fewer strokes, now.

Joanna thought Catherine still had some hidden secrets in her pocket on the game of golf that she wasn't sharing with her and Catherine laughed at the idea, "You'll beat me someday, you wait and see."

The leaves had fallen and the air had turned much colder by the beginning of December when Catherine said one day, " I have to leave for Florida soon. I usually spend six months there but I'm getting a late start this year."

Joanna cringed hearing this. Catherine had spoken of the trip before, but Joanna threw the thought way back in her mind. "When are you leaving?"

"I was thinking about next week."

"Do you drive or fly?" asked Joanna and wished they were talking about something else.

"I take a plane and have a fellow I know drive the car down, which usually takes a few days. Most of the gals from other clubs are already down playing golf. We used to leave after Thanksgiving, but this year it's late. You should come for a visit."

"Thanks, that would be wonderful but I doubt it. With the family it's hard to get away." Joanna also knew with her fear of flying she wasn't going anywhere. She had gotten rid of some fears but some were still around. "We'll see, maybe I'll surprise you one of these days," she said, knowing it would never happened. She had noticed her fears were creeping in if she did think of Catherine leaving. Joanna would stay home with her family and arguing with Ed as usual or Matthew would be in some kind of trouble. Things had gotten so bad at the dinner table, Hope would end up crying because of the three-way yelling match that went on.

Joanna confided this to Catherine and was not ashamed. Catherine listened with compassion and understanding, offering the key to her apartment if it got bad. Catherine asked Joanna if she would take in the mail once a week and leave it on the dining room table.

Joanna was going to be lost without her newfound friend.

Catherine drew on paper, a likeness of the condo she was going to, "See this is where your room and bath will be, when you visit. You'd love it and it's right on the ocean."

All Joanna could say was, "Yes, I bet I would love it."

***

Joanna decided to give Catherine a Christmas present before she left, but didn't know what to buy. She knew she didn't want to buy just anything, and Catherine had everything anyone could ever want. Joanna wanted to give her something special, to show what she felt inside for her, wanting to thank her for all she'd done for her. Taking herself to the mall, which was an oddity, she strolled along looking for something. This is one of the few times she had gone to a mall alone, because of her fears. She had a feeling now, of not being alone any more and felt Catherine was with her no matter where she went. Joanna was now evolving – the one who had hid herself, for so long.

Clothes seemed so impersonal for Catherine, the person who had helped Joanna from out of a hell. She found herself in the jewelry department looking at rings. Catherine didn't wear rings except when she went out and that would be too personal. Also Joanna didn't have much money.

She looked at necklaces and thought Catherine wouldn't wear them either. Then in a tiny box in the glass case, she saw something she thought looked like a rose. Surprised to find out it *was* a rose, when the salesperson brought it out and placed it on the counter. A tiny gold rose. Joanna had goose bumps when she looked at it. How perfect and thought Catherine *might* wear it on a chain around her neck. She wore her mother's Virgin Mother medal and a silver medical alert item that said she was allergic to penicillin, just maybe she'd wear the rose, sometimes.

She asked how much it was and it came to just under what she had in her pocketbook, forty-five dollars. "I'll take it," she told the clerk. "It's a Christmas gift. Could you wrap it in plain gold paper with a red bow?" She was excited, feeling she had chosen the perfect gift and couldn't wait for Catherine to open it.

***

On the twelfth of December, two days before Catherine was to leave for Florida, Joanna said,

"C'mon, let's go get a Christmas tree and have Christmas before you leave. There isn't anything that says we can't celebrate early." She was trying to be strong. She wanted to tell Catherine how much she was going to miss her and feel lost without her. She wanted to tell her that – and more.

They went to the garden nursery and picked out a tree, three feet tall, which had few branches on it and called it their Charlie Brown Christmas tree. Catherine searched the garage for garlands and ornaments while Joanna made Christmas Cookies. Placing it on a table both said it was the most beautiful tree they had ever seen, as they ate cookies and drank hot chocolate. They celebrated their own little Christmas and exchanged presents. Catherine gave Joanna a pair of emerald gold earrings and Joanna gave Catherine the tiny gold rose.

Joanna left for home late that afternoon, crying. She felt part of her being torn away, like a limb being torn from a tree. She fixed dinner for the family while the quibbling continued, but she stayed out of it this time, her mind was with Catherine. Joanna would see Catherine tomorrow, for the last time for months to come. How was she going to get through the winter? She woke in the middle of the night to find she had been crying in her sleep. Her eyes and cheeks were wet, as well as the pillowcase.

COVE

AT SIX the next morning Joanna told Ed, "I'll be home late tonight. Do you think you can take the kids out for dinner? Catherine's leaving for Florida and I'm going to help her clean out the condo."

"Fine," he said. "No problem," and was out the door off to work.

Driving to Catherine's the only thought in her mind was, 'how am I going to live without this woman in my life?' They had come to know each other well and Joanna looked up to Catherine for just about everything. Catherine was older and wiser and knew everything there was to know about life, Joanna believed, but mostly she'd helped her forget her fears almost totally.

When she arrived at the condo five miles away, she was greeted at the door. "Good morning. Would you like breakfast before I throw away the eggs?" Catherine was already ridding the place of leftovers.

"Sure, I'll make the eggs while you finish packing."

Joanna had had breakfast with Hope before the school bus came, but wanted to sit across the table from Catherine and make the hands on the clock stop.

"That'll work. I've started packing but I slept late so I'm way behind." Catherine answered and was off to the back bedroom.

Joanna had been there for lunch a few times before and found her way around the kitchen easily. While making eggs, bacon and toast she thought, 'I'd like to tell this woman what I feel for her but I'm afraid I'll lose her if I do. I've never felt this way about *anyone* before.' She became nervous and agitated, as her brain spun around. 'Should I tell her? When would be a good time to tell her? Before we start working or after?' By now the eggs were overdone and she called Catherine in to eat.

"We'll use paper plates, if it's okay with you? Thank you for giving me your time this morning," then noticing the table, "Look at this beautiful breakfast, c'mon let's sit down."

"I told Ed I wouldn't be home for dinner, so I can stay most of the day."

They sat eating, making small talk about the weather at first then Joanna spoke up, "I hope you'll enjoy seeing your friends again. Make sure you hit a few golf balls for me while you're away."

Catherine didn't answer right away and Joanna wondered if she was feeling the same way.

"Yes, it'll be good to see the ole gals again. I hope the weather is decent here for you and you can get out to play. Bonus days, that's what I'll pray for, for you." And they both smiled, breaking the ice a little. Bonus days where warm sunny days that didn't come often in the dead of winter on Long Island.

"I hope so. It will make the winter go faster, that's for sure."

After breakfast and the plates thrown away, they went to work. Catherine told Joanna what she needed done and Joanna followed directions. During the two hours Catherine packed clothes that she'd be taking, striping the beds and loading the washing machine with towels and sheets. Joanna worked on the refrigerator and freezer and took food next door to the neighbors. Catherine had put a cooler on the floor for Joanna to take home with the rest of the food.

Joanna thought they worked and played well together, but the thoughts of Catherine had to be discussed. She needed them off her chest and to take the consequences whatever they were. Finally, she got up the nerve and called, "Catherine, could you please come here a minute? I'd like to talk to you."

"All right," she yelled from the bedroom. "I'll be right there."

In seconds Catherine was standing at the kitchen entrance, and Joanna was leaning on the sink for stability. Her legs weak and jelly like. She had worked herself into a state of panic, with all kinds of thoughts running through her mind.

"What's up?" Catherine asked.

"Can I talk to you about something that's bothering me?" Joanna's voice cracking like a teenage boy, with almost a stutter. Still at forty-one she was afraid to say what she really felt and guessed it was because of the strict way she'd grown up.

"Sure. What's wrong?"

"Well, I don't know how to say this."

"Just say it – it can't be all that bad. What's the matter? Your face is red and you look upset."

"I am. I've been walking around with thoughts that are driving me nuts and I feel I need to tell you," She got a glass of water to ease the dryness in her throat.

"Okay, then just tell me. What's going on?"

"Well it's hard to say. It' s been on my mind for awhile." These thoughts had become a mountain and she needed to climb over them. "Uh – Ca … I think I love you." There she had said it.

Catherine stood quiet a minute as if she were dissecting what had just been said. Then she walked toward Joanna, "Let's go sit in the living room."

Catherine poured a glass of water for herself, while Joanna walked around her through the doorway into the living room and sat in the nearest seat thinking, 'My God what have I done? I shouldn't have opened my mouth. Who knows what she'll think or say now? I'll probably lose her friendship. She's taking forever.'

Water in hand Catherine appeared and sat next to Joanna on the love seat. They sat without a word spoken, Joanna afraid to open her mouth, fearing she had said too much already.

Then something happened. Catherine took Joanna's hand.

"It's all right my friend. I love you, too."

Joanna cried, finally letting the stress out and Catherine held her. "It's going to be all right, I promise. I don't want to leave you. I'm worried about the fights you and Ed have. I want you to know if you ever need a place to stay you and Hope are welcome here. We've come to know each other well this past year. I've loved watching you play golf with the same enthusiasm I had when I started playing. You have a beautiful spirit, Joanna. Don't let anyone ever break it."

Joanna couldn't believe the words she was hearing. 'I love you too. You have a beautiful spirit.' She'd never heard anyone speak to her this way. This is what

101

she had wanted all of her life – a person who truly cared about her and knew who she was. She had never gotten anything like this from Ed. Joanna was glad she had followed her heart and spoken up. She felt complete with this other human sitting beside her. The demons were gone, snuffed out like a wet match.

***

Catherine asked her to bring in the mail, and told her she would go over it with her on the phone when she called. She showed Joanna a folder in her desk drawer where she had an envelope.

"This is here for you, if you ever need money."

"I won't need it, thank you."

That night after the work was done, Joanna told Catherine how much she'd miss her and hoped she would have a wonderful time playing golf with her friends. With the food in the Joanna's car and Catherine's clothes in the trunk of her car, in the parking lot they hugged each other and said goodbye.

When Joanna pulled out of the driveway, she got as far as around the corner when she broke down crying, missing Catherine already. How would she live the next four months without her? Her friend had become her whole life –her laughter, her happiness, her Savior and now her sorrow.

DECISION

SHE MADE it home wondering how, as she cried the whole way, doing ten miles an hour. Tears and her runny nose had soaked the front of her blouse. Good thing she had paper towels in the car, which she stopped to use along the way.

Joanna saw Ed's car in the driveway. Turning off the engine, she sat a moment trying to compose herself before going inside. She knew he'd be in the den watching television or sleeping in his chair, as usual.

Then she saw he was awake, sitting in his chair, as she struggled inside with bags in her arms. Trying to be as normal as possible, "Hi, how you doing? Everything go all right with dinner tonight?"

"Yeah fine. We went for pizza. Matthew brought his girlfriend."

"Good, I'm glad he went with you. Is Hope still up?"

"No, she went to bed a while ago. What's all that?"

Joanna fumbled with the objects in her arms, setting them finally on the kitchen counter and floor. "Catherine was throwing out food, so I brought it home. She's leaving in the morning."

"Why don't you go with her," he said, in a nasty tone and weird expression on his face.

Joanna couldn't figure Ed out and didn't want to try. She looked at him and had caught the hatred in his voice. She knew he was trying to be funny but to her it wasn't, not now. She unpacked the food and said goodnight. She wanted to take a shower, get into bed and read or watch TV. She knew he wouldn't be up for a while. He'd fall asleep and wake at two or three in the morning, long after she would be into her second dream – she hoped.

She took a long, hot shower, letting the water pulsate on her head to get rid of the headache. She thought of Catherine leaving the next morning and found it hard to believe. It was ten o'clock when she got into bed, turned on the television with the remote and watched some dumb program. Her thoughts were of Catherine till she finally fell asleep, free of her thoughts.

***

The phone rang, waking her at 1:30 a.m. A voice on the other end said, "Mrs. Shaker?"

"Yes."

"This is the Police Department."

"Oh no. Is it Matthew?" being he was the only one not home yet.

"Yes."

"Is he all right?"

"Yes. He was caught breaking in to a toy store with five other boys."

"Oh God, he robbed a store?"

"No, they didn't get that far but they tried," the officer said. "We're keeping him unless you want to bail him out."

"How much is the bail?" asked Joanna, embarrassed

but still shaky, thinking Matthew had been in a car accident or some other catastrophe.

"Five thousand dollars."

Thinking a second she told the officer, "Keep him over night and let him see what it's like in jail." She thought that maybe her son's bad habits had been picked up these last few years, along with his new friends.

Ed woke hearing the conversation, "Give me the phone!" he demanded. "I'll be right down to bail my son out," he told the officer.

Joanna got angry. "You're always rescuing him. Why can't he stay in jail to see what it's like? He broke the law. When is he going to be held responsible for what he does and accept the consequences?"

They yelled while he dressed and Joanna followed him downstairs. "If you bail him out, I'm leaving in the morning for Florida with Catherine."

"Go ahead, do what you want – I don't care!" and he headed for the door.

Joanna was steaming and couldn't for the life of her understand this man. He was so blind to what was happening around him, especially to his own son. He was raising his son so differently from the way *he* grew up. He had grown up a responsible person, even at the age of fourteen was working caddying and as a soda jerk in a lunch establishment, went in the service, then had his own business. Why didn't he want his son to grow up like this?

***

She sat at the kitchen table with a glass of milk, unable to go back to sleep. Hope came downstairs, half asleep.

"What's all the noise, Mom?"

Joanna put an arm around Hope's shoulder and led her back to bed. Kissing her on the cheek, "It's nothing, go back to sleep now. I'll tell you in the morning."

When back downstairs, she thought about what she had said, "I'm going to Florida," and that's when she decided to call Catherine.

Catherine answered with a sleepy, "Hello?"

"I'm sorry to wake you Ca. I – uh – what do you think of me driving your car to Florida tomorrow?"

"What are you talking about? You sound terrible. What's the matter?"

At those words, tears welled up in Joanna's eyes, as she told Catherine what it was like an hour ago.

Catherine, fully awake, asked, "What do you think if we both drive the car to Florida?"

Joanna thought about what she heard. "I'd like that," Joanna said with a sigh. "I'm afraid I'm losing it here, Ca."

"You're not losing it and it's going to be all right. What time do you want me to pick you up tomorrow?"

"I can't leave until Hope goes to school, so probably around 9:30. Is that okay?"

"That's fine. I need to call the airlines to cancel my ticket and then the fellow who was to drive the car. I'll see you in the morning. Try to get some rest."

"Okay, thanks, Ca. Good-night."

"Night." And Catherine hung up.

Joanna went upstairs and packed a few things in a suitcase so she'd be ready in the morning. Getting back in bed, she thought of Hope and how to tell her. While lying there, she listened with one ear for the front door to open and Matthew and Ed to come home.

She slept three hours and woke Hope up earlier than normal. While eating breakfast, she told her daughter what her plans were and what had transpired during the night with her father and brother. Hope said she would be all right and not to worry. Her daughter was thirteen going on thirty. She had a grown-up way of looking at life, sometimes Joanna thought, more than she. Ed and Matthew never came home.

***

As soon as Hope left for school, Joanna took a shower, threw some more clothes in another suitcase, thinking she didn't pack enough the night before. Catherine was at the door by 9:30, as promised. Joanna was happy to see her once again, even under the circumstances. Catherine had compassion and understanding for Joanna and her married life. Distraught over the problems at home, she knew she needed to remove herself from them.

Stuck in traffic on the Beltway trying to get off Long Island, they only made it as far as Virginia, towards early evening. With neither of them liking to drive after dark, Catherine found a place around dinnertime to spend the night. Joanna called Maria to let her know where she was and what had happened, knowing her mother would worry. She called Ed to see how he had made out with Matthew. He told her he'd brought Matthew home an there was to be and arraignment and everything was fine. 'Everything was fine – was he nuts? Joanna wondered. Joanna relayed the news to Catherine then watched television till she fell asleep. Catherine planned the next day's trip.

They left early the next morning, stopping for breakfast along the road. They were in South Carolina by evening, where Joanna made a phone call to her mother, saying everything was all right. Catherine made reservations to play golf the next day at a course in Savannah, where she knew the pro.

The next day was a short drive to the resort golf club in Savannah, where Catherine introduced Joanna to a club pro whom she had known during her tour days. It was a beautiful day of sun, golf and relaxation, just like being on vacation, though it was hard for Joanna to relax. She tried, but it seemed she had forgotten how. Thinking of the problems back home, her body was a mass of nerves – even her jaw and teeth hurt.

***

Late afternoon the next day, Catherine turned a corner and said, "there's the condo."

Joanna saw five high-rise buildings with lights on. "Condo, it looks like a hotel!"

Catherine laughed, "it's called Sea Rise. The first building is the one we'll be staying in."

She was a child compared to Catherine and her travels throughout the country. Joanna hadn't gone anywhere except upstate New York with her mom. Ed and she went on a honeymoon upstate, and then to Florida later with the children, but they always stayed at hotels. To her this *was* a hotel.

Catherine drove up to a guard gate, gave her name to the woman guard who lifted the gate for them and said, "Have a nice stay." She then pulled into the underground garage, where they unpacked the trunk of the car, putting everything on a flat dolly that was there for visitor's to use. As Joanna watched, she felt out of place and fearful. This was all new to her and for a minute she missed her life with Ed and the kids. It was predictable – yelling and fighting – she knew what to do. Here she didn't know how to act.

Catherine unlocked the door from the garage and they entered a large lobby with couches, plantings and a mirrored wall with two elevators. The opposite wall had pink wallpaper that was pleasing and calming to the eye.

Catherine signed a book that stood on a pedestal and asked Joanna to do the same, adding the time of arrival. She hit the elevator button while Joanna watched the numbers light up coming down from the fourteenth floor, hoping she wouldn't become dizzy once inside. She hated them a while back and couldn't go near one because of the closed in feeling she got.

While waiting for the elevator, Catherine asked, "are you okay?"

"Yes, why?"

"You've been quiet and you seem nervous."

" I *am* nervous."

"There's nothing to be nervous about. You're on vacation, so try to relax. It's just the beginning."

"I've never been away before with anyone except Ed and the kids. This is all new to me."

The elevator doors opened and they wheeled the dolly inside. Joanna opened her mouth wide while inside, so her ears wouldn't close. They did it when she flew on planes or rode elevators. Getting off at the fifth floor, they walked along the catwalk to door number 503. Catherine fumbled for her key, opened the door and stuck a suitcase against it, holding it open. Joanna brought her luggage inside, while Catherine took the other things off the dolly and headed for a room to the left. When Joanna closed the door, she stood facing a living room with vertical blinds across the whole wall, two green couches, one along the wall and the other in the middle of the room, separating the living room from the dining room. Standing there, she waited for Catherine. She felt frozen in place.

Catherine came out of the room on the left in front of her, "Come in, put your suitcase down and relax." She then walked Joanna to the other bedroom, where she could unload the cases. The suitcases were heavy. She'd forgotten how much she had brought with her. Placing them on the floor, she saw a room with twin beds, sparsely decorated with white wicker furniture, tastefully done with lavender print flowered bed throws, pale green pillows, verticals over the windows and green rugs throughout.

Catherine opened the verticals in the living room, then the sliding glass doors to the balcony and called, "come and see the beauty."

Joanna, looking straight out, saw black with small lights here and there on the ocean. She walked to where Catherine was leaning on the railing. Looking down, her head began to swirl and she had to step back inside door.

"Does it make you dizzy?" asked Catherine.

"Yes, when I look down. I've always had a thing with heights, even though I like them."

"You'll get used to it. Look straight out first, then slowly lower your eyes." Catherine was trying to help.

Joanna took one step over the threshold and put her hand on the lounge chair, noticing a table with chairs and a lounge to lie on in the corner.

She took deep breaths, smelling the salt air and

noticing how it cleared her lungs. She could hear the waves crashing onto shore, faintly seeing white foam from the moon's light. She began to lower her eyes, not feeling as woozy. She saw a large patio with lampposts along the outside wall, a large lighted swimming pool and a hot tub. She could also see the patio and pool of the building next door.

"It is beautiful," she finally said.

Catherine watched her as she became used to the sight, then Joanna joined her leaning over the railing.

"See, I told you, you would like it. Wait till you see it in the daylight. It's even more beautiful."

After an hour of beauty, Catherine spoke, "Hey, we better get something to eat, I'm starving."

Joanna had calmed down and felt comfortable now, although she wasn't sure she was starving, but was sure she had been filled looking at what was in front of her. "Just give me a minute. I need to use the bathroom."

"Take your time. We'll go around the corner for a quick hamburger, if that's okay with you?"

"Sure that's fine," as Joanna walked to the bathroom.

On their way to the car, they took the dolly back to the garage.

After a hamburger, fries and a soda, tired, they came back to relax on the balcony and listen to the waves. Joanna couldn't keep her eyes open, "I'm sorry, but I need to get some sleep. I'll see you in the morning. Have a good night's rest and thank you. Thank you for everything."

"You don't have to thank me. I'm glad you're here. Have a good nights rest, good night."

Joanna left Catherine on the balcony and headed for her bedroom.

Joanna lay in bed with the sliding window open, hearing the ocean and breathing the fresh salt air. She wondered if Catherine was still outside and thought of the folks she'd left back home, her Mom, Matthew, Hope and Ed. She wished they could share this with her. For some reason, all seemed right with the world here.

***

Joanna slept late the next morning and as she went to see where Catherine was, passing the living room doors, she saw the ocean. It *was* beautiful in the daylight…a blue-green, then farther out to the horizon, a dark, black-blue. A man was doing laps in the pool below and others were in the hot tub. Catherine's bedroom door was closed and Joanna heard opening and closing of drawers.

She knocked, "Come in. Good morning sleepy head, did you sleep well?"

"Yes, I woke a few times, heard the ocean and fell back to sleep. It is as beautiful as you said it was. Have you seen the ocean yet? The color of the water is gorgeous. What are you doing?" Joanna asked.

"I got up early, I couldn't sleep. Yes, it is beautiful out there isn't it? I drank my coffee on the balcony, then thought I'd put clothes away, but didn't want to wake you. I looked in on you once and you were peacefully sleeping. I think we should go food shopping this morning, if you don't mind?"

They'd only picked up the essentials last night while out, milk, bread, eggs, and bacon. There was coffee left in the fridge from whoever was there before them.

"Okay, I'd like to take a shower and eat something," Joanna answered.

"Good, I've already showered, so I'll start breakfast."

While in the shower, Joanna thought how nice this person was and how she treated her. She was a pleasure to be around. Why couldn't life be like this all the time? Dressing in her bedroom, she could smell bacon cooking.

"One egg or two?" yelled Catherine.

"Just one, thanks. I'll be right out."

***

She found Catherine outside seated at the patio table, "Boy, this is something, bacon, eggs, toast and coffee. Thanks, but I could get spoiled if you do this again."

"You're welcome. Just remember this is the limit to my cooking. All done reading the microwave instruction book," said Catherine laughing

"It sure is busy out there this morning." Joanna's chin pointing toward the railing. She ate not taking her eyes off the ocean and the activity below. More people had arrived at the pool for their morning swim.

"Us snow birds get up early to walk and swim laps."

"Oh, am I stopping you from doing all that?" asked Joanna.

"No, not this morning. I usually walk the beach, then it's in the ocean for a swim. Then the pool to get the salt off my body."

"It sounds like the perfect way to live, if you ask me."

They enjoyed their time outside, then put the dishes

in the dishwasher, getting ready for the food-shopping trip. Shopping was fun with Catherine. She bought toilet paper, food, everything needed to fill the household. Joanna felt uncomfortable not being able to contribute money, but she'd left the northern house without any and knew Ed wouldn't have given her any, if she'd asked. She never carried more then twenty dollars with her. In fact her mom had said early on, "you should have a small bank account of your own." She guessed Maria was afraid the same would happen to her daughter that had happened to her – left with no money.

Joanna told her, "there's nothing I need money for, Mom. Ed gives me money for golf." Now though, she wished she had taken the advice and could help pay for some of the groceries.

***

After unpacking groceries, they put bathing suits on and went to the beach, laid in the sun drinking up the warmth, then went for a walk. Joanna tried to relax and not feel as though she was a tag along.

While walking the beach Joanna confessed, "I don't feel right that you are paying for everything, so I'll do the cooking and cleaning while I'm here."

"Would you please stop worrying. You're on vacation and we will clean together. But as far as the cooking – yes, you can cook, because I don't. What you saw this morning is it."

"Good, then it's settled. I'll do the cooking," and Joanna felt better.

"When I play golf with the girls, I usually eat out."

"I want you to do whatever you're use to, make believe I'm not here and don't feel as if you have to entertain me."

Catherine bent down to pick up a seashell. "Look, isn't it pretty?"

"It's beautiful. I've never seen a shell like it. The color is perfect and the size, so small.

"It's for you, to remember the ocean and where you are. Keep it with you and maybe it will help keep you calm."

"Thank you."

The shell Catherine had given her was the color of salmon and as large as the nail on her pinky finger. It was precious. How could something like this be lying here in the sand? When she went back upstairs, she wrapped it and put it in her purse for safekeeping.

***

Around 6:30 that evening Joanna figured Ed would be home and they would be eating dinner, so she made a collect call and got Hope. "No, Dad's not home. He went to play racquet ball with Uncle Marc."

"How was school today?"

"It was good. I still have some homework in science to do."

"I miss you, you know. But I had to get away."

"I know, Ma. Don't worry. I miss you too. I made hot dogs and beans for dinner tonight."

Joanna loved thinking this is right up Hope's alley – master of the kitchen. She'd have the boys in order before Joanna got home. Joanna told her daughter she loved her and would call her tomorrow around the same time.

***

Catherine's little black books were filled with golf dates for the next week, and Joanna had the days all to

115

herself. Catherine left in the morning and Joanna cleaned the breakfast dishes and made the beds. While vacuuming, she heard a loud roar, looking out the sliders, she saw a Zeppelin almost eye level with the floor she was on. "Wow, that's big." She stood in amazement for the full time it took the blimp to clear the building and then went back to cleaning. This was Joanna's way of saying thank you.

Joanna went for long walks on the beach and watched the water-birds look for food and wondered why the gulls faced into the wind. She saw minnows along the water edge, pelicans flying south in the morning then flying back north in the late afternoon. It was interesting to see how nature handled itself. Catherine had told her the water-birds ate twice their weight every day. That meant they didn't have much time for fun, as they were always eating or sleeping. Many thoughts were coming to the surface and her fears of being alone and death were under control for the first time.

The beach wasn't crowded like Long Island and it was possible to do some serious thinking, in a relaxed atmosphere. This was how she spent most of her days. She met people who were staying at the same building and when Catherine came home they went for a swim together, but mostly she tried getting her thoughts together. Even in the rain, she wore a jacket and walked the beach. She found herself peaceful with the answers right there, at her feet.

***

The days flew by and one day around 6 p.m. Catherine came home from golf and found Joanna lying on the lounge on the balcony. She fixed a drink and began telling Joanna of the great golf game she had. Hole by hole she described her shots and Joanna listened, watching Catherine's face light up when she came to the good parts. Joanna enjoyed hearing whatever Catherine had to say, even if she spoke about the weather. She loved the sound of her voice and being in her presence. She was another calming affect.

"C'mon let me take you to dinner tonight. You've been cooking all week. You need a break," Catherine announced.

"That's not necessary. I've already defrosted meat for tonight."

"Then save it for another night. I'm not taking no for an answer. We're going to dinner," Catherine said with authority.

They dressed in blue blazers and white slacks for dinner. When entering the elevator, the mirror on the opposite wall showed their reflections. "My God, we look like twins, except you are the taller one."

Catherine laughed, and said, "No you're the shorter one."

They went to a restaurant on the Intracoastal Waterway where they could see the Jupiter Lighthouse. The red lighthouse reflecting on the water and its light beam directing boaters, was a breathtaking view and boaters were fishing, or just cruising along slowly. Joanna leaned over to Catherine a few times to tell her how happy she was and thankful Catherine had come into her life. Catherine told Joanna she was happy for her.

***

She couldn't sleep the night before her plane trip back to Long Island and thought about leaving this place of happiness and contentment. Ten days had gone

117

by when it felt like two. She lay awake all night
listening to the ocean and going out on the balcony to
see the lights below. She hated to leave. Her plane
wasn't until ten that morning and here it was four-thirty
and she hadn't slept at all. By this time she was crying
and had made herself a nervous wreck thinking about
flying home alone. The calmness she had experienced
had left her. Catherine's bedroom door was slightly ajar
and Joanna couldn't stand the fear any longer.

Gently she knocked on the door and opened it.
Catherine was sound asleep, snoring lightly. Joanna
walked over to the side of the bed and put her hand on
Catherine's shoulder. "Ca – Ca, wake up."

Catherine, waking, seeing Joanna sitting on her bed,
asked, "What's wrong? Are you all right?"

"No," and cried even more now, embarrassed after
waking her.

"What's wrong?" as Catherine sat up and put her
arm around Joanna.

"I can't fly, my fears are back. I'm scared. I don't
want to go back to that house."

Catherine slid over and pulled Joanna next to her.
Joanna lay in Catherine's arms while Catherine spoke
to her softly, "it'll be all right – I promise. Try to get
some sleep." Joanna was asleep in minutes, drained,
and time stopped.

***

When Joanna woke, Catherine wasn't in bed and
the door was closed. She looked at the clock on the
nightstand. It was eleven forty-five. She'd missed her
flight and fear crept in once more. "Ca?" she called.
"Ca, where are you?"

The bedroom door opened, "I'm right here.

Catherine answered. "I've been sitting on the couch. I haven't left – calm down. I've called the airlines and canceled your flight. We're taking the four-thirty afternoon flight today."

"We are?"

"Yes, I'm going back with you."

Joanna looked at her questioning, "Why are you going with me?"

"I have some business to go over and figured I needed to see snow," she said laughing.

"Are you sure?" Joanna was surprised at the answer yet happy she didn't have to fly back home alone and the thought of Catherine being with her just a little while longer was enough.

"We have to be at the airport by three this afternoon. Maybe you should get up and eat something. Why don't you take a shower and I'll make breakfast."

"All right. Thank you Ca – for last night. Sorry I was such an infant."

"Don't think about it, it's over," and Catherine left for the kitchen.

In the shower Joanna thought again of last night, how comfortable she'd felt in Catherine's arms, how safe and secure.

***

On the plane, Joanna talked of the fun she'd had with Catherine and how she had looked forward to every day there with her. How she had learned to relax, except for last night.

After they got Joanna's luggage, they walked over to a van Catherine had called for, to take them back to Long Island, along with other passengers headed in the same direction. The driver took Joanna's luggage and put it in the back of the van. Ready to get in Catherine pulled her arm from behind, "I want to talk to you," she said.

They stepped back a few yards out of passenger traffic.

"I'm not going with you. The van is for you. I'm taking the next flight back to West Palm Beach."

Joanna froze.

"Now don't say anything and get on the van." Catherine directed.

"Oh, Ca, I thought you were staying."

"No, I've got my newspaper and my plane will be leaving shortly, so I'm going to say goodbye for now."

Joanna looked in Catherine's eyes, trying to smile but finding it hard coming and only said, "Goodbye – Ca."

Joanna hugged Catherine then watched her walk away with a newspaper under her arm, back to the terminal. Somewhere in a distance she heard the driver saying, "Miss, we're ready to go. I have a time schedule to keep." She caught the last glimpse of Catherine through a glass door rounding a corner in the building, and she was gone.

***

The trip was cold, seated in the back of the van. On board were businessmen who were tired and smelled of booze, bringing up memories of Ed. She stared out the window dreaming of Catherine on a plane somewhere above her, looking out another window, and she knew they were still connected. The trip home was long, dropping off passengers. She was the last to be delivered.

"I need to run in and get money from my husband," she told the driver.

"It's been paid for," he said. "Have a good night," and he pulled away half an hour to midnight.

Walking up the brick walkway, tired and lonely, she could see the house was dark except for the den light where Ed would be sleeping in his chair. She startled him when she dropped one of the cases on the floor.

"You're finally home. I expected you earlier." She'd forgotten she had called him, telling him of the regular flight time arrival.

"Oh – the plane had engine trouble and left late." Joanna didn't want to go into the bout of fears she had early this morning. She didn't want to go into anything with him and just asked how the kids were.

Once upstairs she used the bedroom phone to call Catherine and leave a message on her machine. Hearing the phone ring twice and then, "Hello?"

Surprised, Joanna said, "Ca? You're home? How did you get to Florida so fast?"

Catherine laughed saying, "I guess you can blame the traffic on the Long Island Expressway." Catherine had traveled over a thousand miles and Joanna less than sixty. They talked briefly, Joanna thanking her for the van trip and how much she missed her already, thanked her for a beautiful vacation and said goodnight.

***

Joanna was back home in the cold, not only because of the weather but also in her emotions. It had been fantastic to get away from the pressures of the house for a while. She had missed the children and there was a lot to do before Christmas. She needed to go shopping and do household chores before the holidays. She'd asked

Maria to go shopping with her because her fears had returned almost as soon as she'd walked in the door that night. She wanted to be in Florida with Catherine, relaxed.

***

At home Christmas Eve, Maria and John had come for dinner, when the phone rang and Joanna got up to answer it.

"Merry Christmas," a voice said.

"Hi, Merry Christmas to you, also." It was a surprise call from Catherine.

"I just wanted to tell you I'm in Texas on my way to California to visit Anne's sister, but wanted to wish you and your family a Merry Christmas."

"Mom and John are here for dinner then we're going to Midnight-mass. If I make it."

"Well, say a prayer for me. I gotta run now, my connecting flight is leaving soon. I wanted to let you know where I would be."

"Thanks Ca. Thanks for calling. Have a Merry Christmas and a safe trip," and she hung up.

After mass and home in bed at two in the morning, Joanna thought of Catherine's call, 'How nice of her to think of me.' And closed her eyes.

***

Christmas came the next day, and all Joanna wanted was to be with Catherine in Florida by the ocean, but Catherine wasn't there. The children had friends over, then went to their friends' houses. Ed was with her in body but not in mind or spirit. He was somewhere else in his mind, just as she.

***

Joanna found it easier to do the normal household

chores now, with Catherine in her mind and memories of her Florida trip. It was so good not to have the fears there all the time.

Catherine called when she got back to Florida the next week and a New Year had started. Joanna was happy to hear that voice once more. Catherine told Joanna she wouldn't want to live in California because of the oil rigs in the ocean and the crazy drivers. She enjoyed her visit with Anne's sister. Joanna chatted about Christmas with Ed and the children and what she'd been doing to keep busy. She didn't mention most of her days were spent thinking of her.

"Think about coming down for a visit with Hope when school is out for spring recess, Catherine said.

"I will, but I'll have to ask Ed first."

"I'll call you every Monday and Thursday in the afternoon at two-thirty. If you can I'd appreciate if you went to the apartment and picked up the mail. I'll go over it with you when I call, Okay?"

"Yes, I'll do that."

"If you want to call me, call collect. All right?" and she hung up. Joanna never answering the question, because she knew she always wanted to call Catherine.

***

In January, Joanna was at Catherine's picking up the mail and watering plants when she heard a call come in over the answering machine from a property broker. The broker said he had found a buyer for Catherine's property on the Island and for her to contact him immediately. When Joanna called Catherine to tell her of the broker, she told Joanna to get back with the broker to see what the offer was on the property and tell him that she had permission to discuss it with him.

"Ca, I'm not crazy about doing this. I don't know anything about selling property."

"Well, just think if you sell it, you can make a commission." She could see Catherine smiling on the other end.

"I don't want anything. Are you sure you want me to do this?"

"Yes, I've had it for years. It's a barren piece of land that I keep paying taxes on."

"Okay, I'll call him, but I'd rather you spoke with him."

"I will eventually. I just want you to do the preliminaries."

Joanna hung up and called the broker to give him Catherine's message, then called her back to say what he had offered.

"Call him back and tell him to sell it. I'll contact him tomorrow." Catherine said. Joanna hung up and followed her directions.

CHANGE

AT HOME the arguing continued with Ed. Matthew gave her more trouble than she could handle. He paid no attention to her when she asked him to throw the garbage out one day.

"Matthew, don't walk away from me," she said.

She went after him before he got to the side entrance. "Where do you think you're going?"

"Leave me alone," was his answer.

"You go out with your friends all night and sleep all day. I won't have this any more, you hear me? Get a job, or go to college, otherwise your clothes are going to be on the front lawn. You got that?"

Upset, she reached up to slap him across the face. He grabbed her arms and held them. Joanna became enraged, not able to move and yelled, "Let me go!"

He grinned at her. She couldn't move. Over night he was stronger and taller. Finally she cried, realizing she was afraid of her own son.

Letting go he walked out the door and she sat at the kitchen table not believing what had just transpired. This was her little friend. What had he become?

***

February twentieth, Hope's school vacation and a possible trip to Florida couldn't come fast enough.

"Hope, how would you like to go to Florida for your school vacation?"

"Really Mom? We're going to visit Catherine?"

"Yes, but it depends on what your father says. Are you sure you want to go?"

"Yeah, I can't wait."

Joanna spoke with Ed and he said it was all right to go. Joanna figured this might be a good time for Ed and Matthew to spend time together. Maybe Ed could talk some sense into their son.

Monday Joanna called Catherine, "Hi Ca. Well, we're coming to visit you."

"That's great. I can't wait to see you both. How is Hope? Does she want to come?"

"Are you kidding? She's told every kid on the block and walking around with a big grin on her face, the size of a Cheshire cat. We're taking the eight o'clock flight Thursday morning. Is that okay?"

"Sure. I'll pick you up at the airport. Is everything else all right up there?"

"Yes, believe it or not, Ed didn't give me a hard time. I'm looking forward to that beautiful ocean and warm weather. I'm going to say goodbye for now. I have clothes to wash and shopping to do. I'll talk to you later."

"Say hello to Hope for me."

"I will, bye for now."

Joanna had heard the anticipation in Catherine's voice, wondering if Catherine heard it in hers.

Joanna and Hope were packing the day before, and it seemed like a day's work.

"Let's use the same tops so we won't have to carry so much luggage," she told her daughter.

"Really, Mom, you're going to let me wear your tops?"

"Yes. You finish picking out the tops you want and I'm going downstairs to call the taxi to pick us up tomorrow."

Hope went to bed early saying she wanted to get a good nights sleep, for tomorrow's trip and Joanna lay there with the vision of her sitting on the balcony watching the ocean.

***

In the morning Ed went to work and Matthew had stayed at a friend's house. Hope and Joanna ate breakfast, talking about their trip, soon to be on their way. Showered and dressed after breakfast, Joanna took the luggage downstairs to wait by the door, ready to go while Hope played with the right hairstyle to travel in.

While waiting for the cab, Joanna started to have second thoughts. She tried to push them out of her mind and think only of Catherine and beautiful Florida.

Now she sat thinking of flying alone, having a panic attack.

Her heart began racing and she started to feel dizzy. 'Oh no, not now please,' she thought

She felt stuck to the point she couldn't move – the feeling her feet were in cement, like years ago. In a fearful moment, she reached for the phone.

Then hung it up, desperately trying to clear her mind of thoughts of terror.

The third time she picked up the phone and spoke.

"This is Mrs. Shaker. Will you please cancel my cab to Laguardia Airport for this morning."

"Mrs. Shaker, the driver's on his way and should be there shortly."

"I'm sorry, I have to cancel because of illness. If there's a problem with the bill, I'll pay for it. I'm sorry," and she hung up.

Hearing her own voice, and falling back to fears, she began to cry, sitting at the desk. She cried uncontrollably and was mad at the same time. She couldn't do anything. The demons returned and she had given in to them once more.

Hope, hearing her crying came and put her arm around her, "What's wrong, Mom?"

"Oh – Hope I'm sorry but I can't go to Florida."

"Why?"

"I can't get on the plane alone."

"You won't be alone Mom, I will be with you," she pleaded.

Hope's words hit home, but the fear was greater and older.

Hope cried when she saw Joanna wasn't going to change her mind and went upstairs to her room. Composing herself, Joanna called the travel agent to cancel, then called Ed, and told him they weren't going.

Joanna dreaded the call to Catherine even more and as she heard herself say she wasn't going she started to cry, knowing then – it was true.

"I'm sorry – I'm so sorry." She wanted to see Catherine so badly but not badly enough to face the fear.

"It's okay, try to calm down. I know your having a bad time of it. Get some rest and I'll call you later," and Catherine hung up.

Joanna had a feeling of relief from the fear, but had let someone down she had come to love, including her own daughter. She hadn't gotten anywhere with her fears and was back to square one. Once again she was sixteen years old and afraid of dying.

Going to her bedroom, Joanna saw Hope lying on the bed in her room, "I'm sorry Hope, truly I am."

"It's okay, Mom" and Hope pulled the covers over her head.

She had grown up with a mother who was afraid of everything and she knew nothing she could say or do could change that. Joanna saw herself slithering onto the bed, like a snake. Her nerves had upset her body, causing diarrhea and nausea, and now she felt like a wet, limp rag. As she lay there, she thought of all she was missing in life, how the fear grips and stops her dead in her tracks. She might as well be in prison and fell asleep sobbing.

The phone woke her at four-thirty that afternoon.

"Do you still want to come down?" asked Catherine.

"Yes, but I can't."

"If I came up to get you both, would you fly then?"

"No, don't be crazy. You can't do that. It doesn't make sense to come up and get us and fly back, like you did when you flew me up last time," Joanna said, feeling the discomfort.

"I'll be up tomorrow and we're taking the plane back in the evening, so keep your bags packed," Catherine insisted.

"Okay," was all Joanna said. She knew when Catherine got something in her head it was impossible to change it. Almost like Joanna and her fears not changing.

Joanna knew now there was hope after all, and went

to tell her daughter. All Hope said was, "I'll believe it when I see it," and turned to face the wall.

***

Catherine came the next day in a black limousine and picked up Hope and Joanna and they were off to the airport. Catherine never gave Joanna time to think. They boarded the plane and were off to Florida. Once in the air, Joanna was nervous but Hope changed her thoughts. Hope had been quiet on the trip and Joanna asked, "Are you all right?" Hope looked at Joanna with glassy, red eyes.

"I don't feel well. My throat and ear is hurting."

Joanna felt her forehead and it was warm, her face getting redder by the second. She had a fever.

"Why didn't you tell me you weren't feeling well before we left?" asked Joanna.

"Because you wouldn't have gone then."

"You're right about that."

Two and one-half hours later they landed and were in Catherine's car, headed to the condo. Joanna had told Catherine, Hope was ill, and they stopped at a drugstore to pick up medicine for gargling and children's aspirin. Catherine and Joanna talked on the way to the condo while Hope rested on the back seat. Joanna felt badly but at least Hope was out of the cold weather and she could breathe the ocean air. This alone would make her daughter feel better.

Arriving at the condo Hope went straight to bed after an aspirin and orange juice. Catherine and Joanna opened a bag of cookies and made coffee then went out on the balcony.

The next day Hope wasn't any better, so they went

to Catherine's doctor. The doctor said she had strep throat, with an ear infection and prescribed eardrops and a prescription for antibiotics.

Hope ill the whole week, Joanna made chicken soup and rubbed her down with alcohol, to keep the fever down. Catherine and Joanna played gin rummy on the balcony after she came home from playing golf. Hope ventured out when she was feeling up to it, sat with them a minute then said, "you two make too much noise. I'm going back to bed."

By the fifth day she was feeling better and was to be back home in three days. Joanna called Ed, "I'd like to keep her out of school another week. She hasn't had any vacation being sick."

"Okay, I'll call the school and let them know." He said.

Hope's grades were good and Joanna would make it a teaching vacation.

They went to the zoo and Catherine drove through a safari with the animals outside and with them in the cage. Joanna dropped to the floor of the car, seeing ostriches taller than the car and rhinos the size of the whole car. Catherine and Hope laughed to their hearts' content. They were making fun of her, but it was in a loving way, so she went along with it. Hope and Joanna played on the beach, while Catherine golfed with her friends. They went shopping and, just like a daughter would, she wanted Joanna to buy everything she picked off the clothing rack. Joanna told Hope she didn't have money to spend, and told her she would buy her one item. Joanna thought for the first time, maybe Hope realized that money didn't grow on trees.

One day on the beach just the two of them Hope

said, "Mom, you're so different down here. You're happy."

"Yes, I am happy. I'm not fighting with your brother or your father."

Joanna was with Catherine and Hope, the two people who loved her dearly and away from the uneasiness of the other household. There was nothing to be sad about.

They lay on the floor one evening 'fighting', playing pick-up sticks.

"You moved the stick." Hope said.

"No, I didn't," says Catherine.

This was the only kind of arguing Joanna wanted to hear.

Catherine took Hope and Joanna to play golf and all they did was laugh. Catherine was good to Hope and she was appreciative of Catherine. Joanna could see the love that had grown between them, and it made her happy.

The last day before Hope and Joanna were to leave, Catherine wanted to make dinner. Catherine knew how to boil water and cook a hamburger or use the microwave for breakfast but that was it. Joanna and Hope weren't allowed in the kitchen and went to the beach for a walk, then to the pool for a swim. When they came back, Joanna peeped in the kitchen door and saw red spots all over the white counter and cabinets. Catherine told Joanna she was making borscht soup, which neither Joanna nor Hope had ever had. Hope and Joanna laughed at the kitchen's mess and said, "here she is, the happy little homemaker at her best." Joanna retrieved the camera and took pictures of Catherine surrounded in red spots. Catherine enlightened Hope and Joanna that night with borscht, which they ate and loved. Daughter and mother cleaned the kitchen because Catherine had cooked; they laughed and wondered how one person could make such a mess.

That night Catherine said she had business up north and was flying back with them.

***

Back home hadn't changed. Ed and Joanna argued constantly.

The marriage had never been a good one, but now it was worse. She hated it and him and wanted out. In a way, she blamed Ed for everything, even her fears, and had the feeling he, himself wanted out of the marriage, but didn't have the nerve or was sticking to his Catholic upbringing. He was seldom home between work, racquetball and tennis and when home, it was a glass of vodka and ice, dinner, then to sleep in his chair. Joanna went out those nights with Rosie to bingo.

Ed and Joanna never had a true partnership. They were two people who lived under the same roof. He wanted a wife who'd stay at home and take care of the house and children. So this is what she did, but always in the back of her mind, was the thought that she wished she had followed her wishes and dreams. She should have left long before, but the fears kept her from doing so. Joanna stayed in a relationship she hated, and was sure Ed did too. Being Catholics they followed their laws of no divorce.

Almost every year she'd say to Ed, "I want a divorce."

And he'd say, "Then go get one."

And she'd think, 'how could I live?'

As the years went by, the hurt carved deeper into her and him, and she was afraid of leaving. Her thoughts for years had been of dying. Little did she know then she was *already* dead – inside.

***

In a couple of weeks, Joanna was back in Florida with Catherine, trying again to relax, walking the beach day after day, looking and hoping for an answer.

She called home and spoke with Hope and Ed. Matthew was nowhere to be found.

Ed asked after her being away three weeks, "are you ever coming home?"

She wanted to say 'no' but knew she had to go back. He had to be having a heck of a time taking the kids out to eat or Hope was driving him nuts cooking. Lord knows how he hated spending money, especially if he had a wife who could cook.

Catherine was returning to Long Island in the beginning of March, her four-month rental up. The last night they sat on the balcony talking and looking at the beauty of the ocean one last time.

Joanna spoke, "I hate to go back. I miss the kids and Mom, but I can't stand living with Ed. I know my fears will come back if I go back there. I married him because of my father. I can't go back."

Listening to Joanna go on about her hurting marriage, Catherine offered.

"I have a golf friend, who is a lawyer, would you like to speak with him?"

"God – I don't know. I'd like to leave Ed, but I have no idea how I would live."

"Think about my suggestion. I'll give you his number and if you feel you want to talk to him, tell him you're a friend of mine. We better get some sleep if we're leaving early tomorrow."

***

Driving back to the Island, stopping along the way to play golf and enjoy the spring months in the southern states. They played a course in Virginia where Catherine played years ago and she showed Joanna where she went to school at the College of William and Mary. She took Joanna to Williamsburg, the town where she spent her college years. It was history, much better than reading a book, Joanna thought. How lucky Catherine was to have parents to send her to this wonderful school. Catherine showed her where she fell off the roof one night, coming in after hours, drunk and thought it was funny.

Joanna hated Catherine spending money on her and again was embarrassed not having any. She had had the money Catherine gave her from the property sale and money Maria had sent for her birthday, but that was gone.

Catherine dropped Joanna off at home and Hope came running out to welcome her, asking if Catherine could come in for dinner. Catherine thanked Hope and said she was tired and pulled out of the driveway, waving goodbye. Joanna waved back and a feeling of hopelessness came on her. Hope and Joanna walked up the brick walkway and when inside Joanna saw Maria, and John, whom she'd missed. Matthew was not there and she didn't know where he was and didn't want to bring up the subject. Ed had sent out for food and everyone was eating. Laying her luggage in the foyer and sitting down, she told Maria and John about the trip and how they would love to live in Florida, with Hope

135

backing her up. When Maria and John left, Joanna cleaned the kitchen asking Hope to get ready for bed and school the next day. Ed was already in his chair with his glass of vodka.

She offered to tell him of her trip and the fun she'd had, but she could see he wasn't interested, and changed the subject to Matthew. "How is Matthew doing? Is he working yet?"

"He's fine," He wasn't a man big on words.

Joanna then said goodnight and went to bed. She didn't want to think of the place in which she was. She wanted only to dream of the place she'd been.

***

As the days and weeks passed, Joanna stayed at home and tried to live her reality family life as much as possible, even though at times it was hard to endure.

Matthew had gotten a ferret as a pet and she'd told him he would have to keep it in the garage. Joanna explained it shouldn't be inside the house, because of the dog and cat and ferrets could become rabid and a danger to the other pets. She found it in his room one day and was upset he hadn't listened to her again. At the dinner table that night, while they were arguing over the ferret, Ed's response to Matthew was, "keep it in the house, maybe *she'll* leave."

This statement hurt, because he had said it in front of the kids. Joanna had reached the point where the only place she had to go for refuge was Catherine's, and began to do this often.

Catherine had patience and understanding. Why should she stay with Ed, to be put down?

***

Ed was home from work due to a late March snow

storm and Joanna said, "Ed, do you think we could talk?"

"Sure I need to go and check the business. Why don't you come along for the ride," he said.

They drove along slippery roads with brown snow left over from the last storm. At least the new snow falling made it cleaner looking. There was silence in the car all you could hear the crunching underneath the wheels.

Once there they had to trudge up the walkway to the front door. Ed unlocked the door, ushered her in, and said, "I'm going to check the back rooms, why don't you wait in my office."

Joanna obeyed and walked down the hallway to his office feeling her stomach churn as she remembered the day he moved into this building. He'd come a long way from a basement office, now having over a hundred employed in the assembly area and others in offices throughout the country. She got a glass of cold water from the cooler and sat down in one of the two maroon leather chairs opposite the large mahogany desk. She remembered the day he bought his office chair facing her now. "Do you like it?" he had said. "Yes," very much she had said back then. She thought he'd deserved this wide, black leather chair that was opposite her now. Behind the chair was a long table full of brochures and booklets to give clients. Years ago there were only a few which she stuffed in to envelopes for potential clients. It seemed ages ago when he asked her, "should I go into business?"

And she had said, "Yes, do it now, or you never will."

He broke her past thoughts coming in the room. He

took his coat off, Joanna keeping hers on still feeling chilled.

"So what's up?" he said, putting his feet up on the desk.

She stammered a little then started. "I did a lot of thinking walking the beach in Florida, and I think we need to separate. I was happy in Florida and know this is not right for you or me to continue as we are."

He sat staring at her, not saying a word. But yet not having a surprised look.

"But, I'm not going anywhere if you won't give me any money."

Then he spoke. "How much do you want?"

"I thought five hundred a month would help."

"I can't give you five. I can give you two fifty and if things get better with the business, I can increase it."

Joanna breathed a sigh of relief and felt he did also. He wasn't giving her an argument, but then he never did years ago, either. They started to talk like human beings instead of animals.

"I'm probably going to stay at Catherine's, then maybe go to Florida. I'm not sure yet." Knowing he would never leave 'his house with his roof and his foundation'. After all she had heard this enough times, how she had everything, because he had worked for it.

When they left the business that day Joanna felt a sense of pride in herself she had never felt with Ed. She felt she was able to do something on her own and didn't need his okay.

***

She stayed with Ed at the house but knew she would leave one day, not saying anything yet to the children. She went to Catherine's friend, the lawyer, and he advised her to stay in the house. He told her, "if you leave, it would be abandonment."

Joanna stayed in the house, unhappy with Ed, and the arguing continued. She and Ed continued to have parties even though the air was filled with hostility whenever they were together. Joanna told Maria of the possible separation.

***

At one of Ed's family reunions, Joanna prepared the food and cleaned the house, playing the dutiful wife she'd always been. While doing dishes and watching everyone in the backyard drinking and playing, she couldn't play the false roll any more. She was unhappy and Ed just carried on like nothing was wrong. Maybe she should have drunk as he did, to blend into the walls. Getting angrier by the second, watching them outside, she called Catherine.

"Hello?" Catherine answered.

"Hi, Ca. Are you watching the golf tournament?" Women's golf was on TV.

"Yes, I am. Are you coming over to watch it?"

Joanna thought, 'I didn't even have to ask her, she already knew.'

"I'd like to, if I can get out of here. Ed's throwing one of his family get-togethers and I've just about had it by now. I'll be over in awhile. Don't worry about dinner. I have lots of leftovers and I'll bring them. See you later."

"Okay then. I'll see you in awhile." And Catherine hung up

Joanna knew she couldn't approach Ed now with his family there, besides it would create a scene. She planned to leave for a few hours, watch golf with

Catherine to get a break and then come back. Sweating from the August heat, she took a shower and dressed, collecting some barbecue chicken and lasagna for Catherine and herself. She hadn't gotten a chance to eat. Joanna was headed to the car when Ed met her at the side of the house.

"Where you going?" he said in his drunken tone, with eyes half shut.

"I'm going to Catherine's to watch the golf tournament."

"You are – are you? Well, maybe you should leave, right now," slurring the words out, but enough so that Joanna understood them.

She stopped in her tracks and thought a moment, staring at him. She saw *he* did mean what *he* was saying through his half-closed eyelids. 'Leave right now.'

"Okay." And she walked to her – not really – *his* company car.

Driving, it took a few minutes to set in, but then she realized what she had said and tears stayed in her eyes most of the way to Catherine's. Finally knowing it *was* time to leave the marriage. He'd made the decision for her and she was glad.

Now the fear was finally going to be faced. Joanna *had* to leave.

***

She called Hope in the morning to say she had spent the night at Catherine's, and would see her after school. Then Joanna called the lawyer to tell him what Ed had said, that she couldn't live with him anymore, "Please serve him with the papers." She said. Everything had been drawn up and she had been holding up the process, telling the lawyer, not yet. But now it *was* time.

A few hours later Ed called and asked to speak to Joanna.

"Hey, I was served with separation papers today." He said.

"Yeah, I told you I was going through with it. I'll be here if you need to speak with me and I suggest you get a lawyer also." Joanna replied with such strength, it surprised her as she hung up.

***

When Joanna went to Catherine's that day, she never returned home to sleep in the house. Joanna told her daughter what she had decided and Hope didn't seem upset over the idea. From then on, when Hope came home from school, Joanna was there waiting for her, or she'd pick her up from school to go to Catherine's, where Hope would do her homework and then swim in the community pool. Joanna cooked at Catherine's, then took the meals home, so Ed and the kids would have dinner, or she stayed home with Hope and cooked, but left before Ed arrived home. It was dreadful going back and forth, for she didn't know where she belonged, but she knew where she was loved, welcomed and understood.

***

Joanna used the guest bathroom at Catherine's and when she opened the medicine cabinet every morning, she read the words taped to the inside, in Catherine's handwriting. 'Don't look forward to what might happen tomorrow, the same everlasting Father who cares for you today will care for you tomorrow and every day. He will give you the strength to bear whatever it is.'

141

One day there was a word taped to her mirror, 'Proboscis'. Joanna approached Catherine with both pieces of paper.

"Ca, thank you for leaving the prayer inside the cabinet."

"You're welcome. I figured you needed reassurance that you're always looked after."

"But what's this one?" showing Catherine the large word beginning with a 'P' which she couldn't even pronounce.

"You said you wanted to increase your vocabulary. What better way to do it than learning a word a week."

"Well, you're right. I did say that. How do you pronounce it and what does it mean?" Joanna asked.

"See the dictionary on the coffee table?" which Catherine pointed to. "Look it up and tell me what you can about the word."

Next, they were seated side by side on the love seat, while Joanna tried to sound out the word, "It sounds like, "Pro boss kiss," then read its meaning. "It means snout, elephant's trunk, that's it. When the heck am I going to use that?"

Catherine, laughing, pronounced it the right way, "You never know, maybe you'll meet someone with a large nose."

Every week there after Joanna found a new word and every morning she read the prayer.

***

Joanna spent time with her mother, trying to explain the reasons she and Ed were separating. Ed had been like a son to Maria, even before their marriage. He'd grown up with the family, playing with Joanna's brother, Marc, and eating in their home. Maria had watched him grow like a member of her own family and this separation was hard for her to understand or accept, but she knew her daughter was unhappy.

That was the summer of 1985.

FAITH

CATHERINE TOLD Joanna she could continue living with her in the condo, even though Joanna thought Catherine felt she was contributing to the break up of a family. Joanna explained this was not true, that Ed and she had a bad marriage from day one.

Joanna's been there since the end of August and now it's September, time for the ladies club championship. Joanna has played her matches and won. Now her opponent is Catherine for the Championship. This will be their last tournament at the club where they had met. For Catherine, she's played it since she was a young woman, and for Joanna, it's been over five years.

Leaving the apartment that morning for the course, there is sadness on the drive to the club. Joanna thinks, 'this is really something. I'm playing against the woman who was the best golfer of all time on the Island.'

Keeping it light, Joanna reminds Catherine, "So you thought there wasn't enough competition for you, hu?"

"That's what I thought but now I know different." Catherine replied.

Once there, golfers and workers wished them luck,

as Joanna, Catherine and the rules person headed for the first tee.

"Good luck, Joanna."

"Good luck to you, also," Joanna says shaking Catherine's hand.

Joanna called heads, when the rules person tossed the coin in the air, and won the honor of going first. Her first drive was off to the right in the rough and Catherine followed with a long drive right down the middle of the fairway.

The first eighteen holes went back and forth, of one up or one down for each of them. The score was tied when they stopped for lunch downstairs in the women's locker room. Catherine ordered her usual, coke and tuna sandwich. Joanna ordered a glass of milk and a turkey sandwich.

Waiting for their food at a round table in the corner Joanna asked, "Ca, it's turning into some match, don't you think?"

"Yes, sure is. Thank God the weather is with us and it isn't raining."

"Oh, by the way, have you noticed I have on Anne's shoes for luck?" Joanna grinning.

Catherine laughs, and Joanna hears, "Yes, I did notice."

Catherine was a good competitor like Rosie, with the same feelings of wanting to win. There was no other way – they both loved the game.

The second eighteen Catherine wins three holes in a row, leaving Joanna minus three by the sixth hole. Joanna tries hard to get her head together and think golf and not who she's playing against. She needs to remember she's playing against the course, only.

Heading into the last nine, it finally comes together; she's remembering the tips Catherine's taught her and Joanna gains back three holes and ties the match. On the fifteenth hole, a par three, Joanna has the honors, and hits the ball onto the green. Catherine also hits her ball on the green. They par the hole and the match stays tied.

The sixteenth, a par four, has members standing behind the green. It seems like the members have come out of the woodwork. People are all over the place in golf carts and standing. There are more people here than Joanna has ever known belonged to the club. They are three deep in spots down both sides of the fairway, standing arm and arm. Seeing so many people Joanna's thoughts turned negative to fear. 'I'm not going to make it to the end of the match. I'm going to pass out, right here and now,' she thinks. Catherine must have picked up on Joanna's feelings and looks her way with a grin and winks. She has been through this many times with Anne, years ago. Joanna also with Rosie, but this is more people than she can handle. Catherine's wink settles Joanna down. She thinks of the prayer inside her bathroom cabinet and she should be enjoying this match with her friend and all she's been through at the club. This is a part of history in their lives, and Joanna wants to remember it like this, as a good memory, not a fearful one. She pulls her golf cap down just above her eyebrows, this way she can see only the spectator's feet and not their faces. It works. She's calmed down and can continue the competition with her friend.

Hitting her drive to the right by a tree, she pitch's the ball out for a clear shot to the green. Catherine drives down the middle, where she's been all day, then hits her next shot on the green. Joanna hits her third shot on the green and two putts for a bogey five. Catherine is on the green in two and two putts for a par, and wins the hole. Joanna is minus one.

The seventeenth hole is a short seventy-five yard par three, a beautiful hole but brutal – tee and green even with the eye and a ditch below you don't want to land in, plus two deep sand traps in front of the green and one behind. Joanna knows she needs to put the ball on the green to have any chance at going on to the eighteenth hole. Catherine hits first, since she'd won the last hole and lands on the green. The crowd cheers and Joanna says, "nice shot."

The pressure is terrible, but beautiful – if that makes any sense. Joanna gets the impression the older members are rooting for Catherine. This is fine, because Joanna knows how much she's loved by them. Joanna takes a nine iron from her bag, swings the club and watches the ball climb high into the sky. It's going to make the green, when out of nowhere a wind comes up and brings it straight down, in the front sand trap. Her anticipation goes from ecstatic to disappointed. She'd forgotten the tip Catherine had taught her; 'if there is wind take more club.' There had been wind with the day's play, but she couldn't feel it standing on the tee surrounded by tall pine trees. Walking down the deep gully, cursing herself for not taking more club. She walks up to the front trap. Feeling her stomach tighten, she knows this is one of the hardest shots in golf. She sees the top of the flag and needs to lift the ball out of the sand quick and high, in order not to catch the embankment. With a sand wedge, she swings and sand flies back in her face and eyes not seeing the ball pop out. When she climbs out of the trap and walks up to the green, she sees she's hit it too far. It's landed in the back trap. Thinking, 'One shot down', as she passes Catherine's ball sitting ten feet from the hole. Joanna hits her third shot, leaving it five feet from the hole and the crowd applauds. Catherine putts, riming the cup, leaving it an inch or two from the hole and Joanna hears the crowd roar. Now Joanna's turn for her fourth shot sees Catherine's inches away for her third. 'Is Catherine going to miss it?' Joanna thinks.

Walking to her ball, Joanna picks up Catherine's ball and decides to give Catherine the hole and the match. She then reaches her hand out saying, "Congratulations Champ. Great match."

Catherine smiles at Joanna and shakes her hand, "It *was* a good match, you played a great game." Joanna knows she tried her best, but couldn't beat Catherine. She's one of the Old Guarde and they know all the shots, but at least she took her to the thirty-fifth hole. The crowd's cheers are loud with whistles in the background.

The folks in the gallery surround Catherine shaking her hand and hugging her, "We're glad you're back, Champ." They approach Joanna, congratulating her, "Job well done." Only a few friends know they're not coming back for next year's Championship.

Catherine gave Joanna a gold pen and pencil set for being runner-up and Joanna gave Catherine the dozen roses in the silver cup that had both their names inscribed on it. Speeches were said, and all was done, now.

It was a beautiful day, celebrating in the clubhouse with old friends and sad with good-byes in their minds.

That night they sat at the dining room table going over golf shots of the day's play. It was a day never to be forgotten for the rest of their lives.

***

Joanna told her family and friends that she was leaving for Florida. Joanna felt she was divorcing her friends along with her husband. She found this harder than telling Ed.

In November 1985 Joanna helped Catherine pack for the move to Florida. She laid everything out for Joanna to put in boxes, later to be sent down to them.

While washing dishes one evening, Joanna spotted a small figurine on the back of the sink splashboard. She picked it up and saw it was a little mouse, sitting up, holding a red raspberry. It was heavy, made of lead and painted gray-brown, with a white chest and neck. Its ears were straight up and its eyes were black beads, with a black beaded nose, standing about one inch high and one half inch wide. Turned sideways it looked as if it had been caught stealing the raspberry and was making its getaway. Joanna called Catherine and asked her where she had gotten it.

"Oh, that's Razzle-Dazzle. I picked him up near the train station at a gift shop years ago. He was so cute I had to have him."

"It has so much character. This has to go with us."

"Ca, how are we going to pack it? He's so tiny, we'll lose him. I'm wrapping him in tissue paper and putting him in my purse. He'll be first, going to our new home."

"Good idea. I wouldn't want to lose him after so many years."

Catherine was keeping the condo and renting it out to a friend. Keeping it they could come back in the summer. Joanna liked the idea, this way she'd be able to see her family.

***

Making dinner for Ed and the kids one afternoon after picking Hope up at school, Joanna started packing her clothes at the house. Hope came in the bedroom.

"Mom, you taking everything with you?"

"No, I'm just taking the things I'll use in Florida. Here, see if these jeans fit you," handing them to Hope. "Here are some blouses too. See if they fit you."

"Thanks, Mom, anything else?"

Pointing to a pile of clothes lying on the floor, "take a look over there. Anything you don't want is going in the garbage."

Hope went to her room to try on clothes and Joanna rummaged through the two large closets. She came across a dark brown wooden box covered with different colored stains on it. Opening it she saw her oils, two palette knifes, brushes, large and small, thick and thin bristles. There were tubes of every color and she ran her hand over them remembering the time she spent at the kitchen bay window, where the light was good. Upon closing it, she brought it to her chest and wrapped her arms around it, tears welling up. It had kept her sane along with the piano, the days stuck in the house with agoraphobia.

Hope came in, "these don't fit," handing some back to Joanna.

"Keep them and put them in your closet. You'll eventually grow into them. Hope, I want you to have this."

"Your paint kit?" Hope said, joy on her face.

"Yes, I want you to have it. Maybe one day you'll get as much happiness from it as it gave to me."

All Hope could say was, "thank you," for she knew, looking at her mother's face, how much it meant to her. They held each other, then Joanna went to the jewelry box on the dresser that Ed had given her when she was seventeen years old. Going through the jewelry, while Hope sat on the bed, Joanna tossed her necklaces and rings she would no longer wear. She wanted her past to be left to her daughter; the good things of her past that Hope's father had given his wife.

It was time for dinner to come out of the oven and she wanted to leave soon, before Ed came home. She had packed two suitcases, all she wanted to take with her.

While upstairs she kissed her daughter, "remember I love you very much."

"Yeah, I know Mom."

"If you decide you want to live with me in Florida you know it's all right with Catherine."

"I know Mom, but I want to stay in school here."

"Okay, if you change your mind let me know."

Hope nodded her head 'yes' and asked if she could go down the block to her girlfriend's house.

Once downstairs Joanna packed the car, then called Ed to ask if she could take the lamp her mom had given them. She was surprised when he said, "Yes." She asked if she could have the cookbook her mom had also given her and he said, "no," and the arguing started, so she let it go. He could have the cookbook and everything else. She wanted no part of this any more.

She feared Ed, not that he would hit her but she feared him like her father. Ed had a way of making her feel that she owed him for anything he had paid for in the marriage. Needless to say, he did pay for everything, since he was the one who worked while she stayed at home. He reminded her all the time that it was his roof over the house and his foundation the house sat on and was doing that now with the cookbook. Joanna was nothing more than the cook and homemaker, as many women her age were made to feel in the sixties and seventies. She felt she hated Ed's face. It wasn't Ed's face she hated, but what she had made it into all the years of trying to know him. She never got to know Ed's true self. He never let her know it.

Her lawyer tried to convince her that her time was worth something, and she was entitled to half of everything. But she was brainwashed to think otherwise, feeling inferior to men, thinking they were smarter, and knew what was best for her. She'd seen her mother treated this way by her father.

She was leaving after twenty-three years, with her clothes, her mother's lamp, and some pictures of the kids. Everything else was left behind. Maybe her fears were, too.

Before Joanna left, one day leaning over the kitchen counter facing each other, she talked to Matthew of what each of them were doing. Their relationship had gotten better since Joanna had left the house for Catherine's the day of the party. She told Matthew, "marry someone whose face you will love, because that's the face you're going to wake up to every morning."

Maybe one day Joanna would get back with her

children in a happier setting, instead of the constant fighting they'd been used to.

***

A few days later, on a Monday morning Joanna called Ed at work.

"I am leaving this morning and I just wanted you to know there are no hard feelings on my part. I wish you happiness and good health, Ed. We have known each other most of our lives and they weren't all bad times. I left the car in the driveway and I'm leaving the phone number on the desk, where you can reach me."

Ed couldn't have been nicer on the phone and Joanna's thoughts were, 'he too, had wanted this, and it was a long time coming.' For the first time they could breathe easier.

Joanna and Catherine left that day for the long drive. Joanna felt happy she didn't have any fears, but as they drove over the Verrazano Bridge off Long Island, she thought, 'What's the matter with you? You're leaving your family – children, husband, mother, brothers, and friends. Are you crazy?' She was leaving everything she'd ever known for forty-two years. She was leaving a life of country clubs and play, the good life, some thought. These were her thoughts, but she had a calmness within, that everything would work out for the best. She had faith what she was doing *was* the right thing. She felt God was directing her back to the center of her path, which she hadn't seen for many years. She would never forget that feeling of peace and calm. She was following her heart.

HAPPINESS

THE FIRST NIGHT they made it to Virginia with Catherine driving all the way. Joanna was not in the mood to talk and Catherine knew it. Joanna called her mother that evening, telling her she was all right but tired, she knew Maria would be worried. Joanna was exhausted after dinner and laid in bed while Catherine looked at the road map, planning the next day's travel. Joanna fell asleep before Catherine had turned out the light.

The next morning they checked out of the motel and were headed to a new life.

Catherine drove sixteen hours, arriving at Estuary Dunes on Wednesday, the day before Thanksgiving. She stopped by the Realtors to pick up the keys for the condo, then the store for Chinese food.

The condo was a two-story, known as a villa, connected to others and Joanna remembered seeing the complex when she visited Sea Trail. Catherine parked the car in a designated spot. Nervous, yet excited, Joanna carried the food while Catherine took a suitcase and clothes on hangers that were lying in the trunk. Joanna followed Catherine up the winding staircase to a double brown door. Catherine opened the door, flicking on the lights at the doorway. She stood aside and let Joanna enter first. Facing Joanna was a foyer leading into the galley kitchen, where she headed to lay the food and drinks. Catherine followed, putting the suitcase on the floor and draping the clothes over it.

Joanna could see into the dining room and living room, then out to the Estuary through the sliding glass doors. She stood in amazement at the view before her. She saw water like a river flowing, with overhanging trees – mangroves, Catherine called them.

Catherine stood in the foyer watching Joanna then broke the silence, "well, how do you like it?"

Joanna, at a loss for words, turned to Catherine with tears in her eyes and said, "thank you Ca. It beautiful." Knowing this was not a vacation but for the rest of her life.

"Let me hang these clothes in the closet and I'll give you the royal tour." Catherine had seen the condo before, when a golfer friend had lived there for six months.

They walked through the archway, facing them was a bathroom, a walk-in closet and a large bedroom done in colors of light rose tones and dark maroon. "This is the master bedroom. It overlooks the river, as the living room." Catherine led Joanna outside to the wrap-around balcony that led to a screened porch off the breakfast nook, then back into the kitchen.

"Do you like the kitchen?" asked Catherine.

"Oh yes, it's great for cooking. Turn three feet and you have everything at your hands. It's beautiful, what can I say. It's all beautiful."

Catherine led her back to the foyer. Facing them

now was a bathroom and to the left was a bedroom with twin beds, done in colors of dark green throw pillows, with pale green spreads. The furniture was white wicker, a chest, long dresser and between the beds a nightstand.

"This is your room. I hope you like it."

"Yes, the colors are light and airy – good for my soul."

"See", pointing to the front window, "if you look out you can see the golf course."

"Yeah, I see. I hope the golf balls don't come through the windows." Three double hung windows in this room and cream colored blinds and cream carpet throughout the condo, except for the kitchen and foyer, which had large, white square ceramic tile.

"This is prettier than Sea Trail. It's more like a home." Joanna had the feeling within these walls; it would be a real home.

Joanna's dreams of inner peace and contentment had come true. There would no longer be the fear of monsters raising their ugly heads.

After the tour, they ran downstairs to get the rest of the luggage. The excitement in Joanna was beyond words, as she hung her clothes in her bedroom closet. When they were done putting plants on the balcony brought down from the north, they sat and had a drink, watching the rippling river.

Later, sitting at the dining room table, Joanna still couldn't tell Catherine in words how happy she was. They were both relieved the trip was over, and the recent memories of leaving Ed, could be put aside, at least for a while. Joanna slept well that night, thanking God for keeping her safe and asking Him to bless her family up north and her other family here under this roof.

***

The next day, Thanksgiving, Joanna was surprised to find the grocery stores open half a day. They bought a small turkey breast, some vegetables and a pumpkin pie for desert.

Around one in the afternoon, Catherine said, "C'mon. Let's go play golf."

"On Thanksgiving?" Joanna asked surprised. She'd never played golf on Thanksgiving. It was a day of work, preparing a large meal for her family.

"Nothing says we have to stay home. Why not do what we love?"

Joanna thought, there isn't anything that says she can't play golf, but was lost without the large preparing of meals, then relieved she didn't have them.

"Okay, good idea, except if we plan on eating around seven, I'll need to start preparing around five."

"Joanna, relax. Remember the course is right out the front door. We'll eat. Don't worry and I can help you," Catherine assured her.

This was going to take a lot of getting used to, having someone else around to help her.

Joanna walked, pulling her cart behind her and Catherine at her side now – not in front of her as in past years, during the team matches. They had fun, seeing different plants Joanna had never seen and Catherine calling them by name.

Thanksgiving dinner that night was shared in love, after saying grace then talk of the days golf game.

In bed she thought of the children and Ed back

north, as well as her mom and the rest of her family. She'd called them this morning wishing them a happy holiday. She was happy here, not having to play the role of a loving wife, and being the fearful fool. She needn't pretend anymore. She had stood up for herself and what she felt. Was it right to do? She felt in her heart it was. She felt inside, that her true self had finally arrived – not buried in some deep, dark, dirt hole trying to get out. Joanna slept without fear or worry – finally relaxed, her body was aware of its own self. She even thought about death and dying without fear and said, "If I were to die right now, it would all be worth it, because I am at peace with myself."

***

Joanna woke early the next morning and made bacon, eggs and toast, looking forward to a new day. They ate on the screened porch discussing what they would do. Food shopping had to be done, then afterward they were free to do what they loved most – golf. Tomorrow the movers would be delivering some items from Long Island – Catherine's desk, a television and other things. While sitting talking, Joanna suddenly jumped up and ran to her room, coming back with Razzle Dazzle. "Look now we have a real home, Ca. Razzle Dazzle is in his place on the back of the sink."

Around three that afternoon, they grabbed their clubs and golf carts out of the storage closet outside. They headed for the first tee, enjoying the breeze that was coming in off the ocean and a fairly empty golf course to boot, what could be better.

On the back nine, when walking past a pond, Joanna noticed in the brackish water, tiny bubbles rising to the surface.

"Hey, Ca, look over there. Do you see that?" Pointing to the bubbles.

"Yes, I wonder what it is?"

They walked down the slight embankment to the water's edge to get a better look.

"It sure is weird looking. Look at the gray strip behind the bubbles."

"I wonder what it is? It could be a pipe for water to keep the pond flowing," said Catherine.

"Maybe it's an alligator or a snake," Joanna laughed, with her vivid imagination. Who knew what lurked in these dark waters? She thought.

Staring at the water, the bubbles followed by something silver, came toward them. All Joanna could think was, snake or alligator and she hightailed it up the fairway, not looking behind her. Then she saw a flash of Catherine's long strides pass her by. When they reached the front of the green, eighty yards away, and turned around, they saw a person climbing out of the water wearing a wet suit and air tank. He had been searching for golf balls at the bottom of the pond and then sold them to northerners, like them. They stood laughing at themselves saying, "Boy, we sure are brave northerners, aren't we?"

***

The days that followed were *all* good ones and Joanna wondered at times, where Catherine got the words she taped to her mirror every week for her to learn. Joanna had taped the prayer inside her medicine cabinet to remind her the Almighty Father looked after her every day. Then they'd be off to play golf or rearrange the furniture, brought down by the moving men. It started to look like a real home, with flowers on tables and colored plants on the balcony and kitchen porch. After walking the beach and sitting on the sand in front of the condo Joanna had first visited, Sea Trail, she would come home and cook their meal.

***

Cleaning floor tiles while Catherine played golf one morning, Joanna thought, 'I have a smile on my face – scrubbing tiles – boy, that's a first.' She realized how happy she was, or the first time since she was a child climbing trees.

Joanna called the kids telling them she missed them and Hope said she would be down during school recess. Matthew called one night at one in the morning to say he and his girlfriend were in Jacksonville, on their way to surprise Joanna, but his car had broken down and he was fixing it. Joanna tried to convince him to spend the night in Jacksonville, but Matthew wanted to drive so at eight the next morning, Joanna was welcomed with her son's face. Happy, she hugged him and said how much she missed him. He looked good, except for needing a shave and his girlfriend was pretty. Joanna gave them her room to sleep in and said, 'no hanky-panky.' They looked tired and she didn't feel anything was about to happen, and he had been driving with the girl for twenty-one hours, so if it had happened he *was* a grown man now. They stayed for three days talking, and having dinners together, enjoying one another like years ago when he was her little friend, which Joanna missed. When it was time for them to go, she said goodbye, giving him a kiss, telling him to be careful driving home and telling his girlfriend she was happy to meet her. He looked good and she had enjoyed the brief time with him. Maybe he was growing up after all and she thought that night after he'd left, 'maybe that's all we ever have is brief times.'

***

With Christmas approaching, they made room in the corner of the living room near the sliding doors for a tree, then went to the local supermarket to purchase one. The trees were lined up outside in front of the store, different from up north, where they went to nurseries or Christmas tree lots to buy them.

Catherine held a small one up, "How about this?"

"It's kind of small. With the cathedral ceiling, we could get a real big one, maybe eight feet."

"Sure, and how are we going to get it upstairs?"

"Good thinking," said Joanna. "Okay – let's take that one, it's cute," reaching for the small one.

The young man at the store tied up the five-foot tree and put it in the trunk of the car. At home, Catherine cut a two-inch slice off the bottom to absorb water and last longer. Then with Catherine taking the back end and Joanna the front, they carried it from the car to the staircase and up the first landing. Making the turn for the second landing, they almost lost it over the railing, juggling it back in position. Finally, reaching the top landing they laughed so loud it brought the neighbors out.

Joanna opened the front door placing it in a stand at the end of the living room. Catherine held it while Joanna turned the screws, making sure it was straight.

Christmas Eve they decorated it with the box of ornaments that was shipped down from the north. For dinner Joanna made Coquille St. Jacques, shrimp with linguini, a salad, pumpkin pie for desert, with whipped

161

cream, and coffee with anisette. Sitting on the couch with an after-dinner drink, they admired the tree they had decorated and played Christmas Carols. They agreed it was a beautiful tree. This was just what they needed, after so many months of unsettled times.

Later they went to midnight-mass and then exchanged one present, before going to bed. Joanna gave Catherine a box of notepaper for the letters she wrote to friends and Catherine gave Joanna a picture of a lighthouse. It was the same red lighthouse she had seen on her first visit. The picture had an inscription by Albert Camus, *"Don't walk in front of me I may not follow, Don't walk behind me I may not lead, Just walk beside me and be my friend."* Joanna put the picture on her dresser in the bedroom and reread it several times thinking how true it was.

The tree stayed up for a week, but by the fifth day it was turning brown. Every time the front door opened, it caught a cross breeze. If the back sliding doors were open you could see the needles fall, as the breeze blew through the apartment. The next two days they kept the lights off, for fear of fire. The day after New Years, they tried to figure a way to get the now totally brown tree out of the apartment without dropping needles all over the place.

"We'll wrap it in a sheet and carry it downstairs," said Catherine.

"No, let's wrap it in a sheet and throw it over the balcony," which was only a few feet from the tree.

"Good idea, I'll get the sheet." And Catherine ran to the linen closet.

Wrapping it in a sheet they carried it out to the balcony railing. Catherine went downstairs and looked up at Joanna, "Let her go," Catherine sang out.

"Stand back Ca, I don't want to hit you," and Joanna lifted it up over the rail letting it drop. It hit the ground trunk first, like a dart, stood straight, then fell on its side.

"Are there any needles left, Ca?"

"Not a one." Again they brought the neighbors out with laughter.

***

After the holiday Hope and her school friend, Ginny, came to stay for a week. Joanna and Catherine picked the girls up on a late night flight from Long Island after Ed called to say what flight they'd be on. On the ride back to the condo, even though tired, they were excited about being in Florida and out of the cold weather. Joanna and Hope talked about her school and Catherine asked Ginny questions about her school.

Catherine and Joanna walked the girls to the beach the next day where they had brought sandwiches and sodas, then made a mad dash for the waves. The older girls sat in chairs watching the young friends play in the waves.

"Ca, I think Hope has gotten taller since I saw her in November. She's turning out to be a beautiful young woman, isn't she?

"Yes she is and she seems to like the school she's in. I like Ginny too. She's quiet but funny."

Later afternoon Joanna walked down to the water where the girls had been most of the day, "Girls, we're going back to the condo."

"Okay, Mom. We'll see you guys later. Bye Miss B."

"Bye girls, be careful," Catherine yelled back.

"Make sure you two get back before dinner," said Joanna. "I'm making chicken and rice with brownies for desert, so no later than five o-clock. You hear Hope?" as Hope jumped back to catch a wave.

"Got ya mom, bye."

Joanna walked back to Catherine, turning to see the girls having fun.

"Ca, you get the towels and basket. I'll get the chairs, leave two towels for the girls."

Joanna and Catherine walked passed Sea Tail along the path to the back of Estuary Dunes to their condo. "It was fun with the kids today, wasn't it, Ca?"

"Yes, they're good fun to be around."

***

The girls came home almost on time, only a little after five and at the dinner table they talked of the two boys they'd met after Joanna and Catherine had left. They were excited as young teenage girls are. "Oh, he had such a cute smile, Mom," Hope said. "But the one Ginny spoke to was even cuter. We're going to meet them again tomorrow afternoon."

"How old are they?" asked Joanna.

"I don't know, around our age, maybe sixteen," Hope answered.

"You girls be careful, and I don't want either of you in anyone's car."

"Oh Mom, stop worrying," and she rolled her eyes.

***

The days went by, taking the girls to the zoo and movies and dinners and of course the mall. What teenage girls' vacation would be right without a mall visit. Catherine and Joanna went food shopping one day while the girls played golf. Ginny came back with a bad

164

sunburn and during dinner her forehead swelled up like an egg. Hope noticed it first and started laughing which embarrassed Ginny and Catherine got an ice pack to bring the swelling down. It turned into a large blister and one of the girls popped it with a pin while they were watching TV in bed.

The girls decided to cook for Joanna and Catherine one night and told them to leave the house for a few hours, but first asked, "do you like Mexican food?"

"Yeah, it's good," answered Joanna.

Neither cared for it at all, but they didn't want to hurt the girls' feelings. When Catherine and Joanna came home from golf, the girls were on the floor cleaning up a mess of brown mush. They had dropped the glass dish containing the whole meal of meat and brown beans and it had splattered all over the white floor. They were embarrassed, but argued back and forth as to who was to blame. Catherine chimed in quickly with,

"Girls, I think hamburgers out will be fine."

With a fast-food meal and great conversation, Hope told Joanna about school and Catherine talked of her younger days as a teenager and the trouble she'd gotten into.

"You, Miss B?" asked Hope. "I don't believe it, you were probably a star pupil."

"Well, not really. I had my problems too, especially being taller than all the boys. I'd have to beat them up when they made fun of me," said Catherine.

"Ohoo – I don't believe it. I bet you were a nerd," answered Hope.

The night the girls cooked for Joanna and Catherine was special, even though the meal was a disaster, it was prepared with love. This was the best food, food from the heart even though they didn't eat it.

The week passed quickly and Hope and Joanna had a wonderful time together, as did the two with whom they shared it. Joanna called Ed to tell him the time the girls would be returning home. Hope was teary eyed and tried to act as if she wasn't. Joanna was worse and *did* act the way she felt. She told her daughter again if she wanted to come to live with them, she was welcome to and again, Hope said no.

***

Joanna loved to go out on the balcony and watch the river flowing in and out with the tide. This late afternoon, Catherine was at her desk doing paper work, while Joanna watched the white egrets on the over hanging trees looking for food. Then she heard a chirping sound directly in front of her where two trees stood off the balcony. Straining her eyes, she saw a large black bird. No, wait, it wasn't a black bird, and looked closer and saw another bird on the branch above. She also thought 'black birds don't make chirping sounds'. Moving slowly back inside the doors, she went to Catherine's room to get the binoculars where Catherine was seated at her desk.

"Ca, there's two birds in the tree out back. Come and take a look," grabbing the binoculars hanging on a hook inside the closet. They crept out to the balcony where the birds were.

"They're large crows," Catherine said.

"I don't think so. They look different." Then Joanna noticed the beaks were different. "See the beaks, they're hooked." The two birds chirped, enjoying these humans observing them going about their business of eating.

"Get the book, let's see what they are," said Catherine.

Catherine and Joanna sat on the couch opposite the sliding doors looking in different bird books. Catherine knew her birds and had tracked many of them over the years. She didn't go duck hunting or bird watching like some of her friends, but she had introduced Joanna to the different variety in Florida and up north.

Looking through the pages, Catherine found one, "This is it. I think it's the same bird."

Joanna went to the doors to look at them again, while she called out the looks of their beaks and their dimensions.

"It's called an Ani, Joanna. Listen to the sound it makes. In the book it shows the same sound. You've spotted a new bird. Let's circle it and put today's date next to the picture."

From then on, wherever they were, if they spotted a new bird, they'd write what it's looks were, then come home and look it up in the bird books and write the date it was seen. They spotted Green Herons, Kingfishers, Ibis, which Catherine called partner, for some reason of her own. Joanna loved the Gallinules and Coots at the golf course. They reminded her of the Bantam chickens she grew up with and Matthew had had one as a pet. They became the bird watchers of the condominium complex. Any time a neighbor saw a bird they didn't know, they'd come to Joanna and Catherine's door and say, "hurry, get the book, we spotted a new one."

***

Having breakfast one Saturday before housework, Catherine and Joanna were in the screen patio enjoying their last sip of coffee before the vacuum and sponges came out. Looking down, Joanna saw a woman she'd seen before, walking a small white poodle.

"I see her in the mornings walking. I think she lives in the building over there," Joanna pointed to the building catty corner to them.

"I'm going down to throw the garbage out and introduce myself." Joanna got the small bag of garbage out of the kitchen and cleaned off the table for more.

Walking to the garbage dumpster, where the woman was now getting rid of what the poodle had deposited, "hi there, beautiful day isn't it?"

The woman, turning around when she heard Joanna, "yes, it sure is another beautiful day in sunny Florida."

Joanna detected a New York accent. "Hi, my name is Joanna," reaching out her hand and then bending down to pet the dog.

"Pleased to meet you, I'm Jan."

"I see you almost every morning and I thought I'd come say hello this time," said Joanna.

"I work nights and Muffin usually likes this time of day to go for a walk, so I get the job."

"She's beautiful, especially with the pink bow in her hair. What kind of work do you do?"

"I'm in nursing and have been working the night shift since the beginning of the year. I hear a New York accent, where do you originally come from?"

"It's really a Long Island accent, we just moved in this past year," said Joanna turning around pointing to where Catherine and she lived.

"Oh, my friend and I came down from Jersey two years ago and love it, here."

"Yes, it is beautiful. Do you or your friend play golf?"

"No, we both work, hardly any time for play, but I would love to learn."

"Catherine, my friend, and I can take you out one day if you'd like. Why don't you both come over for cocktails tonight?

"That would be great. I'm off tonight and don't have to work so, yeah, that'd be great."

"Good, around five o'clock, if that's okay? I need to get back, we're cleaning today and if I'm not there she'll have the house done in no time."

"Great, see you then. You're in that building right?" pointing to Joanna's building.

"Yes, number eighteen, upstairs. See you later. Bye Muffin," and Joanna tasseled the dog's hair then walked back to the condo and up the stairs.

Telling Catherine they were having company tonight, Catherine said she would make hors d'oeuvres. Next on the list was cleaning. Joanna started from her bedroom and Catherine from hers and they met somewhere in the middle till the whole place was done.

***

At five that evening, when Jan and her friend came to the door, Joanna greeted them and Jan introduced Hazel. Joanna hadn't known any women who lived together, all her friends were married, living with their husbands up north. These women were roommates sharing a life together trying to make ends meet, just like Catherine and she.

During that year, they became good friends and had many laughs together. Jan was a great cook and loved to have people over for meals. Catherine and Joanna never turned down an invitation. Jan made an eight-course meal from drinks to desert, and laughs that could be heard through the whole complex. They played scrabble and card games and had nights of enjoyment with their new neighbors.

Joanna and Catherine had other neighbors with whom they became friendly, also. Florida was a friendly place to live, because everyone came from somewhere else. There was always lots to learn about each one, and what state of the country they came from. One of their neighbors Sam, Shelly, and Tim came from England trying to make it in this country. They shared many dinners together and learned about England, where neither Catherine nor Joanna had been, even though they discussed going to Scotland to play golf. But that was just a dream some time in the future. Sam and Shelly owned a florist, and would bring the leftover flowers to neighbors, which Catherine and Joanna got to share in, and Tim got to meet Hope when she came for her second visit. They were the same age and had things teenagers have in common, music especially.

***

The year was a learning experience for Joanna, getting to know her own self. She learned she was able to live with someone else in harmony without arguing or fighting. She and Catherine never fought, but had discussions if they felt differently about something.

PREMONITION

THE SUMMER CAME with Catherine and Joanna playing golf using two balls at a time, because the snowbirds had finally left for home. They loved the summer in Florida, and when Catherine said they needed a vacation and Joanna asked,

"Vacation? Why? We're on vacation all the time."

"Well, I feel we need a small trip for a change. We haven't been away in a year," replied Catherine. She was dead set on going somewhere.

"Can we go to Disney World?" asked Joanna.

"Disney World? Don't you think I'm a bit old for that?"

"No, Ca, you'd love it, especially Epcot, where you can visit countries. It's just like going to Europe or China."

Catherine was under the impression it was just for children, so at dinner Joanna told her of the trips she'd made with Ed and the kids.

"We enjoyed it more than Hope and Matthew. The first time we went Hope was around five and Matthew was twelve. I have to say it was one of the best trips we had made through our marriage. Wait'll you see It's a Small World and Pirates of the Caribbean. It's amazing how they set it up to look so real. We went about four times when the kids were young, and then when Matthew was seventeen, we went for Christmas. At first he said he didn't want to go and would stay at a friend's house. It wound up we all went with our neighbors that he had grown up with and I was so glad he'd gone, because I knew it would be our last trip together as a family. I think he got more fun out of that trip than he'd gotten from all the others. You'll see, Ca, you're going to love it."

"Really? Okay, you convinced me. You make the reservations since you've been there before."

Joanna reserved a motel off the grounds where the rates were cheaper for Florida residents in the summer months, and in a few days they left for their first real vacation together. Catherine did the driving and Joanna was the map-reader even though she had a pretty good idea of where to go.

They stayed outside the park, and hopped the hotel bus, staying at the park five to six hours. They walked all day between Disney and Epcot, Catherine saying she liked Disney the best, even though Epcot was a learning experience. As Joanna had said, Catherine loved *It's a Small World* and *Pirates*, but when she wanted to ride the *Tea Cups*, Joanna cracked up.

"So you're the one who said you were too old for this?" as they rode high above the park.

"What can I say? I was wrong. I'm glad you talked me into coming."

After two days they'd seen enough and drove the two and a half-hours back to Jupiter, Catherine thanking Joanna for introducing her to Disney.

***

Their year's lease would be up in November and Catherine said it wouldn't be a good idea to stay where they were permanently, because of the hurricane season and everyone leaving in the summer months. The condo was too close to the ocean, so they started looking for another place to call home. Her broker had advised her to sell the Long Island apartment and buy something in Florida before the winter months, when the northerners returned and the prices went up. Catherine wanted a larger place so they could have company during the winter months. Joanna had to admit the condo was small and too close to the ocean, but she'd grown to love it and it felt like home. She didn't want to make it known to Catherine, for after all, it was Catherine's money that was being used. Joanna got a small amount from Ed each month, when he was ready to send it. They looked at places together and when Catherine joined her golf friends for a game, Joanna went alone with the Realtor.

There were condos on the other side of the main road that were large but Joanna didn't care for them. They reminded her of long dark bowling alleys.

When Catherine was playing golf one day, the Realtor called and said she had a three-bedroom, three-bath that just went on the market. The owner had become ill and the daughter was living there now, would we like to see it? When Catherine came home they met the Realtor at the condo. It had a large screened porch off the back and a split floor plan, two bedrooms and two baths on one side of the condo and one bedroom and a bath, on the other side of the living room and dining room.

Catherine liked it, Joanna could see. "Do you like it?"

"Yes, it's not as dark as the others we've looked at, but it's awfully big, Ca."

The Realtor said it was a good buy and you could offer less because they were in a hurry to sell.

"Okay Ca, I like it." Joanna said, and Catherine gave the Realtor an offer of twenty thousand less than the price. The Realtor said she would run it by the owner and get back to her.

On the ride back home Joanna said, "Ca, we're never going to go to the beach anymore."

"Why do you say that?"

"Because we'll have to drive to get there."

"I promise we'll go to the beach, just like we have been," replied Catherine.

But in Joanna's mind she doubted it. They were now going to live a 'normal' life with a large place to keep up. It wasn't that Joanna didn't like the place, because she did. It was close to shopping and they could ride their bikes or walk to the stores. Still, she felt there was something wrong when she walked into the place, but couldn't put her finger on it. It was just a feeling or premonition she had. She said to herself, 'We'll just have to eat and sleep there. Most of the day we're out playing golf anyway, so what's the difference?' Catherine was buying it and Joanna didn't want to say anything of how she felt. Catherine was the smart one and Joanna had to trust that she always knew the right thing to do.

So in November of '86 they moved Razzle Dazzle with them to Garden Parks. The rest of Catherine's furniture was shipped down from Long Island to fill the large three, three and they started a new home again.

***

They looked in the yellow pages and found a place not far from where they lived, and met a couple, Linda and Ray, who owned and handled the upholstery shop. They set up an appointment with them to come and measure for drapes. Catherine and Joanna picked the material for the drapes, couch, and Catherine's mother's chair, a beautiful a light pink, with light green running through it – a soft look – a Florida look – light and airy. They found a dining table with a pale green glass top, with a darker green pedestal.

Before Christmas the condo was looking like a home, except for a few small things. Even Joanna thought it was home and Catherine enjoyed the space because it felt like her house in the north.

Christmas Eve came and they bought a Christmas tree from the grocery store and decorated it, playing Christmas Carols just like last year. Joanna prepared a wonderful meal and then it was off to midnight mass, and back home to open one present, then to bed to wait for Santa.

***

The first winter a cardinal came to visit them and hopped along the wall, chirping and begging for food. Catherine spotted him and bought sunflower seeds leaving them along the wall for the tiny red bird to eat.

"He's much smaller than the cardinals we have up north," she said as she placed the seeds along the wall.

"Yeah, he is. I guess they don't need as many feathers down here to keep warm."

"I'm going to put some seeds on the patio table to see if he'll pick on them."

175

Sure enough in the late afternoon that day, he'd eaten the seeds on the table under the kitchen window.

The next morning Catherine put more seeds out on the wall and table. When Joanna was cleaning up the morning's breakfast dishes, there in front of her on the wall was the brilliant red creation of God. He began chirping as she crept away from the window to summon Catherine, who was in her bathroom brushing her teeth.

"Ca, come and see, the cardinal is back."

Now in the kitchen, they both crept slowly toward the kitchen window. With the front door open, they could hear his voice loud and clear.

"Shhh, we don't want to frighten him off," whispered Catherine.

They stood like statues afraid to breathe for fear of having him fly away. The red bird hopped along the wall, back and forth, trying to figure a safe way to get the seeds that were on the table.

"Look he's about to make his move to the table," Catherine noticed. He then took one large hop and glided down on the white patio table underneath their eyes. They didn't move as he looked up towards them, tilting his head every which way to see what was around. Scared, he jumped back up on the wall when Joanna tried to get a better look, leaning forward straining her neck.

"Oh darn," she said, mad at herself for frightening him.

"He'll come back, watch and see," Catherine declared with confidence

"I'll try to be more careful next time."

Soon he was back on the table picking at the seeds

and eating. This time, he'd turn to look towards the window not bothered by Catherine nor Joanna. Smiles were all over their faces.

"I think we'll name him Geech," Catherine said,

"Geech? What kind of name is that? How about Reddy, since he's so red?" asked Joanna.

"I used to call my Uncle George, Geech. He was my favorite uncle."

"Okay, then Geech it is." Joanna confirmed.

Geech was there every morning and afternoon, chirping, saying he was hungry. In the weeks ahead he brought a female friend, his partner, they supposed, and he led the way for her to follow. After his partner, they noticed he brought his family. He just added a little bit more love to their lives.

***

They have spent their days playing golf and enjoying each other and friends who come down from the north for the winter, to play golf. At night over dinners they'd talk of the day's golf games and enjoy their friends' company.

Catherine spends time at her desk, working on investments and writing letters to friends and family, while Joanna enjoys cooking, reading books on golf and playing the keyboard piano Catherine gave her for Christmas. It's fun playing the piano again as she did when she took lessons, while living with Ed. This was another way to survive those days of agoraphobia in the house a few years ago, which now seemed like a century ago.

Summers they play golf with other die-hard women golfers traveling from Ft. Pierce to Ft. Lauderdale on a league. Catherine still beats Joanna just like up north,

177

winning tournaments as partners and alone. They spend time at the beach, but not as before. They walk and talk, searching for shells and wave-worn glass to add to their collection. They ride their bikes to the store and go on nature walks on the two and half mile heart trail. They also attend plays at the teaching theater, around the corner from their condo.

In August, they drive north playing golf along the way and see family and friends, staying until Joanna's mother's birthday in November. Joanna helps Catherine plant flowers at the gravesides of Anne and other friends and family. They go back to the Sound, where they sat on a log, eating ham and cheese sandwiches and drinking lite beer, thinking of the first time they were there and still enjoying each other's company as much today as they did then.

***

Joanna invited Maria and John to visit them in Florida for the months of December and January. The condo association says you're allowed guests thirty days out of the year, so Catherine comes up with the idea of December in one year and January the next year.

Catherine and Joanna pick them up at the airport and drive back to the condo. Joanna is happy to see her mom, but she looks pale and tired. She tells her mom "you are here to relax and enjoy the warm sunshine." They had left Long Island with seven inches of snow.

Maria and John spend the days enjoying the warm winter air at the pool on the days Catherine and Joanna play golf. Maria and John walk around the corner to the stores and have lunch at one of the small cafés. Occasionally Maria picks up something to cook, like

Joanna's favorite spaghetti and meatballs or one of Maria's great soups. Joanna wishes her mom and John would find a place to live, so they could live close by. Catherine loves having Maria and John around because they are so easy to entertain, or maybe it's because she doesn't have to entertain them. Catherine and Joanna take Maria and John on the golf course, even though they don't play. John handles the golf cart while Maria directs him. John becomes friendly with the neighbor upstairs, Jay, who plays the organ. They sit and play as young boys while Maria and Bea, Jay's wife, discuss recipes. Joanna is happy her mother and John are feeling at home where Catherine and she have made their home.

Catherine and Joanna came home from golf one day and Maria and John are not there. It's around four o'clock and Joanna says to Catherine "it's odd they're not home yet."

"Don't worry. I'm sure they're around the corner shopping."

"Yeah, I guess your right. I just hope nothings happened to them. You're right Ca, knowing mom she's trying on clothes, in one of the stores.

An hour goes by when Joanna, quite nervous now yells to Catherine, "I'm taking the car around the corner to look for them."

"Okay. Call me if there's a problem," Catherine calls out from her desk.

Joanna searches from one end of the shopping center to the other and sees no sign of them. 'Where the heck are they?' she wonders, frantic, knowing John's heart is not in the best of shape and her mom is not in good health either. After three runs through the shopping center she thinks 'maybe they're up visiting Jay and Bea' and she heads home.

Nearing the condo complex, she spots them sitting on a bench, and thinks 'John's having heart trouble or is out of breath.' As she pulls closer and puts the window down, she sees they're holding hands. They look so happy, content and in love, that a smile crosses her face. She knows they are all right. " Where the heck have your two been? Don't you know what time it is?"

Looking at each other as if they were little children, they smile back, "we didn't know we had to be home at a certain time."

They were just two eighty year olds, in love, sitting on a park bench, without a care in the world.

***

Four years have passed - where have they gone?

It' been a happy time – living in the condominium, with wonderful neighbors – New Year's Eve parties, barbecues in the summer and just meetings at the pool everyday for exercise and chatting.

Joanna has a life unlike she could ever have imagined. It's a simple life, with none of the difficulties she had in her marriage. The time had come to forgive her past mistakes and move forward in her life, wherever the path would take her. Every night her prayers were answered as Catherine and she prayed together. This was something she had always wanted – someone who shared her beliefs – and now she had it. She thanked God every day for putting Catherine in her path.

***

The months went quickly by, as they shared happy

days with each other, until one night at the end of 1989, when Joanna woke at 1:30 a.m. with a racing heart.

Sitting on the edge of the bed, the feeling in her chest was like a racing train. She began to sweat profusely, getting more and more out of control with each labored breath.

'What's happening to me?'

'Am I having a heart attack?'

'I'm not in pain, so it can't be a heart attack', she thinks.

She's having trouble thinking clearly, with thought after thought racing through her mind – racing along with her racing heart, similar to her old panic attacks, yet different. She had almost forgotten as it had been years since they were with her.

Catherine hears her and wakes up. "What is it? Are you all right?"

"Ca, something's wrong. My heart feels like it's beating out of my chest. I can't catch my breath," speaking as if she'd just run a race.

Catherine takes Joanna's wrist and checks her pulse. "C'mon, let's go to the hospital."

"No ... no. It's probably nerves. Will you get me a glass of ice water, please?"

"I'd rather take you to the hospital."

"I'll be all right, just get me some ice water. It's probably a panic attack."

While Catherine goes for the water, Joanna makes her way to the bathroom, to throw up. She's afraid again and having trouble handling it. Joanna has been in control since the therapy, which taught her to hypnotize herself.

"Dear Lord, please make this go away," almost the

same prayer uttered years ago.

Catherine comes back with water and Joanna sips it slowly, while propped up in bed. She can feel her heartbeat slowing down, and her stomach making noises as if she's hungry. Catherine sits on the bed next to her and holds her hand and Joanna doesn't feel alone as she once did. She's connected to someone.

"I'm feeling better Ca, I think it's passed."

"You sure?" as she checks her pulse. "Your pulse is down to 85. I couldn't count it before, it was beating too fast."

Joanna can feel her insides settling down and Catherine goes back to her side of the bed. A short while later Catherine has fallen asleep and is snoring lightly while Joanna wonders what had just attacked her body. Joanna laughs because the snoring always bothered her, but tonight it's a pleasure to hear, since she thought she was dying just a few hours ago. The last thing she hears are the birds chirping outside and falls asleep.

***

The next day Catherine talks Joanna into going to Dr. Ban, to check last night's attack. Running some tests, he finds nothing. "Just a panic attack," he says. "You're under a lot of stress with your divorce still going on and sometimes nerves can affect the heart."

"Yes, I guess that's it. But are you sure?"

"I'm sure. I'm giving you a prescription for a tranquilizer to take when needed." he says and Catherine and Joanna leave for home.

***

In the weeks ahead Joanna decides to quit smoking, because she's having more of these so-called panic attacks. She's waking in early morning hours out of a sound sleep, feeling the same episodes of her heart pounding out of her chest. The doctor puts Joanna through more tests and finally one comes back positive. She has gallstones and they should be removed. The doctor feels this is upsetting the stomach, which is making the heart beat fast and irregular. Something called the Vegas nerve, he says. She agrees to have the gallbladder removed, but she's afraid, because the only time she ever spent in a hospital, was when she gave birth to Matthew.

Doctor Ban knows Joanna's history of panic attacks and tells her, "if Catherine wants to stay in the hospital with you, she can. I'll arrange for a cot to be brought to your room."

"Ca, will you stay with me?"

"Of course I will."

With it settled, the doctor arranges for Catherine to stay with Joanna at the hospital.

The drive to the hospital on a December morning was quiet, Joanna thinking she is going to be fine in a few weeks, able to play golf again and well for Christmas.

At seven-thirty she says goodbye to Catherine, with tears in her eyes. They haven't been separated for four years and Joanna's slightly afraid she may never see Catherine again.

"Ca, if anything happens to me, will you call Ed and the kids?"

"Nothing's going to happen. Everything's going to be all right. I'll be here when you get back from surgery. I promise. I love you."

The nurse preps Joanna and asks her to sign a permission form for the doctor to remove her gallbladder and appendix.

"My appendix. Why? There isn't anything wrong with my appendix."

The nurse says it's a normal procedure that goes along with gallbladder surgery.

"I don't want anything done that isn't necessary." Joanna says, wanting to be playing golf and swimming in a few weeks.

Ten o'clock after surgery, Catherine is waiting in Joanna's room with a smile on her face. Joanna is wheeled back, feeling no pain. She's a bit drugged and in and out of sleep. The nurse tells her if she has any pain, to push a button and the machine will administer pain medication to her.

She nods her head, 'yes' and she's off to dreamland. When Joanna wakes later in the afternoon, Catherine is there, reading the paper.

"Hi, you still here?"

"Yes, I promised you I'd be here," with a smile on her face.

"Boy, I sure am hungry."

"I'll ask the nurse if there's something you can have to eat."

Catherine comes back with the nurse and says, "you can have ice chips."

Finding it hard moving in bed, because of the large incision below her right rib cage, she doesn't have the strength to pull herself up or move. She had no idea it was going to be like this.

Catherine later gets the nurse to bring Joanna some broth, which she proceeds to throw up. The nurse says it will take a while for the anesthesia to wear off and soon she would be feeling better.

Catherine stayed with Joanna, running home only for mail and a change of clothes. Joanna was glad Catherine slept in the room with her. The nights when she needed to get out of bed to go to the bathroom would have been hard without Catherine's arms helping her out of bed and walking with her.

Five days later, on December 10, 1989, Catherine drove Joanna home. All she wants is to look around the condo, and thank God she's all right and that Catherine is here at her side.

She's in bad shape and nothing like she expected. She is not able to cook and it's hard to lie in bed, move around or get out of bed. Catherine rigs up a rope that attaches to her dresser so Joanna can hold onto and pull herself up. The neighbors bring them meals because they know Catherine doesn't cook. They're so blessed to have such great neighbors and friends. The days pass and she gradually gets better each day.

***

With Christmas approaching, Catherine and Joanna go to get a Christmas tree so it will be ready to put up Christmas Eve, a tradition that Joanna has always kept. It was in her childhood, then her life with Ed and the children and now with Catherine. Always decorating the tree Christmas Eve afternoon, then having dinner and going to midnight-mass. Catherine has to do all the decorating this year since Joanna can't be doing any bending, because of surgery. Catherine's doing the bending with those lanky legs and doing a grand job. They play Christmas Carols, sit back and admire what a beautiful tree it is. Every year they say the same, "Boy, this is the best tree we've had yet." Joanna didn't cook and they ordered takeout this year and later, after dinner, were off to midnight-mass. They need to be there early by 11:00 p.m. because it gets so crowded and they want to be there to sing carols. When home, as usual, they open one present then it's off to sleep to wait for Santa Clause.

***

Months before Christmas, Catherine had asked Joanna to put something in her file cabinet and while doing so, Joanna found behind the file cabinet, a rolled up piece of canvas. When she unrolled it she found a beautiful oil painting of Catherine. Bringing it to Catherine at the desk she had asked, "What's this? I found it behind the file cabinet. Did you know it was there?"

"Oh that. Yes, I knew it was there. I put it there after we moved in."

"Ca, it's beautiful. It should be hanging up."

"Oh no. My parents had it painted when I was just out of high school. A neighbor artist wanted to try out his portrait painting with me as the subject. In fact, there should be a newspaper clipping attached to it, telling the painter's story."

It took awhile, but that year Joanna had had the picture framed without Catherine's knowledge and on Christmas morning Catherine spotted it hanging on the wall in the living room.

"You son of a gun, how did you get that there?" pointing to the picture. "How did you keep it from me?"

Joanna laughed, "Oh, you think you need to know everything that goes on in this house?"

Joanna could see Catherine had a tear in her eye, and guessed it reminded her of the past when her parents had it hanging on their walls. Joanna could see how happy she'd made her friend.

And, so, another year of happiness passes and Joanna looks forward to feeling better.

HEART

JOANNA'S HEART PALPITATIONS continued into 1990, waking her from a sound sleep in the middle of the night, frightening her out of her mind, and disrupting Catherine's sleep. The doctors couldn't find anything wrong and blamed it on her nerves, again giving her more tranquilizers with other calming medications, none of which worked. She sensed something was seriously wrong and they weren't finding it. Catherine also came down with palpitations and Joanna wondered, could it possibly be something in the household that was making them ill? Now they were going to doctors instead of playing the game they loved – golf.

The doctors finally determined Catherine had a prolapsed Mitral Valve, which was causing her feelings of skipped heartbeats. She was put on medication and it worked the first time she took it. Joanna thought, 'How great it would be if I could take the same medication.' Doctor Ban tried, but it didn't work, and the palpitations were almost daily, along with dizziness.

After many tests of heart monitors – twelve to be exact –they decided to go to Long Island to Joanna's former doctor. They were on a train headed north within a month.

Joanna spoke with her former doctor who sent her to a heart specialist. The cardiologist read the reports Joanna had brought with her from the doctors in Florida and ran more tests. He gave her a monitor the size of a pack of cigarettes and told her, "when you get palpitations, place the monitor on your chest and it will take a recording of your heart beats, which will be sent to me by phone."

It sounded easy and she couldn't believe how small the monitor was. She hadn't had anything like this in Florida.

They spent a few days visiting Maria, John, Matthew and Hope while there, but Joanna was anxious to get back to Florida. With the cold weather, neither of them wanted to stay, and were missing the clothes for it. The winter jackets and boots went to the needy before they left Long Island to live in Florida.

***

Not a month back home and Joanna wakes at 1:00 a.m. with an attack. Getting out of bed and going into the kitchen, she places the monitor to her chest and prays she will stop hearing the galloping going on in her chest. She feels the fear of death at her door again, reliving the fears of the sixteen-year-old. Finally, after a few minutes, it stops and she sends the monitor's recording over the phone. The company, which handles the monitor, calls her right back, "how are you feeling?"

"Awful, this was a bad one. It felt like it lasted a few minutes."

"If the sensations come again, call emergency, 911. We will send the recording to your doctor immediately and he will call you back."

189

"Okay, thank you. Goodnight." Joanna went to bed totally drained.

The doctor called early the next morning saying, "You need to have an EP study done."

"I don't know what that is?"

"It's called an Electropysiology study done." He explained

"I can't go north now."

"I don't want you to travel north. I want you to see Dr. Luchi in Ft. Lauderdale," he said. "I will call him myself today and let him know you will be calling."

"Okay, I'll give him a call. Thank you for helping me," and Joanna, feeling down, hung up the phone.

***

Three days later Catherine and Joanna were in a hospital in Ft. Lauderdale for an EP study.

Dr. Luchi arranged for Catherine to stay in the room with Joanna while she was in the hospital. Joanna told him she was afraid and worried there was something terribly wrong with her heart. He spoke with her at length and had a way of relaxing her. He told her he was good at what he did and would try to fix what was wrong with her heart. Joanna was won over by him, and just wanted to be helped. This was no way to live a life, constantly at doctor's offices. Thank God Ed was holding up the divorce proceedings and she still had his health insurance.

***

After they had prepped her for the study, the doctor came in and she could see him across the room talking with others. She called out to him, "you better not let anything happen to your piason!" – which is an Italian word for friend. She knew he was Italian by the sound of his name and his nurse had confirmed it.

Walking over to the operating table where she was, "you're not Italian, your name sounds German."

"My married name is German, but I'm Italian. My dad came from Italy," she answered.

"Then I'll take good care of you, my piason, don't you worry."

After a small dose of a sedative, but still awake, she felt him make an incision in her right groin then thread a wire up into each chamber of her heart. She watched the screen and could see exactly what he was doing. She was relaxed while this was happening and felt complete confidence in Dr. Luchi. He then took control of her heartbeat and it went into the same rhythm that scared her out of her wits in the middle of the night.

"That's it," she yelled.

"What are you feeling?"

"It feels the same as the attacks at night. I'm starting to feel lightheaded."

"Try to relax. If you black out I'll bring you back. Just lie still."

Even with him telling her this, she was scared and hated the train that was running through her insides. She felt her heart was going to explode or stop.

"Please make it stop," crying now, she started to move.

"Stay still!" he yelled. "We're almost done."

He tried different medications on her in the IV and the heart rhythm went back to normal. He jumped up and down as if he'd just hit a home run.

"We've found it and I've given you the medication to control it."

"You mean I'm not nuts – there *is* something wrong with my heart and it isn't just nerves?"

"No," he said, "you're not nuts. You have a non-malignant arrhythmia, called non-sustained Ventricle Tachycardia.

When Joanna heard this she cried with happiness and wanted more information from him. Gently taking the wire out of her system, he told her, "lie still and don't bend your leg. I'll see you in your room later."

March 5, 1990, she had just turned forty-eight years old. Happy Birthday, Joanna! There finally was an answer.

They wheeled her back to her room, where Catherine was waiting and Joanna told her everything that happened downstairs. They were happy the doctor had found out what the crazy heartbeats were and could fix it with a drug.

When Dr. Luchi came in to see Joanna and Catherine, he sat down and chatted about what he had found downstairs in the operating room.

"When you had the flu years ago it apparently damaged cells in your heart. That's why you've had palpitations all these years. Sometimes they go away, but in your case they didn't."

"So I haven't been just a nervous wreck all these years? There really was something giving me the crazy heart beats?"

"No, you're not a nervous wreck and yes, there was a reason. With the medication you shouldn't have any more trouble. You'll stay here for five days on the medication so it can be regulated, then we'll bring you down on Friday to try induce an attack."

"I have to go through the same test on Friday?"

"Yes. We need to see if the medication is controlling the arrhythmia."

Upset and fearful of the heart sensations again, she gave in, knowing he was doing it to help her. "Okay, I guess I don't have a choice, if I want to get rid of the attacks."

"I'll see you tomorrow to see how you're doing on the medication."

"Thanks doc."

He shook their hands and left the room.

For five days Catherine stayed by her side, sleeping at the motel across the street. She stayed and ate dinner with her in the hospital room then left after visiting hours. Joanna was thankful to have her there.

Joanna's body had trouble adjusting to the medication. First her blood pressure went too low and when she sat up in the morning for the nurse to take her pressure, the room spun around. Until they found the right dosage, whenever walking she felt as though she was on a swirling ship. Dr. Luchi met her sometimes and walked in the hall with her, discussing her illness. He introduced her to a young man across the hall from her room, who was twenty-four years old and had the same tachycardia, with one difference. He had passed out during the test. His was a sustained VT and would need a defibrillator implanted in his chest. Joanna was thankful hers wasn't that bad.

Five days later she was brought downstairs for another EP test and found the medication had worked. Dr. Luchi could not produce an arrhythmia and she was allowed to go home on Saturday morning.

She'd have to take a pill a day for the rest of her life but was glad he had found what was wrong with her heart. Just to think it had all come from the flu.

Driving home, Catherine asked, "Do you want to stop for lunch?"

"Yes, I'd like that. I'm so happy Dr. Luchi found the problem. For years I thought it was nerves."

"I bet you're glad. He's a nice man as well as being a good doctor."

So Catherine and Joanna stopped at a diner in Lake Worth and made it back to the condo around four that afternoon.

All the troubles were behind them now. The doctor said no pool or stretching for at least two weeks, because of the puncture wound in her thigh. She didn't mind at all, if the heart beat problems were gone.

How good it was to be alive and healthy. Catherine and Joanna were back doing their favorite pastimes – playing golf, riding their bikes and swimming. The summer was hot as usual and they loved it, playing two balls at a time, as the snowbirds were gone and off the roads.

JUST A WORD

YES, everything was back to normal, playing golf in leagues from Ft. Pierce to Boca Raton, winning and loving every minute of it, meeting and playing with new friends and old.

Hope came for a visit with another friend from school and they did the routine of going to the zoo, beach, playing golf and movies. Catherine's friend, Pat, came and stayed for a week of golf and Joanna stayed home and rested. She cooked while Catherine enjoyed seeing her friend from school. She cooked making dishes she'd never tried before. She liked using others as guinea pigs to try her new dishes. She thought she'd try floating islands for desert one night, which turned out to be a real disaster. They were so hard they could have been used as Frisbee's, and sailed across the room. Apparently the egg whites were in the oven too long or the oven had been too hot.

Geech came for visits along with his family and Catherine continued to tape new words to Joanna's mirror, where inside her cabinet door she still read – Don't look forward to what might happen tomorrow. The same everlasting Father who cares for you today, will care for you every day… So yes, everything was normal. This seemed to be the way life was or maybe Joanna never thought about it before, when fear blocked her thoughts. She knew she *did* have more faith after the heart problem was solved. Maybe you don't come to know the good, until you've known the bad, to compare it to.

Catherine bought Joanna an attachment to the mixer to make pasta dough, and she went to work making pastas of every color and shape. Catherine rigged a drying area, putting two chairs back to back, stringing twine between them to hang the pasta to dry. For the next two weeks they had pasta coming out their ears, as did the company they invited over. They made spinach, broccoli, and carrot pasta, any vegetable they could get their hands on to blend with flour. They finally became so sick of it they stopped eating pasta.

Catherine surprised Joanna with a new sewing machine and she made cornices for the bedrooms to match the bedspreads. Catherine made the wooden frame and Joanna quilted the material over the wood. They not only had fun working hand in hand but also were happy with the end results of their joint efforts, or laughed at their mistakes. Like Joanna accidentally hammering a nail in to the kitchen table. Thank god, Catherine filled the hole with wood filler.

Matthew called one night to say he was marrying the girl he'd brought to visit and Joanna stressed again the importance of loving the face you see every day, and his answer was, "Yeah, okay Mom."

The only problem that still existed was Ed. He fought Joanna on everything pertaining to the divorce and didn't want to pay his lawyer any billable hours. God help him if he gave her anything but half of the tax refund. She remembers him calling, asking her to sign the income tax forms. He was so nice over the phone. Her answer back to him was, "I'm not signing a blank form any more. If you want me to sign the form, it has to be filled out." When he sent her the tax form to sign, it was the first time she'd actually seen how much he had made, and realized how stupid she had been all those years. It was a lot more than she ever had imagined, being in the six digit numbers, and she wondered where it had all gone.

But she *did* have health insurance, so there was something to be thankful for.

Joanna never got used to the idea of Catherine paying for things and buying her small presents, but she tried to make up for it by working around the house, by making pasta and sewing for them. Catherine said, "That's what money is for, to spend and enjoy. Stop worrying."

***

On a Tuesday at the end of September 1990, Joanna had made a quick meal of left-over ham, cabbage, carrots and potatoes from the fridge, for dinner and Catherine was out on the porch reading the paper. Walking toward the porch to call Catherine for dinner, she noticed how tan she was. They both had taken showers and changed into shorts to relax after perspiring on the course. Catherine's long legs had a beautiful bronze tan and with her haircut short, she looked like the picture hanging over the couch. She hadn't changed in looks at all, Joanna thought, as she passed the picture. Joanna on the other hand, was turning gray and had put on weight. She blamed it on the heart medication, fooling with her metabolism.

"Ca, dinner's ready. What are you reading?"

"A story about the pelican lady. She saves pelicans who have swallowed fishing hooks, or have broken wings, and keeps them in cages at her home until they're better, then lets them go. Here look at the picture."

Joanna looked at the picture, "that's' great. I don't think we'd be reading anything like that back in New York.

"Yeah, I guess you're right. It surely is different down here. That's why I chose to be here, in the first place."

Walking to the kitchen table, Joanna asked, "Ca, what would you like to drink?"

"Think I'll just have water with a slice of lemon."

Joanna went to the cabinet, took two glasses out, then opened the fridge for ice and water and filled them, putting a slice of lemon in each. She enjoyed making their nightly meal look appetizing.

They said a quick prayer and started eating, talking of the day's golf shots and the other women they played with. Almost through with dinner, Catherine began staring up toward the ceiling, shaking her head. Joanna saw this and asked if she was all right. Catherine didn't answer and kept shaking her head as if in a trance. Joanna got up and touched her shoulders, "Ca. – Catherine!" trying to get her attention. Finally Catherine looked at her.

"Are you all right?" Joanna asked.

"Yes, why?" snapping out of it.

"Are you sure you feel okay?" Joanna repeats.

"Yeah, I'm fine. Why, what's the matter?"

"You were shaking your head and staring towards

the ceiling. I couldn't get you to look at me."

" Oh? I don't feel anything different. We were talking about today's golf, right?"

"Yes, then you were somewhere else. You sure you don't have pain anywhere or a headache?"

"No, I feel fine. Hmmm – maybe it's from not drinking enough on the course today. I was thirsty all day."

"You have to stop drinking sodas and drink more water when you play. Would you please do that, for me?"

"I'll try ... okay, let's forget it," and Catherine ended the thought.

Joanna was frightened, because something *had* happened with her friend, but she seemed okay now. They finished eating and Joanna poured decaf coffee and got two chocolate chip cookies for each of them. She couldn't get her mind off what she'd just seen minutes before. Something had happened. She had never seen anything like it before, with Catherine or anyone else.

***

Weeks go by and while playing golf, Catherine doesn't remember where she hits the ball. Joanna sees Catherine's ball slightly off the fairway, when she's always been down the middle since their first game together, years ago. They walk to Catherine's ball and Joanna points it out to her.

Joanna starts beating Catherine at the game, which had never happened before. She notices Catherine's backswing is shorter, but still she's out-driving Joanna and is as graceful.

She starts having more head tremors and Joanna convinces her to see Dr. Ban. He's been their doctor for three years now since he came to the town to practice. At the doctor's, they go in together and the nurse checks Catherine's blood pressure and pulse and writes it down. A few minutes later the doctor comes in and shakes both their hands.

"Hello, how are you two doing?"

"Good and you?" Joanna answers as he turns to Catherine.

"And what's happening with you?"

"Joanna is concerned something is wrong."

"Oh … and what is that?" he said looking at Catherine, then at Joanna.

"She says my head shakes and I stare at the ceiling. She says I forget where I hit the golf ball when playing golf."

Joanna, seated in a chair, watches Catherine to make sure she tells him exactly what she's observed and waits to see the doctor's reaction. He then turns to Joanna and she explains what she had been noticing in Catherine.

"Let me check your lungs and listen to your heart … sounds all right, now your reflexes." Catherine's foot jumps as he strikes her knee with the rubber hammer. "Watch my finger." Joanna watches Catherine move her eyes back and forth, then up and down, after his finger. He asks her to lie down and presses on her stomach, checking her armpits, and ankles.

"I'd like to do blood work, just to make sure everything's okay. It's probably your heart medication for the Mitral Valve. Sometimes heart medications can make the brain do strange things. In fact, let's change it to something else," and pulling out his script pad he writes a prescription. He shakes both their hands and says goodbye, and sends the nurse in to draw blood.

"Oh, boy. I hate this."

The nurse assures her it will only take a minute. But after the third try Catherine is making faces and hates every minute of it. Joanna watches, feeling badly for her, knowing she is in pain. The nurse repeats, "I'm sorry. Because of your roll-over veins, they collapse. You just have tired veins that roll over and want to sleep." This gets a smile from Catherine. Finally the nurse finds a vein and Joanna watches the blood flow into the small tube while Catherine looks the other way.

On the way home, they stop by the drugstore to fill the new prescription and feel Catherine deserves an ice cream after the tension she'd been through. A feeling everything will be okay comes over them as they chat and enjoy their ice cream.

The nurse calls the next day. "Your blood work came back fine. The doctor wants you to take the medication he prescribed."

A few days on the new medication and Catherine is worse. When she goes to get up out of a chair after sitting, she's dizzy, with heart palpitations, feeling she's going to pass out, and falls on the floor. She doesn't want to go out of the house because of the way she feels and Joanna knows *exactly* how she feels.

Doctor Ban tries another medication. "We have to find the right one that will stop your palpitations," he says. He orders more blood work and more extensive testing – neurological tests, cardiac test, and an MRI of the brain. They spend almost a month going from one doctor to another, taking test after test.

One test, an EEG without sleep, from the neurologist, Catherine had to stay awake for twenty-four hours. Joanna wanted to be awake with her, and did until 2:00 a.m., when she could no longer stay awake. Joanna came out of her bedroom at 4:30 a. m. to go to the bathroom and saw Catherine sitting in the living room watching television.

"See, I'm not sleeping. I'm wide awake and bright eyed," smiling at Joanna.

"Would you like a cup of tea? I'll try and stay up with you and lie on the couch."

"You don't have to. I won't go to sleep. Go back to bed."

"I know you won't but I'd like to stay with you." Like the saying in the picture – she wants to be 'by her side'. Joanna made tea and they played gin rummy for an hour and a half, then at six o'clock she made pancakes and eggs for breakfast.

At 8:30 a.m., Catherine went for the brain wave test, which was normal. All tests were coming back normal, but Catherine was still having head tremors and once in awhile forgetting where she'd left a glass of water or her car keys. But, then again, Joanna forgets where she puts her keys at times. Maybe it's nothing. She tries to instill this in her mind.

***

A few days later Joanna and Catherine are at the hospital for the final test, a spinal tap, checking for encephalitis. The neurologist enters the hospital room where Catherine and Joanna have been waiting for two hours.

"Sorry I'm late. I had an emergency," as he greets both of them. "Catherine would you please lie down on your side and pull your knees up to your chest. This will only take a few minutes." When Joanna sees the long needle, she heads for the hallway.

The neurologist finishes the test and meets Joanna in the hall.

"What do you think is wrong with her?" Joanna asks.

"I don't know. If this comes back normal then I would suggest a PET scan."

"What happens if this shows something?"

"Then she will be treated with medications and hopefully she will be all right."

"Then I hope this test does show something."

"I have to go. I'm late. I'll call you when the results come in. It should be a day or two."

"Thanks doc."

***

The office called to say the spinal test came back normal and in a week they headed to Long Island for a PET scan. Catherine got the name of a neurologist from one of her golf friends and made an appointment to have the test done. They decide to take the train as Joanna didn't feel confident driving the distance. With all they had been through, they decide it would be better to leave the driving to the engineer. The train was full of people headed north before Thanksgiving and it was a fun way to travel. They played gin rummy to pass the time and ate in the dining car, sitting with other people. Catherine met a fellow she had played golf with in a tournament years ago at Pinehurst, North Carolina. They talked golf and the twenty-one hour trip to Grand

Central Station went faster.

***

Once on Long Island, they see family and friends before going to the hospital. It was good to be on the Island again for the first time since Joanna had gotten the heart monitor.

At North Shore Hospital, the receptionist shows them to a large waiting room. They're in a huge New York hospital and have forgotten how many people there are, compared to their small town of Jupiter. They feel they're only a number without a face. Sitting quietly but nervous, Joanna looks at Catherine once in a while and sees a worried look on her face. She smiles back at Joanna, but still Joanna sees the look, or maybe Catherine is seeing Joanna's worried look. They are at a loss for words, not knowing what to expect, when the nurse calls them in to meet the doctor. Following her down the hall to an open door, they see a good-looking young man with curly dark hair sitting behind a desk. He has a smart look about him that makes him look like top-of-his-class smart – it's just a feeling Joanna has. Dr. Greenberg seems pleasant and welcomes them, making them feel at ease as they sit opposite him.

Many questions are asked about what brought them to him and Catherine talks of her golf friend who sent her. Giving him all the reports from Florida, he settles back in his chair studying them.

"This is good. It looks like you've had everything done to you," looking at Catherine.

She smiles and says, "yes, you could say that."

"We won't have to repeat any tests you've already had. Right now, I'm going to ask you some questions." Catherine nods her head, 'okay.'

"Do you want me to leave?" asks Joanna.

"No, you can stay," he answers.

"Catherine, I'm going to give you three words to remember. Then I'll ask you to repeat them later. The words are: Boat, Pencil, TV.

"Boat, Pencil, and TV," she repeats.

"What day is it?"

"Tuesday."

"What month is it?"

"November."

"Who is the president?"

Catherine answers, "President Regan."

"What season is it?"

"Fall."

"Starting with one hundred, subtract seven from the last number."

"93...86...79..."

Joanna sits in amazement as Catherine subtracts seven from every last number while Joanna counts on the fingers in her lap, thinking that if she were taking the test she would have failed already.

"Very good," as he stops Catherine from counting, and gives her a sheet of blank paper and asks her to draw the face of a clock, with the hands on 2:30.

Joanna watches thinking, 'how stupid. She knows how to tell time. Why isn't he doing some other kind of tests?'

Joanna looks at the clock Catherine has drawn. It's small but the hands say 2:30.

"Can you tell me the three words I asked you to remember?" he asks.

Joanna watches Catherine put her finger to her lips, looking a little nervous and then down, closing her eyes.

"TV, boat and uh ... car."

Joanna didn't know if she was right or not, but it sounded right. Joanna remembered two of the words, TV and boat, but wasn't sure of the third, she didn't think it was car, though. The doctor says she did fine. Joanna, on the other hand, has already failed the number test and some of the other questions.

"We're going down the hall to the next room where the PET scan will be taken. Joanna have a seat here outside the room," and he opens the door as Catherine follows him.

"Okay, see you later, Ca."

She turns around, "yep, see you later."

Joanna takes a seat just outside the room and picks up a magazine to wait. The doctor said it would take about forty-five minutes, she thinks, as she searches through the pictures not reading. She can't concentrate on anything except Catherine in another large tube. She got a glimpse of it as she walked by the room.

She wonders what it will find and if she is seriously ill?

Why haven't they found anything yet?

What more is there to look for?

Maybe there's nothing wrong. She's so tired of doctors and tests for the both of them for the past year.

The technician comes out, "You can come in now we're finished."

Catherine is sitting on a chair tying her sneakers and sees Joanna walk in, "Thank God that's over with." She says.

When Joanna sees how long the tube is, "I don't blame you, Ca," pointing to the tube. "I couldn't have gone in that one either."

206

"The doctor wants to speak with both of you in his office," the technician tells them.

'Catherine looks so healthy. How could there be anything wrong with her?' Joanna thinks, while Catherine walks by her side, to the doctor's office. Catherine tells her about the loud noises that she heard while in the tube.

Dr. Greenberg greets them again, "you did good Catherine. After I have a chance to look at the PET scan, I'll call you on Monday with the findings."

Today is Friday, Joanna thinks. They shake hands, thank him and are out the door into a cold wind that has picked up since three hours ago. The weather report this morning said there's going to be frost tonight.

***

They drive a few miles away to Joanna's mother-in-law's house, to say hello and have lunch with her. Joanna has stayed in phone contact with her through the years since leaving Ed. She was like a second mother when she was young, living only a few doors away. She has become almost blind now and can barely make out Joanna's face. Joanna's happy to see her again after many years and introduces Catherine. They have lunch together, remembering the old days – the fun and the dinners she would cook – then say their good-byes and leave for their one-hour trip back to the motel. Joanna's only thought is 'I want to keep busy this weekend and spend time with family and friends.'

***

Once off the Long Island Expressway, Joanna has a thought, "Ca, I think we need some chocalotta ice cream right now."

"I agree. Make mine a hot fudge sundae."

"You're entitled, after all you've been through today. I don't know how you stood it so long in that tube."

They still remember the times they went for chocolate ice cream sodas after a hot day of golf, but Catherine would be the one to say, "I think we need some chocalotta ice cream," and Joanna thought it a neat name for chocolate.

They brought the ice cream back to the motel only a few miles away, talked of the day's events, and how they needed the ice cream to lift their spirits.

Joanna's mother has left a message for them at the motel to call. When she returns the call, Maria asks, "How did it go with Catherine today?"

"It went well mom, I guess."

"How about coming to dinner tonight? Paul and Donna are going to be here."

"What are you making for dinner, Mom?" Joanna asked, loud enough so Catherine could hear. Ca nods her head yes.

"I've put sauce on to cook with meatballs and sausage. Do you want linguini or spaghetti?"

"Wait, I'll ask Catherine."

"Mom wants to know, do you want spaghetti or linguini for dinner?" smiling at Catherine.

"Oh … spaghetti, I guess." She was happy Maria treated her as a second daughter.

"She said she wants spaghetti, Mom, and we'll bring desert."

"No, don't bring desert. The freezer is full of pie and cake."

But Joanna could hear John in the background

208

saying, "tell her to bring cheese strudel."

"Hush, John," Maria snickered. "Be quiet."

"No, tell her to bring strudel." John yells louder.

"It's John again. Okay. John says bring strudel … cheese, preferably."

"Good, I like the cheese also. If you need help, Mom, let me know. We'll be here for the rest of the afternoon. We got up at six this morning and we're bushed."

"Tell Catherine we said hello."

"I'll, see you later." And Joanna set the phone on the nightstand.

They laid down for a nap and Catherine was snoring within ten minutes. Joanna also stressed from the mornings adventure stayed awake thinking.

***

Dinner that evening was just what they needed. While John played the piano and sang, Maria ran around making sure everyone had enough to eat. She loves to see people enjoying themselves. The spaghetti and meatballs were delicious, just as Joanna remembered them as a child. Maria was a good Italian cook and she had taught Joanna everything she knew, but Joanna didn't have that special something, a touch of this and a touch of that. No measuring cups with Maria.

Afterward, while Donna and Joanna did the dishes, Donna asked, "when will you find out about the test?"

"The doctor said he would call us on Monday."

"How is she doing? She looks a little nervous."

"Yeah … well, I'd be too, if I were her. She's not though. You know Ca, she takes anything as it comes."

They could hear Catherine in the living room

laughing with Paul, talking golf. Donna and Joanna joined them when finished in the kitchen and Maria brought out a photo album of when her children were small.

"Hey Ca, look at how much hair Paul used to have." Joanna said laughingly, looking at her brother, who was almost bald now.

"Wait, you're going to lose yours someday." He retorted.

"No I won't," as she ran her hands through her thick dark brown hair, that had a hint of gray.

Everyone laughed while Paul and Joanna discussed their heads. At ten o'clock they said goodnight and left behind a stressful day taken over by a lovely evening.

***

Saturday they played nine holes at St. Andrews with friends, then ate dinner out and another day had passed. Sunday morning they picked up Hope and went to church, meeting Maria while John sang upstairs in the choir. It was just like old times for Joanna, everyone together in one pew. Prayers went up for Catherine that when the phone call came tomorrow, she wouldn't be seriously ill.

They went to the diner for breakfast after church and after a meal of pancakes and sausage or eggs and bacon, Hope spoke up, "when are you going back to Florida?"

"We're probably going to leave in a week or two. It's getting too cold here," Joanna replied.

She could see Maria's face drop and Joanna knew her mom hated to hear the word 'leaving'. Almost every year they had come back to Long Island around the same time to visit family and friends, except for the past few years, since Joanna's heart problems.

"When are you going to hear from the doctor?" Maria changed the subject.

"Tomorrow morning some time. We'll stay at the motel till then. That's the only number he has. Maybe we can get together later in the day, Mom."

Hope spoke of school and when she'd be coming down to Florida for a visit, during school recess. She was in high school and was in her own little world of boyfriends, trying to decide which one to go out with. She had met many interesting kids from all over the world at the new boarding school, and Joanna could see she was happy there. It had opened a new world for Hope, away from her brother's and father's arguments at the dinner table. She was also looking forward to college.

After two hours of chatting, Joanna and Catherine said goodbye to Maria and John, who were ready for naps, took Hope to a movie and then home.

***

Monday morning Joanna went down to the motels' continental-breakfast bar and brought food back for herself and Catherine. They could eat downstairs in the living room-lobby but didn't want to miss the call they were waiting for. They were just finishing their coffee when the phone rang. Looking at each other, for what seemed like a long time, Joanna sat on the bed and answered the phone.

"Good morning. How are you this morning?" Dr. Greenberg asked.

"Fine thank you. Do you have any news for us?"

He went into a long diagnosis of Catherine's PET scan and Joanna understood some of it, but not all. She wanted to know if it was thumbs up or thumbs down, clear and concise.

Then she heard the words, "I'm sorry to tell you this. Catherine has a dementia disease known as Alzheimer's, possibly Multi-Infarc."

At first it didn't register and she asked him to repeat it. All she heard was the word – Alzheimer's – once again. She couldn't think of anything else to say, and wanted him to take the word back, as she stood up in shock.

"Thank you" and she hung up.

Catherine, sitting in a chair by the window, stopped reading, seeing the blank look on Joanna's face.

"Who was it?"

Joanna didn't answer.

"Was it the doctor?" Again she spoke.

Joanna trying to get her thoughts in place couldn't think of anything to say. She didn't believe the word she'd just heard.

'Alzheimer's? How can it be? How bad is it and where did she get it?'

Again she heard Catherine's voice, as in the distance. "What is it?"

Finally, "oh, it's nothing." She finally put the words together, "Yes, that was the doctor."

"Well, what did he say?"

Joanna then looked at Catherine feeling pity, no – sorrow, no – there wasn't any feeling.

"It's…. Alzheimer's," not thinking of anything else to say, except the truth.

"Alzheimer's? … Oh God, no … I'll need to go to a nursing home," she cries.

Joanna, walking to Catherine, pulls a chair up next

to her friend and puts her arms around her.

"No, no. We'll work this out. We'll go through this together." With both heads side by side, tears flowed like tiny rivers as they sobbed, not believing the word.

"Everything will be all right Ca, you'll see. Besides, maybe he's wrong."

They held each other for what seemed a long time as Catherine cried. Joanna wanted her to know she would never abandon her. They would go through this together as Catherine went through Joanna's heart problem with her.

At the same time, somewhere in the back of Joanna's mind, she was saying to herself, 'I know the love we have for each other is stronger than any illness. That alone will cure her'.

'I know *YOU* will hear our cries, Dear Lord, to cure her.'

***

Joanna held Catherine, lying together on the bed, with a spread pulled up, to keep them warm. It felt as if ice water were running through their veins and all the blood had drained from the both of them. Dr. Ban called from Florida a few hours later.

"Yes, hello Joanna. I just got off the phone with Dr. Greenberg. I am so sorry to hear the news. If there is anything I can do, please call me."

"Thank you doctor. Thank you for calling. We'll probably be home in a few days," was all Joanna could say.

***

For the next few days they tried to continue their visits with family and friends, both of them trying quietly to accept what had happened. But Joanna felt

213

they should go back to Florida, where they could be in their home instead of a motel room. She canceled the rest of their family gatherings, explaining to everyone over the phone about Catherine's diagnosis, and that they were leaving for home. Family and friends were surprised, sad, and offered their help.

They left two days later, on the twenty-one hour train trip. Both of them were still in shock and stayed in their compartment playing cards or staring out the window, going out only to get their meals.

Once home, they lived as if the word Alzheimer's didn't exist, at least until they became used to it. They did their normal everyday living, going to the store, playing golf and seeing friends and neighbors, who were also surprised over the word. No one could believe it, least of all Joanna and Catherine.

***

As the holiday approached, they went all out on decorating the condo inside and out. They had just had a terrible year, with Joanna's heart condition and Catherine's diagnosis. It was as if they were living a nightmare that wasn't going away. They felt they deserved to have a Christmas with nothing but happiness and laughter. They had forgotten *how* to laugh this past year.

Catherine walked down to the storage room to get ornaments, and Joanna moved furniture to make space for the tree. They decorated, playing Christmas Carols and singing, tossing tinsel on the tree, like kids at play. Neighbors came to the door with fruit cakes and candy canes and the phone rang with well wishes from Long Island. Joanna made Cornish hens with rice stuffing, browned and cooked in peaches and prunes, with green

214

beans, salad, fresh rolls and chocolate cake for desert. They invited Ileen, who had just had a knee replacement and her nurse, Doris, who was caring for her. Helen, another friend, who lived alone and didn't have family, also came. The table was decorated in sprigs of pine needles and pinecones, with a large glass bowl of different colored Christmas balls in the center. Catherine had shined the silverware and the brass candlestick holders and filled them with red candles. The wreath on the door was made of fruit of every color. They had bought a teddy bear, wearing a red Santa hat and scarf that played Christmas Carols when you pressed his foot.

A beautiful evening was had by all, especially Catherine and Joanna, because they were able to share it with friends. When everyone left, Catherine and Joanna got ready for their tradition, attending Christmas Eve mass. They were tired this year, not like other years, but they knew they needed to go to church, to make the evening complete. That night in church, Catherine and Joanna out sang everyone. They sang from their hearts and souls and wanted all illnesses to be gone.

***

The next few weeks were spent talking to the Alzheimer's Association for information on the disease, since neither Catherine nor Joanna knew anything about it except it was bad. They were told of a support group near their home that met once a week. Catherine and Joanna spoke of going, and Catherine made it clear she wanted to attend. She wanted to know what to expect with the disease, and to see if there was help for her.

In February, they went to their first support group meeting, held at the hospital. Two familiar faces were there, Linda and Ray, the couple who had helped them decorate the condo. Ray's brother had Alzheimer's, and Ray was there for support, and also facilitated the meeting. It was good to talk with old friends that they had something in common with. It was a small group of maybe ten or twelve people and all were caregivers. Melinda, a nurse, was the guest speaker this day and greeted everyone.

Catherine and Joanna sat and listened to what people had to say as they went around the table asking how everyone's week had gone. They listened to horror stories, such as people running out of the house in their nightgowns in the middle of the night, and having to call the police to help find them. One woman, Leone, told of her father breaking the water pipes, because he thought he was still a plumber. After listening to only three caregivers, Joanna wanted to leave. She felt they were in a place they didn't belong. These folks were speaking of people, not like Catherine, and Joanna wasn't like the caregivers. 'Why did we come here? This was not for us' – it felt foreign to Joanna. Then Melinda came to them asking their names.

"My name is Catherine and I have Alzheimer's disease."

Joanna looked at Catherine in surprise. My God, she didn't think she was going blurt it out like that, so blunt. Joanna knew Catherine to be open, but didn't expect her to say it the way she did. But somewhere inside Joanna was proud of her for saying it like she did.

"Good to have you with us, Catherine," Melinda said.

Next, all eyes were on Joanna.

"My name is Joanna and I live with Catherine." that wasn't too hard, she thought.

Melinda smiled, along with a few others and said, "Welcome to the group girls. You'll find we have a lot of fun here. How can we help you?"

"I want to know if there is a cure for this disease?" asked Catherine.

"No, there isn't a cure yet, but they're working on it. There is a research center in Tamarac doing studies. If you call the Alzheimer's Association they can give you the number."

"Thank you, we will," answered Catherine.

Joanna spoke next, "What is the age a person gets the disease? And could a person have a wrong diagnosis?" Joanna noticed Catherine was the youngest in the group, diagnosed with Alzheimer's at age sixty-four.

"It was once considered a young person's disease – as young as age thirty, but they're finding more elderly people now are being diagnosed. The name used to be called senility." And every one in the room shook their heads. "As far as diagnosis, the only one I know of is a brain biopsy after death."

"Thank you, Melinda."

After that, Joanna and Catherine sat quietly, listening and watching others in the group. The stories were almost impossible to believe. Joanna remembered an old woman that lived across the street from her, when she was a child. Joanna would see a black car coming for her when she yelled and everyone said she was crazy. Her son then put her in an institution, Joanna remembered. Could this be the same disease?

They had coffee and cake with the rest of the group but didn't want to stay after hearing the stories. Joanna was sorry they had gone and on the way home no words were spoken. Joanna didn't like what she had seen and heard.

At dinner, Joanna said to Catherine, "Ca, I don't think we should go back to the meetings. You're not sick. We still play golf and swim and ride our bikes. You're not like those people they talked about." Catherine agreed.

***

Catherine's birthday came on February 14th. She turned sixty-five and looked more like forty-five. Her hair was without gray and she was tan from golf and swimming, she looked the picture of health. At Catherine's request, Joanna made shrimp and spaghetti and a chocolate cake with all sixty-five candles. Friends were invited to help blow out the candles and enjoyed every minute.

They got calls from the Alzheimer's Association about Catherine going to a Day Care Center and Joanna told them she didn't need a center, that they were doing just fine. Catherine was active and they didn't even think she had the disease. The association was nice, telling her to call if needed. They went to church every morning, as usual before golf, and prayed a lot this year about Catherine's illness – to cure it, make it go away, or that the diagnosis had been wrong. They decided not to go north this year, as Maria and John had been down for a few weeks visit and Hope and her girlfriends had spent their school holiday with them. Matthew came with his fiancee for a few days, also.

***

218

Catherine had handled all the household finances and now she wanted to teach Joanna. She had an investment broker in Florida and an accountant up north, whom she had used for years. Joanna had spoken with the accountant when Catherine had introduced her to him and she'd met the broker, since he had taught a class in finances they had taken at the local high school when they first came to Florida. Catherine had wanted Joanna to know where everything was in case of an emergency.

She had made Joanna power of attorney and health care advocate back in 1986, and at that time Joanna had wanted no part of it. Joanna told her then she was worrying about something that wasn't going to happen and she would probably drop dead before Catherine. She knew Catherine was always prepared and had everything under control. She said it came from being a Girl Scout. Now, Joanna was glad she had done this, if she needed to act on Catherine's behalf, it was all in place. She had wanted to put the condo in both their names but Joanna's lawyer was against it, saying it would be considered personal property and Ed would be entitled to half. So Catherine left it in her will, if anything happened to her, it would all be passed on to Joanna.

Joanna had no experience with handling household finances. Ed and she had life insurance policies and some mutual funds that Ed handled, but there were no other financial records or important documents that she knew of. There wasn't anything else needed, because they were husband and wife. The little money she got from Ed she used to buy gifts for her mom or items for Catherine and their home.

Her divorce was still going on and the lawyer said her husband was not cooperating. She told the attorney to please do whatever necessary, because she wanted it over. Joanna didn't have to worry about paying the lawyer, because he said he would take a percentage of the final money awarded, which was expected to be more than enough for her to live on for the rest of her life. She *was* starting to worry now about Catherine's health.

TRUST

AS THE WEEKS and months went by, Catherine had more head tremors and started to leave clothing, or personal items and her paperwork around the house. Before this, she had been neat and organized in every way, and had taught Joanna to be. Now she'd look for the items, not knowing where she'd left them. She drove wherever they needed to go, and drove well, but Joanna was starting to worry about this. One night at dinner Joanna approached Catherine.

"Ca, I think we should discuss your driving."

"Yes, what about it?"

Joanna tried to think of the right words to say without hurting Catherine's feelings.

"I've been thinking, if you're in an accident and they find you've been diagnosed with Alzheimer's, you will be held responsible. I'm not saying you would cause it."

"You want me to give up driving?"

"Well no not really. Maybe it's a good idea to ask your advisor about this. Okay?"

Catherine agreed and spoke with her accountant, who recommended that she no longer drive. Joanna was right and hated the idea, but everything could be lost if she were driving and had an accident.

***

Joanna called the research center in Tamarac and made an appointment with the hopes of getting Catherine on a drug that would stop this disease.

Catherine writes in her little black book: 7:30 a.m. Dr. Mike, Neuro Med. Center for Res.

Anticipating the trip to the center, they didn't get much sleep, hoping for a cure for Catherine's illness. If you wanted to know anything about Alzheimer's this was the place to go. But in Joanna's mind, Catherine didn't have Alzheimer's. It's just something else they haven't found a name for yet.

The drive was over one and a half-hours, because of heavy commuter traffic. They planned on making a day of it, lunch after the meeting, possibly some shopping and then home.

With Joanna driving and Catherine the map-reader this time, they found the research center easily, located in front of a large hospital. The waiting room was small, with maybe ten chairs for patients and their loved ones.

They signed in and the receptionist opened the sliding glass window.

"Hi, first time here?" she asked.

"Yes," came two voices in harmony.

"Please fill these out," handing Joanna and Catherine at least ten sheets of papers. "There's a wait and we're backed up, so please have a seat and make yourselves comfortable."

With papers on their laps, they started with the first page. Catherine filled in her name, address, social security and insurance numbers, while Joanna watched.

Then came papers asking who your doctor was and past history, which Joanna helped Catherine with. They had brought all records, lab work, Dr. Ban's reports and everything else with them, just in case there were other questions. When done Joanna delivered the papers to the receptionist and they sat and waited. Joanna picked up a magazine she used to read with her children, while waiting at doctors' offices years ago. Pages full of pictures where you had to find the hidden hammer or pineapple among everything else on the page. This kept them busy and laughing as the time slid by.

When they were called in to meet with the doctor, Joanna could see a long hallway with doors jutting off from it. They were led into a room, asked to sit in two chairs in front of a large mahogany desk and the nurse said, "Dr. Mike will be with you shortly."

Joanna looked out the window with Catherine's eyes following.

A young man in his late thirties or early forties came in and introduced himself.

"Hello, I'm Dr. Mike."

"Nice to meet you. I'm Joanna and this is my friend Catherine."

"Hello." Catherine answered.

He seemed pleasant and friendly, and made them feel at ease. Sitting down, he opened the folder the nurse had left on his desk.

"How was the drive from Jupiter this morning? Do you live there year round?" he asked.

"A little heavy traffic, but not bad. Yes, we're there most of the year except for two or three months we go to Long Island." answered Joanna.

"Jupiter is nice, not like down here. It's a city. I

take my wife and son up on weekends to fish off Jupiter Inlet."

"Oh, do you? That's not far from where we live. We like Jupiter and have been there since 1985," answered Joanna. She could see Catherine was nervous, yet smiling.

Then he started with medical questions. "Why did we want research? What led us to him?" And more, as he went over the paperwork.

"Joanna, will you please wait in the other room while I talk to Catherine?"

Getting up, Joanna turned to Catherine, "See you later, kiddo," she smiled and left.

A half-hour later Catherine came out, joined by a nurse in a white uniform.

"Joanna, would you please come in?" asked Dr. Mike.

"Catherine's gone down the hall to take tests. She's very nice, but she *is* confused at times."

"I think I'd be too, after all she's been through the past few months. Doctor after doctor and no diagnosis, then up north where she was diagnosed with Alzheimer's. I think we're both confused and in shock."

Then Joanna spilled her thoughts of the past few months.

"Where did it come from? How did she get it? Could it be something else?" On and on she went, almost happy to vent to a professional in the field.

Dr. Mike let Joanna go on, but couldn't answer the questions.

"What is she like at home?" he asked.

"She's fine, except for her head shaking and leaving

some things out of place around the house. I don't think she has Alzheimer's."

"I'm afraid the PET scan shows she has some form of dementia."

"But she is *so* organized! I do the cooking and we clean the house together. She's never cooked, not even when I met her. But she handles all the bills and finances. How is it possible for someone to be so organized and have dementia?"

"She is in the very beginning stages. The disease can go from three to twenty-one years. We don't know that much about it."

Joanna went on telling him Catherine still did all the normal activities they'd always done – golf, swim, shop, read the paper, watch TV, go the movies and more. He asked what her food habits were like.

"We eat all fresh foods, vegetables, fish, all the right foods you're suppose to eat. We don't eat red meat or fats, because of my heart problem."

"Does she smoke?"

"No. We both quit in 1988 when I started having palpitations. You know that was weird, we both had the same type palpitations. Hers followed mine by a month or two and that's when they found her Mitral Valve Prolapsed."

She mentioned she felt it had been caused by something in the air they were breathing or in the apartment, or they had possibly picked it up on the golf course. One day in particular, fish were lying dead on the shore and floating in the ponds.

"Joanna, you know there is no medication for Alzheimer's."

"Yeah, that's what our doctor told us. That's why

we're here, hoping *you* can help us."

"What we'll do after her blood work and other tests, she'll be put on a drug of her choice. It is a double-blind study which means you don't know if you're getting the drug or not, until after a number of months."

"You mean she won't even get the real drug?"

"We won't know at first. It will either be a placebo *or* the drug. The only people who know, is the company who makes the drug."

"You won't know either?"

"No, only the drug company knows. She will be tested each month, when you come with her. She'll have blood work and testing done then it's sent to the drug company."

This was all new to Joanna. She understood it, but then again, she *didn't*. She asked as many questions as she could think of, but was starting to feel stressed and tired. God knows what Catherine was going through at the same time.

Dr. Mike finished questioning Joanna and was behind schedule with his other patients, so he led her back to the waiting room.

Joanna, afterward, was allowed to go into the room where Catherine was having blood work done. Poor Catherine, she hated blood work, because of those rollover veins. But she hung in there like a real trouper – she knew it had to be done. After that, they were sent to the hospital behind the building, which Joanna had seen driving into the doctor's offices.

"So how did the testing go, Ca?"

"Not too bad, but some of the questions were pretty stupid. The woman asked me if I could tie my shoes laces."

"I guess they're set questions, for everyone who comes to the center, not just you." Joanna reinforced.

Taking the stairs to the third floor to get some exercise, Joanna and Catherine entered another office. This was where she would have an EEG to check the brain waves in action. Joanna was allowed in the room with her, watching her friend on a table, wondering what she was thinking looking at flashing white lights, while a machine spit rolls of paper all over the floor. All Joanna could see were rows of straight lines or wavy, up and then down. She had had all of this done before without the flashing lights. This had to be repeated to be part of a study. Thank God she didn't have to repeat the MRI.

Dr. Mike saw them back in his office at the end of the day and told them of his plan of attack

"There are three studies Catherine qualifies for," handing them three manila envelopes.

"Read over the material and pick the study you want to go on."

They listened with a hopeful feeling now and Joanna knew Catherine was going to be cured, if not through medicine, then through their nightly prayers.

"We're staying at a motel on the beach tonight. Do you think you could set us up with an appointment in the morning?" asked Joanna.

Joanna and Catherine followed Dr. Mike to the receptionist. "Is eight tomorrow morning too early?"

"No, that'd be fine." And the receptionists handed Joanna a card.

"Thank you, we'll see you in the morning," Joanna answered, knowing surely that Catherine was tired after three hours of testing.

They went to Denny's for an early dinner and then got a room at the beach. After putting their belongings in the room, they retrieved the beach chairs out of the trunk of the car and went to sit by the ocean. They went for a short walk along the water's edge and then settled down facing the waves. High tide was beautiful and soon the sound of the waves put them both to sleep. Joanna opened her eyes every once an awhile to gaze at the waves, then at Catherine, who *was* in a deep sleep. She looked so peaceful here. Joanna wondered, 'Why was that other life out there, thoughts, full of worry?' She wished life could always be like this, as it was in the beginning.

Before sunset, they went back to their room to go over the studies handed them earlier. They read two studies from Europe and one from the United States, which told of a drug, called Nimo. It had been used for another illness, but they were doing new testing to see its effects on the Alzheimer's brain. Dr. Mike had told them sometimes there are drugs used for other illnesses, but, by chance, are found to help different diseases.

Joanna called Paul and he reassured them Nimo was a safe drug to use. Catherine and Joanna discussed it and picked the drug Nimo, because it had fewer side effects and they didn't want to pick a drug from another country. The only side effect of Nimo was possible stomach nausea, depending on the person. They were confident they had made the right choice and slept well that night.

***

The next morning they ate breakfast at the motel, then on to the research center, telling Dr. Mike which study they had decided on. Joanna and Catherine had to sign many papers, as if their lives depended on it and in a sense, one life did.

He explained how the study worked, as far as office visits for blood work, then gave them boxes of the medication. They made their next appointment with the receptionist for a later hour, to miss the heavy traffic next time, and said their good-byes. They left with a feeling of new hope hidden inside the boxes.

Starving, they stopped at a luncheonette to eat tuna sandwiches and lemonade and Joanna could see the look of happiness in Catherine's eyes and felt it within, knowing all was not lost. They finished lunch and went shopping to look at clothes, then stopped at a bagel shop, buying enough for them and the neighbors at the condo unit. The bagels in South Florida tasted just like the ones in New York. In Jupiter there weren't any bagel shops. The only bagels were frozen in grocery stores.

Taking the long way home on Route One, driving through small towns and seeing beautiful homes on Palm Beach Island, for the fifty miles stretch, relaxed them. It was a longer way to travel, but it was a beautiful day and they didn't have to hurry home for anything. Arriving home late that afternoon, their neighbors, Jay and Bea, were standing on the catwalk when they pulled up. They were nice neighbors and good friends. "Welcome home," they said, as they did almost every year, when Catherine and Joanna came back from their northern trip visiting family and friends.

"Hello, wait till you see what we have for you," Catherine yelled out.

"What is it?" asked Jay.

"Bagels from South Florida; all kinds, onion, poppy seed and more. I'll bring them up in a little while. We need to get in and unload right now. See you later," answered Catherine.

Later, Joanna separated the bagels into bags of five for their neighbors and Catherine delivered them throughout the condos while Joanna made a light meal. They said grace and Catherine took two little white pills before dinner, and Joanna's own little prayer was, "Please cure Catherine."

***

Catherine and Joanna went to the beach during the next few weeks, played golf, walked the heart trail near their home – two and a half miles, three times a week. They rode their bikes around the neighborhood after dinner and swam in the pool in the morning hours. The exercise made them feel better mentally, and they thought if they kept the body in good physical condition, it would never break down to a disease. 'Why then had this happened?' Joanna never stopped thinking.

And then on March 5, 1991, Catherine took Joanna to play golf at a club she belonged to before Joanna met her. She played it in the winter months when she came to Florida for six months in prior years. Joanna came once in a while to play and it was always a treat. It was an exclusive club, ranking among the top ten clubs in the country. President George Bush was a member and when he came to visit his mother on Jupiter Island, he would play here. Catherine had told Joanna he'd flown in by helicopter and while he played the course, his guards were posted all over the roof of the clubhouse.

You needed to have a caddie and Joanna also knew it cost Catherine one hundred dollars to have her as a guest.

"I'll pay the caddie fee," she said to Catherine.

"No you won't. It's your birthday and I'm taking you out."

And Joanna accepted graciously.

They played with two women Catherine had known for years from the clubs up north and in the winter months playing here. They were likable but Joanna had a hard time in conversation with them. Having grown up poor and being limited in grammar and expressing herself, she felt inferior in their presence. She was grateful Catherine had brought her to play this great course, though. It was a glorious day for her forty-ninth birthday and a honor to play the course.

***

Joanna cooked a St. Patty's Day dinner and both dressed in green and white. Catherine wore her kelly green pants and a white blouse and Joanna wore white pants with a green blouse. They invited their neighbors and friends for corned beef and cabbage, with green Jell-O for desert. Things were going well.

Later in March, a good friend of Catherine's passed away and she asked Joanna to take her to the memorial, for she was no longer driving. It was held in a small chapel on Jupiter Island, which held about two hundred people. The church was packed and it seemed Catherine knew everyone there. Joanna watched her as she chatted with her friends and telling them all, she had Alzheimer's. Again Joanna was amazed how open she was about it.

***

Friends, Rosie and Carla, came for a visit to play golf one day and stay for lunch. Joanna noticed a difference in Catherine's playing during golf. She had trouble keeping score and said her eyesight was going bad, making a joke of it.

Rosie and her husband Jeff, had bought a condo just north of Joanna and Catherine. They rode in golf carts, Rosie with Joanna and Carla with Catherine. After golf they all went back to the condo for lunch. Joanna had prepared carrot soup and french bread the night before, so Rosie and Joanna went to the kitchen to make a salad, while Carla and Catherine sat on the back porch.

"I can see a difference in Catherine," Rosie said.

"Can you, honestly?"

"Oh yes, Joanna. She's changed since I last saw her. Her look is different. She doesn't have that soft smile she used to have. She looks worried and is much thinner."

Joanna wondered what Carla was thinking since she had known Catherine at West Meadow Beach years ago.

"I guess I don't see it, being I'm with her every day. Rosie, I don't know what I'm going to do without her."

Rosie put her arm around Joanna's shoulder. "She still plays a good game of golf, but she's not the old Catherine I remember."

"I guess we should call them in to eat now, before the carrot soup simmers down to nothing. Thanks for coming Rosie, it's great to see you again."

***

In the beginning of April they went to the research center for testing and were back home early in the day. Catherine worked on the Florida intangible taxes and tried to teach Joanna. It was Greek to Joanna. She'd never done anything like this before. Catherine showed her the statements that came in each month, how to make entries on sheets of paper to see how much money was coming into the household and how much was going out to pay bills. She taught her how dividends come in on a monthly, quarterly or yearly date and where to pencil it in on the graphed sheet. Out of this, she got the yearly income, which needed to be sent to the accountant for taxes. It was hard at first, but Joanna eventually got the hang of it, as she sat week after week working at the dining room table with Catherine. She didn't want to learn this part of their relationship, but she had a feeling she needed to, for the both of them. Joanna also figured that when her divorce was final, she would at least know what to do with her own money.

Joanna talked to Dr. Mike about learning the household finances and how hard it was. He suggested they get a computer and put all the records on it, to be able to track the investments and bills. Catherine agreed, if it would be easier for Joanna but she would keep doing it her own way. They bought a computer that both of them had no knowledge of. Joanna read instructions and recorded all investments and bills on machine while Catherine continued to do it her way, and then they compared both ways at the end of each month. Joanna found she started watching the stock market on television to learn how the economy worked. She had always hated money and what it did to people, especially her own father, because he was so cheap, while his wife worked her heart out. All the arguments were always over money in the household where she grew up, then with Ed she had no knowledge, and didn't want to. Money had left a sour taste in her mouth. Now, though, was the time to learn how it affects one's life and Catherine wanted her to learn it, which is the reason she tried.

***

Joanna noticed while Catherine was on Nimo, she was having a lot of stomach discomfort and trying different stomach soothers, drinking milk, and other things to help with indigestion. On April twentieth, they had an appointment at the research center in the afternoon. This time they didn't leave home until 11:00 a.m., so they'd miss the heavy traffic. Once there, they put Catherine through testing and asked Joanna questions similar to the ones before, though not in so much detail.

"She's having stomach problems and the heart palpitations are back," she told Dr. Mike, while Catherine was being tested.

"Well, it could be the medication but we don't know for sure. If she's having that much discomfort then she *is* on Nimo and not a sugar pill. Let's see what the blood work shows and, if it gets worse, we'll switch to another study."

They were going to Tamarac once a month where Catherine was having cognitive testing and they were asking Joanna how she acted at home. For awhile, Joanna told Dr. Mike she didn't see any difference, except she would get dizzy in the morning before eating, and that she was leaving things out of place around the house still. Other than that, they were playing golf and she was doing her chores, though she was noticeably slower now.

***

Joanna got a call from her mom saying she needed surgery to remove part of the colon because of cancer. Afterward Joanna spoke with the doctor and her brothers by phone, finding the operation turned out fine and they would reattach Maria's colon in six months.

Joanna felt bad not being with her mom, but knew her brothers would be close by and John was always there for Maria. Joanna, still afraid to fly and didn't want to leave Catherine, now. Joanna and Maria spoke daily, on the phone, which was of some comfort to the both of them.

***

Back to the research center in the end of May 1991 and Catherine was given a new drug because of her stomach upsets.

Joanna feels, 'Am I losing hope?'

'Is Catherine losing hope?'

They didn't talk about it, but tried to keep an *up* feeling between them. Joanna felt, if they didn't talk about the disease, then it wouldn't be there.

***

Joanna made reservations for them at the Dora Golf Resort for two days, during their visit to the center. Joanna had been there many years ago with her husband and remembered the great golf courses. She wasn't into golf back then but this would be a nice surprise for Catherine, since she had never played the courses and Joanna knew she would love them and the resort. The main thought was they would have something to look forward to, after their visit to the clinic.

When they got to the resort, Joanna remembered

seeing the building with Ed for the first time, especially the brass railings leading up brick steps. How beautiful this place was, again she thought. A valet came to park the car and Joanna and Catherine went inside. Giving the woman behind the desk their names, she got a bellhop to take them to their room. Joanna looked at Catherine a few times and saw the happiness on her face.

"The room is beautiful. I love the colors," was Catherine's first words. It was a large room with cheerful colors of light blue and yellows, her favorite.

"C'mon, Ca, let's change our clothes and go play nine holes." She didn't give Joanna any discussion about that subject and was ready before Joanna came out of the bathroom.

"Boy, that was fast. How'd you get dressed so fast?"

"You said the word golf. I love to play this time of the day, with shadows on the greens."

It was late afternoon, the best time to play, with the course empty and a cool breeze. They kidded with their usual match of one up or one down or tied. This time they weren't playing for who was going to cook dinner, which was always a laugh because Catherine didn't cook. They were just happy to be there to play.

When they came back they took showers and were down to dinner by eight-thirty and seated near an open French door. Catherine ordered steak and Joanna ordered the same, they felt on vacation. A kitten came over to the opened door, and Catherine talked and played with it. As usual, the animals always came to her. She told the waiter she thought the kitten was hungry and needed some milk. While they were having desert, the kitten got her milk.

Joanna looked at Catherine and saw the softness on her face. "You having fun Ca?"

"Oh Yes. This is a lovely place and the golf course was great today. Are you having fun?"

"I sure am. Wait till you see the Championship Course tomorrow, you're gonna love that even more. Ed and I were here in the 60's and I didn't have as much fun as today with you. Just watching you, makes *my* fun."

***

The next morning they got in line for a breakfast buffet, then out to play the course. This was a real treat since the pro golfers had just played a tournament here and it was in great shape.

"These greens are sure interesting. You're on the green, then you have a forty foot putt, to get to the hole," Catherine announced.

"Now you can visualize what we watched on TV last month. It sure is hard in person and they made it look so easy."

After play, they sat on the open patio overlooking the course, sipping lemonade going over their scorecards.

"Well, it's not too bad. We both shot in the eighties, but I beat you by four shots. Ca, look behind you at the impatience hanging under the trees. Isn't that a brilliant idea?"

Hanging from the trees, in pots, were flowers of all shades and colors.

They sat outside until the sun started down, enjoying the scenery overlooking the golf course, then showered and went to dinner. It had been a gorgeous day and it was good to be close to Catherine. She made Joanna feel complete, even with her illness. They had dinner in the same dining room, at the same table, as the night before, with the same kitten, but this time she had her milk before they got there. After eating, they walked through the complex and looked in the golf shops. Catherine bought Joanna a small white straw hat, with a wide brim and a red and blue colored band. The next morning they had a quick breakfast and started on the road home. It would have been a memorable mini vacation – almost normal – if it hadn't been for Catherine trying to add up the scorecard.

***

A month later they were off to the research center to visit with Dr. Mike. The trip down was slow, because of construction.

Again, they went through the same testing, with the same people. They took Catherine in one office and Joanna in another and they met later on. While Joanna was waiting for Catherine to finish her test, she met a gentleman who had been there at their last visit. He was with his wife and told of how she had been a songwriter years ago, and couldn't remember anything now. He told of how she would write and then put music to the words. He mentioned songs that she'd published, but Joanna didn't know them. He was in his eighties and Joanna was still in the end of her forties. Joanna saw in his eyes, what she was sure he saw in hers – the tremendous fear of losing the person that once was.

Joanna enjoyed the people she met in the little waiting room and found that they had a lot in common. Was she just being polite, chatting with the other caregivers, because actually, this is what she had become? Had she given in to Catherine's illness – that, she wasn't going to be cured?

The nurse called Joanna in with Dr. Mike, while Catherine was still going through testing. "Catherine didn't do well this time on the one of the tests," he said. "She's dropped a few points in the cognitive behavior test."

"Oh?" She's heard him, but not really – or maybe she just didn't want to hear him. Then Catherine came in, all smiles,

"C'mon, let's go eat something. I'm starving." She was smiling and had that bouncy look about her.

Joanna looked at Doctor Mike and he gave the okay to leave. "See you next month."

Together Joanna and Catherine said, "Goodbye."

They stopped for something to eat and then for bagels as usual, then started the drive home. They didn't speak much on the way, probably, Joanna thought later, because of what she had heard – 'Catherine didn't do well on the tests.'

A CURE

ON OCTOBER 16, 1991 Joanna's brother, Marc, pulled up to the condo for a visit. Seeing him was great, but having another human being in the house was even nicer. The three sat in the living room talking.

"Hey girls. Let me treat you to dinner tonight," he said.

"We'll see. How are the kids?" Joanna asked, as Catherine got up to go to the bathroom. Marc had five children, all close in age and all adults now.

"Good, everyone's fine up north. They're all doing their own thing, between school and work. Where do you want to eat tonight?"

Joanna thought then spoke, "there's a place around the corner that is noted for its fish. I think you'll like it. If we leave soon we can catch the early bird special. Let's see what Catherine thinks."

"That sounds great. I eat fish all the time since my cholesterol's gone up, and you know I gotta watch my waistline." Mark had had a heart attack in his early fifties, but you would have never known it to look at him. He was slender and kept himself fit. He still worked as a pharmacist and played golf and tennis.

"You're still trim and good looking, too bad I don't

240

look like you any more." Joanna was getting a small pouch for a stomach and wasn't proud of it. You'd think with all the exercise that she and Catherine did, she'd still be thin. Catherine was still slender, but the ice cream as a steady diet now, to keep them happy, was all going to Joanna's belly.

"So where are we going for dinner?" asked Catherine, coming out of her bedroom.

"I thought we'd take brother Marc over to Harpon Harry's for dinner. What do you think?"

"Good idea. He should like the scenery and the food."

"I'm going to freshen up a bit first." Marc went into the guest bathroom.

Harpon Harry's was the first restaurant Catherine had taken Joanna to when they dressed in blue blazers, not long ago.

Marc appeared, "Okay girls, we ready to go? I'm starving."

Joanna drove to the restaurant and Marc loved the look of the red lighthouse across the waterway, taking pictures of the boats docked at the restaurant. He loved to dabble in photography and the camera he was using had a night lens. Explaining to the girls, after a few martinis, what the camera could do, Joanna thought it could probably walk and take its own pictures.

Joanna and Catherine spent the next few days showing Marc around the town and driving to Jupiter Island to see where the elite lived, in homes that looked like pictures out of magazines. Sitting in the back seat Marc said, "I notice everyone is looking at me."

"What are you talking about? Who's looking at you?" asked his sister.

"Don't you see the car next to us? They're looking at me." Joanna looked to the car next to them and Catherine, in the passenger seat, did also.

"No one's looking at you, Marc."

"Sure they are. They're wondering who I am, being chauffeured around by two gorgeous women."

Joanna couldn't help but laugh out loud, while Catherine stifled hers. "He's a great guy, this brother of mine, always full of compliments."

During his visit, they played golf and Catherine taught Marc how to hold the club and swing it.

"Hold it like a baby bird," she said, "and swing like a rag doll."

These were the same tips she had given Joanna a long time ago at St. Andrews.

Joanna watched and saw how her brother loved the attention Catherine gave him. He knew the tips where coming from the best. Marc made them forget their troubles and was great to have around.

One day while Catherine went for the mail, Marc and Joanna were left alone at the dining room table and he asked his sister, "What are you going to do with her?"

"What do you mean, what am I going to do with her? I'm going to take care of her like I promised her," Joanna said, impatiently.

"Are you crazy? Do you know what's in store for you? She's changed a lot Joanna, since I last saw her."

"I know she's changed. Marc. Let's not talk about it right now. I've made up my mind to care for her, and I will. You forget how much she's helped me."

Marc stayed four days, then drove south to Ft. Lauderdale and on to Miami. He was on vacation and wanted to see Florida. Joanna hated saying goodbye to him, even though at times he drove her nuts. She didn't know when she would see him again and she missed her family very much.

***

It's been a year since the diagnosis and Joanna notices Catherine is writing less in her little black book and she no longer has words taped to Joanna's mirror to learn, but Joanna still reads what's inside her cabinet, trying hard not to look forward.

Thanksgiving came and they had invited neighbors in for dinner but Christmas was different this year, going to the Methodist church at 8:00 p.m. instead of the traditional Catholic midnight mass. It was easier on Catherine, as she didn't have to remember to sit, stand, and kneel. There was standing and sitting only and singing of carols and hymns. The Christmas tree was decorated on the Eve and one present exchanged later in the evening before bedtime.

The new year began with them playing nine holes of golf, instead of usual eighteen. Most of the days were filled with doctors and taking Catherine to the clinic. Joanna had begun to have skipped heartbeats again. They still tried to keep their schedule of swimming, and walking the heart path when they weren't at medical offices. It was as though their lives of yesterday had stopped and all they had to look forward to each morning, was illness and despair. Catherine was getting worse by the minute, mentally.

Joanna bought a videotape of Tia Chi to learn exercises, while Catherine stood behind her watching

243

and trying her best to make the movements.

"Now your arms, Ca. Up, down, now to the side. Let's work on the legs now. Lift them high, like walking up stairs," Joanna would say, and Catherine would follow.

Joanna makes shakes of ice cream and bananas to keep weight on Catherine. She's losing for no reason and the doctor says it may be the brain shutting down. Joanna doesn't want to think along those lines and tries her best to keep Catherine healthy.

They've started attending the Alzheimer support group, going every week and every time they attend, they come home more depressed, hearing stories of how the disease robs the brain of everything.

LOST

IN THE SUMMER, Joanna spoke with Dr. Mike about Catherine's heart palpitations waking her every morning and he said they should switch the trial drug. Now the study was the Italian one, taking one pill three times a day. The good thing was, they didn't have to make the trip south every month – now it was once every three months. Catherine liked the idea for it meant she didn't have to be stuck with needles as often. Her arms were full of black and blues marks, and now they could heal.

***

Just shy of two years after the diagnosis in '92, Joanna took it on herself to rent a house on Long Island for three months, one block from where Catherine had lived with her parents. Joanna did it as a surprise for Catherine, then thought it might upset her, so she decided to tell her.

"Ca, how would you like to go to Long Island for a vacation?" They hadn't been back in two years.

"Sure."

"I thought we could rent a house in Stony Brook for three months."

"Sounds good."

Catherine's words had decreased over a short

245

period of time. Joanna thought seeing old friends and places would bring her back and there would be happiness for both of them once more.

***

Hope was having her first child and wanted Joanna there for the birth. Joanna couldn't leave Catherine to go north for the wedding last year, so this way they could spend time together with her first born. Matthew was married with two children and she could also see them. It seemed as though the children, and life, had gotten away from her within two years. She thought renting this house, the family could come and visit like old times.

Getting out the door was a little harried, but once they were on the road for the two and a half-hour drive to the auto train in Sanford, it went well. Catherine looked out the window, making comments on the fast traffic and the different trees she saw, while Joanna drove. Joanna had brought a book on tape along, to listen and occupy both minds.

They stopped at a small restaurant in Winter Park to have something light to eat and then boarded the train at four-thirty. The auto train shortened the drive by nine hundred miles and it was enjoyable meeting other people traveling north.

The next morning around eight-thirty the train pulled into Virginia. The car trip from the station wasn't a bad drive and they could make it in one day to Long Island, but first they stopped in Connecticut to see friends of Catherine's mom that she had grown up with.

Helen and David, who had known Catherine since

she was a baby, were in their eighties. David played the piano and Helen was an artist and Joanna saw how they loved Catherine, as if she were their own child. While David cooked dinner, Helen set the table. Catherine and Joanna tried to help, but they wouldn't hear of it.

"Sit, and tell us about Florida," Helen said.

Catherine had kept up with them through the years, calling them on all holidays and writing birthdays. She had told them she had Alzheimer's, when she had written to tell all her friends.

Helen, at one point, called Joanna aside, when Catherine had gone to the bathroom.

"She's really gone, isn't she?" Helen said.

"No – she's changed, but she's still the same old Catherine. She just has trouble getting her words together," Joanna responded, hurting for her friend.

They understood, but Joanna knew they hated to see their little Catherine, helpless in so many ways.

They slept in the guest bedroom that night, with the bathroom adjacent to the room. The room had two high, four-poster beds with down mattresses. Catherine was tall and had no problem getting in her bed, whereas, Joanna needed a stool to get in – up one step and she was in bed, but sank deep into the feathers.

"Hey Ca, can you see me?" as Joanna was sucked up by the mattress. "I feel like I'm in a hole," laughing so hard but quietly, afraid of waking the rest of the household.

In the middle of the night, Joanna got up to go to the bathroom and fell flat on her face. She had forgotten to use the footstool.

Sitting up Catherine asked, "Are you hurt?"

"No, I'm fine, but remind me never to buy a bed full of feathers."

The next day, as they were saying goodbye, Helen took Catherine and Joanna by the hand and led them to the curio cabinet filled with cut and colored glass.

"Pick anything you want," she said.

"Oh, no, we couldn't," said Joanna.

Again Helen directed Catherine, "pick anything you want."

Catherine reached for a glass bluebird, and Helen remarked, "that's the bluebird of happiness. It's yours."

Pulling away from the Connecticut home, laid-back in the woods, they waved goodbye to Helen and David, with Joanna thinking it would be the last time that Catherine would see them.

***

The trip to Long Island took three hours and driving was easy. They stopped by Maria's and John's apartment. Joanna had told her mom she was coming, but not the exact time, and wanted to surprise them.

Joanna knocked and John opened the door.

"Oh, look who's here. Maria – Maria, come here." Maria would get mad at him at times when he joked around with her, which he did most of the time, and she thought he was now.

"Who's here, Santa Claus?" Maria called out from the kitchen.

Joanna crepe up behind her mom, cooking at the kitchen stove. "Hi, Mom,"

Maria at a loss for words hugged her daughter.

John and Maria were happy to see them. John loved Maria and made her happy in every way he could. He was a marvelous husband and father.

Catherine went to Maria, giving her a big hug, looking like Mutt and Jeff.

"Stay for dinner," Maria said right away.

"No Mom, it's been a long trip and we want to see the house before dark."

"I'm glad you're staying for awhile. It'll be good for the both of you."

The house was about ten minutes from the apartment, so they could visit anytime.

"I just wanted to stop by and see you first, Mom, and make sure you are all right. I'll call you tomorrow."

After twenty minutes Catherine and Joanna left. As they approached Stony Brook, Catherine's hometown, Joanna could see the excitement on Catherine's face and hear it in her voice.

"Look, there's the country store."

"Yeah Ca, and the ice-cream parlor right next to it. Yippee. How about we stop in the chicken place and bring a bite home for dinner?"

"Yes."

Catherine recognized the stores and knew where she was. Joanna had new hope. Perhaps this is what Catherine needed, to see her old hometown again.

The house was a ranch style, with an attached garage. A young man met them outside.

"Hi, I'm Jim. The owners told me you would be coming."

'Who was this guy?' Joanna thought.

"I rent the basement apartment and if there's anything I can do for you, just let me know."

Joanna had not known about this and was upset. The Realtor should have told her over the phone. His entrance was in the garage and she saw he had no way of entering their part of the house, so she decided it shouldn't be a problem. He seemed likable enough.

"Here, let me get that for you," as he took the luggage out of Joanna's hands, bringing it into the house.

"Thank you Jim. By the way, I'm Joanna and this is Catherine," not shaking hands, because all hands were full. He carried large suitcases and the golf clubs in the house.

Once inside, unloading everything, he told them if they needed anything to call.

"Thanks a lot Jim. We appreciate it. Goodnight."

Joanna walked him to the door, then started to unpack.

Catherine, not saying much, but looking happy, went from room to room, finding all different items of interest. Decorated similar to her parents' home, with mahogany furniture, printed fabric on chairs and window treatments, Joanna thought Catherine should feel right at home. One room had twin beds, and Joanna thought this would be a good room for them to use.

After unpacking, they sat and ate the pieces of fast food chicken they had picked up.

"It's a nice house, isn't it Ca?"

"Yes, I like it."

"It's amazing that it's almost around the corner from your old house."

"I know the people across the street, but I can't remember their name." Catherine tried, but couldn't remember.

"I wonder if they still live there?" Joanna said.

Finished eating, Joanna was tired from the long trip

and needed to rest, so they turned in early.

Joanna woke in the middle of the night hearing noises. She looked over at Catherine's bed, and saw it was empty.

"Ca." She called. "Where are you?" She checked the bathroom. Not, there.

She found her in the kitchen turning the faucet on and off, mumbling to her self, very agitated.

Putting her arm around Catherine's shoulder, "It's all right, Ca. You're just a little confused. After a day or two you'll be right at home. You wait and see," calming her down, then leading her to the bathroom.

Catherine looked at her and nodded, 'Yes,' and Joanna felt compassion and sorrow for her friend, for she saw fear and confusion for the first time – similar to her own years ago.

When Catherine finished in the bathroom, Joanna led her back to bed, where she fell right to sleep. The next night was the same and the night after that. Joanna then decided; since the den had an adjoining bathroom and the sofa opened into a bed, they would use it as their bedroom for the next few months. This was much easier on Catherine and therefore easier for Joanna.

***

During their time there, they went to the house Catherine had once lived in with her parents and met the new owners. They were not the folks who had bought the house in 1982, when Catherine sold it and moved into her apartment. These people had bought it recently. Before they left Florida, Catherine had wanted to bring old pictures of when the house was being built, pictures of the original vacant land and the design plans of the house. She thought the new owners would like to have them. They served tea while Catherine reminisced about the past and living in the house with her parents. Joanna sat in amazement, watching her go into great detail about what had gone on in all parts of the house, when she had lived there. She told of the home fires her father would build, and how the swan smacked her mom with its wings, when she went down to the pond one day. (The swans had had babies and they didn't want her mom around.) She spoke of her whole family, even her grandmother, Chris, who was living there with them when she had her stroke. Even spoke of her portrait that hung over the fireplace and the artist down the block.

Catherine had many stories and, as Joanna listened with the owners, she felt this was the old Catherine again, and decided it *was* good she'd rented a house close by.

How is it she remembers this and doesn't remember where the bathroom is now?

***

In September of '92 they went to the club to watch the Ladies Club Championship, remembering their last match there in '85. They had Catherine's old friends over for dinners, as well as Joanna's family. They watched the birds in the bird feeder in the morning and after a while were able to call them by name. It was like old times again. They went to Marc's house while Maria made dinner and Marc teased her about too much salt in the tomato sauce. One has to be Italian to understand when there are too many cooks in the kitchen. Catherine, Marc's children, who were all in their twenties, and Joanna, sat at the kitchen table and laughed at them bantering back and forth. "Marc, listen to your Mother," said Joanna.

***

The first month went well, but late afternoons and nights were chaotic. Catherine was up out of bed headed for the bathroom at all hours of the night. Joanna could see she was having trouble finding the right words to say, both with her and with others, and this embarrassed her. Joanna felt bad for her friend and helped her find the missing words, which made it even worse. Catherine was angry she could no longer carry on a conversation. If they went out for dinner with family, she would become upset, excusing herself from the table and Joanna would find her in the bathroom, asking if she was all right, and knowing that she wasn't. She couldn't tell Joanna what was wrong and got angry with her, which was not like Catherine at all. Joanna knew something else was wrong.

Could it be the Italian study medications? Joanna called the research center, and they said it could be, but not likely. The medications shouldn't have that affect on her, so maybe they should see a doctor and have him call, if there was another problem. Joanna suggested to Catherine she visit her former doctor in town. When they went he found she had a urinary track infection and said that could account for the confusion, not being her self and the constant trips to the bathroom. Thank God – an answer.

***

A month and a half into the trip, Joanna had become discouraged and wanted to go home to Florida. She saw it wasn't any better after antibiotics for the infection. They made her confusion worse, and Joanna thought it best to go back home. Maria was upset, because she could see what her daughter and Catherine were going through. She had loved Catherine as a daughter for the past years.

They left for the auto train the middle of October and were home in Florida the next day.

SPEEDING TRAIN

BACK HOME, living was getting harder for Catherine. She got urinary track infections constantly, and was always on medications. Plus, she was losing her vocabulary at a steady pace and most of the time couldn't express her self at all. Joanna filled in for her, either with words or by action. Catherine became depressed and Joanna knew it was because she was losing herself.

Catherine cried, "I can't *do* anything."

"Yes, you can, Ca," feeling the pain along with her friend.

"No I can't – I hate this. I can't do the paperwork. I'm useless."

"No – no you're not useless. I don't want to hear that. You write out the birthday cards and all the anniversary cards. I don't do that stuff, *you* do." Joanna had made it easier for Catherine by typing the names and dates on the computer and printing it out. "We still do the bills and investments together. You do other things, also. Please don't be upset."

Joanna tried to convince Catherine she wasn't useless, by having her dry dishes, sweep the patio and other small jobs around the house, that she *could* do.

Joanna wanted her to keep busy and not in this depressed state.

She knew her hands were tied and could only help Catherine a small amount. To really help her was the medical field's job; all she could do was be at her side. Catherine would sometimes sit at her desk with papers in front of her, Joanna thinking she was working on something, and would find her crying, instead.

"I'm losing my mind. I can't think any more," she'd tell Joanna.

"You're not losing your mind and the medicine is going to help. Wait and see – it will."

Was Joanna fooling herself and Catherine by telling her this? But she needed something to go on. She needed something to believe in.

Catherine would calm down and Joanna would end up in the bathroom crying, cause it hurt so much to see her declining so fast. Catherine was never a depressed person. She was always up on life and people. She found the good in everything she came across, even if it was negative to someone else, but now she was down and Joanna didn't know how to make it better. The support group said, "It's a stage of the disease and it will leave soon."

Her question was, "what are they going to find in the next stage?"

How could she be *so near in body, yet so far away in her mind*?

The only happy moments are when Geech and his family come calling.

"Ca, get the seeds. Geech is here."

"Okay" and she'd run to the closet for the

sunflower seeds, putting them on the table in front of the kitchen window and on the wall, where they could watch. Even into the disease, she's able to understand Geech needs to eat. This little red bird brings them happiness.

***

By the end of 1992 they were living each day as it came and not looking to the future at all. It seemed all was dark ahead of them. The support group helped Joanna to understand a little better, and know that Catherine and she were not the only people going through this terrible time.

Then, Catherine started doing new things. She'd ask Joanna, "what time is it?"

"It's 3 o'clock," Joanna would answer.

A few seconds later, "what time is it?"

"It's 3 o'clock."

"What time is it?"

"Ca – It's 3 o'clock, I just told you a minute ago."

Catherine would forget and ask again and again until it drove Joanna nuts. Joanna eventually learned to let it go in one ear and out the other. But why is it she remembers the question, and doesn't remember the answer? Joanna thought.

Joanna had to start lying so Catherine wouldn't get agitated and Joanna could keep her own sanity. Making a simple mistake like telling Catherine, "we're going to the research center tomorrow" would keep them up all night, as Catherine asked over and over, "When are we going?" She'd look at her black book or a note she'd scribbled on a piece of paper on her desk. Catherine had forgotten the concept of time and day. Joanna finally learned not to tell her they were going anywhere, until it came time to go.

***

Today was the first day Joanna has had the desire to write. She's been thinking about it for months, even years, but this is the first time she's had the need. She wants to write about the struggle Catherine's going through, with this horrific disease and wants people to know of it. She also wants to write about what she's going through with Catherine, and how the caregiver loses herself, along with the victim. This is the first time she's even thought of this word, victim, but there isn't any other word that best describes it. Catherine is a victim of time.

***

Joanna has lost any feeling and thought that Catherine will get better. She has come to the conclusion that she's living alone now, even though Catherine is with her in body. She doesn't talk to Joanna in any understandable conversation. Usually they play charades to discover what she is trying to say or what she wants.

Joanna's depression has come back. She's not able to go out and walk for exercise, or do any activity and the agoraphobia is returning, or has it always just been hiding? She doesn't want to go to the store because she's basically alone, even though Catherine's still by her side. Joanna's beginning to hate life again and is eating all the wrong foods with fat, hoping to bring on a heart attack and die. Then she won't have to face Catherine dying in front of her, inch by inch or minute by minute.

Joanna cries when she watches Catherine read the same sentence, over and over, not knowing what she's read. She used to think Catherine understood what she was reading, but one evening while reading the paper Joanna asked her, "Ca, would you tell me the story?"

"Oh, you know, you know," she said, flailing her arms about.

Joanna knew then – what she'd thought was true, and gave up on any miracle.

Joanna asked one night. "Ca, are you happy?" Catherine shrugged, and motioned toward heaven as if to say:

'Yes, what else can I be. I can't do anything about what's happening to me.'

Those pretty much were her words, as Joanna perceived them. Joanna thought she's still happy and leaving it all up to God's plan. She takes whatever life has to offer her. She is a greater person than Joanna could ever hope to be, that's for sure. Joanna wished she'd had the disease so she wouldn't remember what Catherine was like before, the fun they had playing golf and watching the animals' outdoors. Joanna watched her talk to the butterflies and lizards that were outside the condo. She whispered to the flowers, so they would grow healthy and feel loved. Some people would have thought she was nuts back then, but not Joanna. She knew Catherine was a true part of nature and God's creation.

She was a pure child of God.

Joanna feels she's up against a brick wall and can't do anything for Catherine except to make sure she is clean and fed.

Thanksgiving and Christmas have come and gone

and they didn't even know it.

The urinary problem keeps getting worse and the Urologist says Catherine may have to be catheterized regularly, because of her enlarged bladder. He says, "it usually happens when we don't take time out to go to the bathroom." Joanna thinks back to the times on the golf course when Catherine wouldn't stop after nine holes. Joanna would go to the bathroom and Catherine would get a coke instead. She thought, 'it's catching up with her.' They have stopped playing golf entirely now, because of this, and it seems everything else is stopping too. Catherine is starting to walk around the condo constantly for no apparent reason, and is on her feet most of the day. Her ankles are starting to turn purple.

She begins loosing weight and goes from 175 to 130 pounds in a short period of time. She is starting to look ill. Her rib cage is showing and you can see the spine down her back and count each vertebra. Dr. Mike and Dr. Ban ask, "Is she eating?"

"Yes, she is eating everything in sight," Joanna tells them.

Dr. Ban says the brain may be shutting down and telling the body it doesn't need food. Joanna, in her heart, doesn't believe this, and makes banana milk shakes, with an egg thrown in, for Catherine to drink three times a day. Joanna also orders Choline from the drugstore, because she's reading where it is good for the brain and memory.

After one month, Catherine gains back some of the weight and Joanna feels better; again there's hope. Even the urinary problem gets better, because Joanna reminds her to go to the bathroom and drink cranberry juice.

***

It's March 21, 1993 and Joanna doesn't want to write today. She's feeling depressed, mad, and lonely. She misses her friend. Catherine isn't here mentally, any more. She doesn't even remember Joanna's name.

Looking at Catherine, Joanna asks, "Where is Joanna?"

"She's here," Catherine utters words and motions with her hands and arms and Joanna deciphers that she means, 'Joanna is around here somewhere.'

'But, how can that be, when I am standing right in front of her?' are Joanna's thoughts.

***

Joanna's looking into a full-time retirement facility where they could rent a two-bedroom, two-bath apartment and have one meal a day. On the property is an Assisted Living and a Nursing Home for Catherine, when she will need it. Joanna thinks, this may not be too far in the future. Just a feeling she has, even though she still has a slight faith that God will intervene and cure her, but she's losing it fast, and tries hard to fight the thought.

Joanna has slowly brought her down on the research pills, because there is a new pill coming out that shows some promise of help. She's scared, because she's playing with a life – to give a pill or not to give a pill. The new drug has shown some promise in people with memory difficulties and they are a little better physically.

Joanna reads in the newspaper about a man shooting his wife, who had Alzheimer's. Could *she* do this? And thinks, 'no, not after all Catherine has done for her in time of need and Joanna's love for her'.

261

Why doesn't the government do more to help with the research of this disease so the drugs will pass sooner for a cure. So much money goes into the wrong hands and pays for beautiful offices and trips made by the CEO's. Joanna never felt this way about her country before, but she's afraid she won't be able to get health insurance after her divorce because of her heart problem.

Joanna can see the pain and terror on Catherine's face and it reminds her of her own panic attacks and the agoraphobia. This is why she stays close to her all the time. Joanna knows Catherine is afraid to be left alone and wants her to know she will always be there for her. Joanna is no doctor, but she knows what Catherine is feeling because she's living with her twenty-four hours a day, seven days a week. She is never out of Joanna's sight.

She's losing weight, again. Five months ago she was 130 pounds and now she is 126 and looks like skin and bones. She reminds Joanna of children she sees on TV in other countries, who are starving.

Joanna tries to make her eat, but she's lost her appetite and doesn't want to come to the table any more for a meal. Joanna bribes her, saying, "No chocolate pudding or chocalotta ice-cream if you don't finish your dinner." It's like she's raising her children all over again. Catherine likes sweets almost all the time, yet when she was well she rarely ate them, except for ice cream. Joanna wonders if the brain is craving sugar for a reason, and buys a juicer to make fresh vegetable and fruit juices. She reads everything she can get her hands on at the bookstore and library on nutrition and getting the body well.

Joanna's going crazy with the chores around the house, bathing Catherine, keeping her clean and washing clothes. Catherine's changing during the middle of the night, and putting clothes on top of clothes. Joanna sleeps with her at times, softly rubbing her arm, as it helps calm her to get to sleep. Then around 2:00 a.m. Catherine starts to stir and fiddle with her clothes and Joanna leaves and goes to her own room, where she can rest. The burglar alarm is on and Catherine can't go out the door without Joanna hearing. Joanna needs to sleep if she's to care for her in the right manner. Catherine's hair has started to fall out for no obvious reason, black circles are under her eyes, and sores are on her lips and inside her nose. She's even stopped yawning, Joanna notices. Even at night when she's very tired; she doesn't yawn. Strange, and she wonders if others also do this. The doctors have no answer.

Catherine is going downhill fast, like a runaway speeding train, and there is no stopping it. Hating this disease, all Joanna wants to do is love and comfort Catherine in any way she'll let her.

She still wishes something else would show up in the tests that she has every few weeks at the clinic, even wishing it were Cancer, instead of this dreaded disease of losing her mind.

ANGUISH

BY JULY OF 1993 they're shopping for food around the dinner hour, when the store is empty of people. Catherine pushes the cart while Joanna pulls it.

"We need cereal, Ca. You get your shredded wheat and I'll get the oatmeal." Joanna watches her go for the yellow box and put in the basket, while Joanna reaches for the oatmeal box.

Forty-five minutes turns out to be a good exercise as they walk from aisle to aisle. They're outside – somewhere different from the walls they are coming to know so well – then they head for home at 7:30 p.m.

Walking through the dining room after putting the groceries away, Joanna notices a stain on the ceiling. Catherine has gone off to her bedroom to pace, her usual habit now, especially later in the afternoon. The support group calls it sundowners. Joanna finds the room behind the dining room also has a stain on the ceiling, and calls Jay, upstairs.

"Hi Jay. We have a problem down here. Would you check your floor in the dining room and see if it's wet?"

"Sure hang on…" he comes back. "No, nothing here. Maybe it's the seal under your toilet. We've had a lot replaced over the past few years. I'll come down and check."

"Thanks Jay, I appreciate it." Joanna hangs up the phone and Catherine joins her in the dining room.

Joanna leaves the front door open for Jay and seconds later he comes in. Looking up at the stain, then looking at the wall where the pipes are hidden, he puts an ear to the wall.

"Uh oh … sounds like you have a leak. Come here and listen."

Joanna puts her left ear to the wall and sure enough hears water dripping.

"I'll call Henry and see if he has anything upstairs." Henry is on the third floor.

Joanna overhears Jay talking with Henry and when off the phone says, "Yep, Henry's rugs are wet. We better call Ben and Sophie." Jay dials Ben and Joanna hears him, but is more interested in the spot, which is growing by the second.

"Ben says no, he doesn't have any wet spots." Ben and Sophie are on the fourth floor.

"I think I'm calling the plumber, Jay," Joanna says as Catherine moves back away from the scene knowing something is wrong.

"Okay, I'm going upstairs to make sure it's not wet in my place. Odd, the third and fourth floor are wet and mine isn't."

Joanna calls the plumber and Jay returns saying he has water also in his condo under the piano organ. Henry and Ben have joined them downstairs to wait for the plumber and Catherine has gone into her bedroom to pace and talk to herself. The neighbors look at Joanna for an answer, wondering why Catherine is talking aloud.

"She'll be all right. She's just upset seeing so many people here." Joanna brings chocolate chip cookies in to her, which Catherine takes with a smile.

Thirty minutes later the plumber knocks on the door and by this time the stain is larger and now is in three rooms. The plumber checks all the condos and says, "I can't tell where the leak's coming from. I'll have to come back in the morning and check the roof in daylight. Shut your main water valves off tonight."

Joanna thought it would be better for them to sleep in Catherine's room. She woke three hours later to the sound of water running into Catherine's shower, cascading down where the ceiling meets the wall. Water was everywhere when she went to check the dining room and guest bedroom and bath. She felt she was walking through a carpet swamp. Thank God it was staying in the one area. The room that was the worse was the guest bedroom and bath, which had five inches of water. Apparently the condo floor was sloping in that direction.

At daylight the plumber and neighbors gathered on the roof, while Joanna called the insurance company to come and take a look.

When they came down from the roof, the plumber said it was from a drainpipe that was closed off by mistake, when the new roof was put on three years ago.

The condo insurance company said they would cover it and the private property insurance which, Catherine and Joanna had, would cover the insides.

Joanna started making phone calls while Catherine paced through water agitated, not knowing what was happening. Joanna contacted a main contractor, given to her from the insurance company, who would handle the work, the new rugs, the new walls and whatever else that had been destroyed. They first tried to vacuum up the water but said, "you'll never get rid of the damage that has already been caused." The insurance company said they would pay for ninety percent for new remodeling.

As the workers started coming, Catherine was impossible to handle, running outside every chance she got. A door was opened for a worker and Catherine was out the door, with Joanna running after her. Since it was so upsetting to Joanna and Catherine, she called the nearest motel and got a room for home base. She got Catherine ready every morning to meet the workmen at the condo to let them in, then they would to go back to the motel. When four-thirty rolled around, they went back to the condo to lock up after the workmen left.

Carpet was ripped up, walls were broken through. When the workers lifted a credenza, the bottom fell off because of rotted wood. How long had it been like this? Because it was a heavy piece, it was never moved to see behind. The molding behind it was doubled in size. When they broke through the wall, Joanna saw all kinds of colored mold – black, red, and white dots. The water had laid behind the wall for years. As this was the ground condo, it got all the water. Under Catherine's file cabinet, the carpet was soaked, with black mold – another piece, that was never moved from the day it was delivered.

A few days later they were in the grocery store, to bring some items back to the motel they were now calling home. Catherine's confusion was worse than ever and Joanna's wasn't far behind. While waiting at the deli area for two turkey sandwiches to go, they heard,

"Hello, you two."

Joanna turned around to see their old neighbor Bob, from Sea Trail.

"Hi Bob. Long time no see." At this, Catherine takes notice of someone she knows and smiles.

"What are you both up to? I thought you left town. I haven't seen you in years."

"We've been living at Garden Parks. Catherine bought a place back in '86. How have you been with your diabetes? Is it still acting up, or are you eating all the right foods now?" Joanna asked with a smile.

Living next to Catherine years ago when she was down on vacation for six months, Bob was known to have great parties and when Joanna came down with Hope, he took the girls out fishing. He was a good neighbor and friend, with whom they had lost contact. Catherine liked Bob back then and now she couldn't think of anything to say to him. Joanna said in a whisper, while Catherine was looking at something on the shelf, "she has Alzheimer's."

"Oh no … I thought something was wrong when she didn't say hello or talk to me."

Then a thought came to Joanna, "Bob, is there anything for rent in your building?"

"I'm not sure, but I know my neighbor isn't coming down this year. Her husband died on February fourteenth." Joanna thinks, umm, Catherine's birth date.

"Bob excuse me a minute, I've got to get Catherine.

Don't go away." Catherine headed for the doors to go outside in the split second Joanna had turned to talk to Bob.

Coming up behind her slowly, then in front of her, "Catherine, would you please come with me?" Seeing a familiar face, Catherine smiled, as Joanna took her hand and walked back to Bob.

"Bob, do me a favor and ask your neighbor if she would like to rent the place out. You know we're good tenants and won't destroy it. We've had a flood and are staying at a motel at the moment, and I don't know for how long. Here's the phone number." Joanna wrote the motel number on the back of a piece of paper.

"Will do. You both take good care now and I'll call you tonight. Goodbye Catherine." And Catherine waved back.

"I look forward to hearing from you, thanks Bob."

A lady behind the counter handed them their sandwiches, with something to drink, and they headed for the inlet to watch the boats come in and eat their lunch.

Bob called around 8:30 p.m. and said, 'yes,' his neighbor was willing to rent the condo for a year and he would meet them there in the morning, to see the place.

***

The next morning Joanna and Catherine left the motel at 9:00 a.m. after a buffet breakfast and Bob buzzed them up to the third floor. Joanna had Catherine under the arm just in case she got confused and wanted to leave in a hurry. Joanna didn't know how Catherine was going to react, being at the same building she had lived in winter months, years ago.

269

"C'mon Ca." Catherine held back, looking fearful, as Bob opened the door to the condo. "It's okay Ca, relax. Everything's all right." Joanna took her hand, walking inside the condo, slowly.

The place was dark; the hurricane shutters were closed across the full balcony and Bob turned on lights.

"Bob, would you please open the shutters?"

As Bob rolled the shutters back, the ocean came into site, and Catherine's long stride pulled Joanna behind her.

"Ohoooo … " Catherine said with feeling, and Joanna held back tears as she saw her friend come to life. She knew by the look on her friend's face that she had to take this place for a year.

"We'll take it Bob. I think Catherine just made the decision *for* us."

The three of them leaned over the balcony watching the ocean and people below swimming in the pool. Joanna watched her friend, full of happiness.

"Bob do you think we can move in soon, because of our situation?"

"I'll talk to the president of the board. There shouldn't be a problem since Catherine has lived here before."

"Thank you, Robert. You've been sent by God, I'm very sure."

Joanna had a hard time pulling Catherine away from the beautiful sight. "We're coming back later, Ca, I promise," and Catherine let her take her hand.

Later that day after getting a few things from home, Joanna was sitting on the balcony over looking the blue-green water, while her friend lay on the lounge chair smiling with her gaze towards the ocean. Joanna thought, 'it's going to cost a lot of money and Catherine will be paying for it, but this is what her lawyer said to do.' "Do anything that makes her happy."

***

So in summer of '93 Joanna and Catherine went from condo to condo until most of their clothes were with them at the ocean. Joanna gave the house key to the contractor so she wouldn't have to meet them every morning and every afternoon. The work was going well, but it was going to take several months before the place would be livable. It didn't matter now how long it took since this would be their new home for a year.

One of her first jobs was to hang the portrait of Catherine over the couch, so she could recognize herself. Besides, Joanna loved it. Catherine loves lying on the lounge out on the balcony. They eat breakfast, lunch and dinner outside, like years ago when Joanna came from the unhappiness up north. As they swim in the pool and walk the beach, their skin goes from a sickly white to a bronze tan and Catherine looks almost healthy again.

***

This morning the ocean is beautiful and they've decided to go for a swim. Catherine is first in, being the best swimmer, and starts swimming out to sea, while Joanna stays in the shallow water. Joanna knew Catherine was a great swimmer but she's gone out much too far now, and Joanna knows she won't be able to save her if anything happens. Joanna can feel fear, and yells to her, "Catherine, come back. You're out too far." Catherine, not listening, swims farther out.

271

Cupping her hands to sides of her mouth, Joanna yells louder, "Ca, You get back here, right now!"

Catherine turns, smiles, and waves as if to say, "I'm all right, it's fun," laughing like a child at play.

Joanna, upset and ready to call the lifeguard, sees Catherine has turned and *is* swimming towards her. It's like watching her children years ago, when they were young. Now Catherine was her child.

Catherine, back to where Joanna is, splashes her. "Cut it out. Don't you dare go out that far again. Stay with me. You know I can't swim in water over my head," and Catherine nods her head, 'yes.'

Later they walked up the wooden staircase like years before, except this time Joanna has Catherine by the hand and leads her to the tar station.

"Ca, sit down. I need to clean your feet." A bench was there by the condo so they could remove the tar that had accumulated on the bottoms of their feet. Ocean barges had a habit of spilling small amounts of oil that would wash up on shore.

Catherine listens to Joanna and sits on the bench while Joanna reaches for the mineral spirits and a cloth to clean her feet. Bending down to clean Catherine's feet, out of the corner of her eye she sees a woman standing, waiting. Rising up to face the woman, "We're going to be a while, so if you want to use the hose, go ahead." And hands the woman the hose.

"No, that's okay. I'm in no hurry."

Extending her hand, "Hi, I'm Joanna and this is Catherine. We're up in 305."

"Hi, I'm Debbi on the 10th floor. Nice to meet you."

Joanna bends down to finish Catherine's feet. "We moved in a few days ago and couldn't wait to get to the ocean. Catherine used to live here in the winter months years ago, on the 5th floor."

Joanna thinks Debbi is probably wondering why Catherine isn't joining in the conversation. Catherine is reading their faces, and Joanna knows if she sees doubt, she will react with fear and run. Joanna is aware Debbi has picked up on Catherine's illness, but doesn't know how much. Ready to go, Joanna reaches for Catherine's hand and says, "Goodbye Debbi. It was nice to meet you."

"Bye for now. Good to have you back in the building again, Catherine," and she smiles back at Debbi. 'She does know, what people are saying to her.' Joanna thinks.

***

In the days and weeks ahead, Joanna finds out that Debbi is a psychotherapist and tells her about Catherine's illness, their living conditions and how she's having trouble handling it. Debbi offers her help and gives Joanna books to read on encouragement and faith and tells her, if she needs to talk with someone she will help in any way she can. Joanna can't thank her enough, because Catherine and she have become loners, except for Bob who stops in once in awhile to say hello. They've found because of the illness, people talk around it, or make believe it doesn't exist. Friends have told Joanna they will call and never do. This makes her feel they both have been abandoned.

***

Catherine's happy living at the ocean and they both enjoy the bird life and lying on the balcony lounge, where they can smell the clean, fresh salt air. Catherine has been on Cogne a couple of months now; the only drug passed by the Food and Drug Administration for Alzheimer's. She started on ten milligrams, slowly worked up to forty milligrams, four times a day. Joanna has seen a difference in her, after only a short time on the drug. She's more alert, washing herself and she has also started to read again, but still can't talk in sentences. This Joanna doesn't understand.

Christmas this year they are invited to go to a country club with one of Catherine's long-time golf friend. It's a different Christmas. Joanna puts on a table a small fake tree; about two feet high, already decorated, and cooks a simple meal. It's memorable but not for the usual reasons they knew. They go to Christmas day mass and Catherine can't sit through the service, so they leave.

***

The improvement of the drug for Catherine lasted only a short time, maybe two months. She had prayed Catherine would get better on the drug and be cured. But that didn't happen.

Joanna hates the thought of losing Catherine bodily, as she's lost her mentally already. Every morning she wakes and still doesn't believe what has happened – Catherine with this frightful disease that rids her of her dignity and being.

It's getting harder and harder.

December 29, 1993 and Joanna hasn't written in a while. Having bouts of confusion, she thinks she's getting Alzheimer. The doctor claims it's only depression.

Joanna still doesn't have a divorce, and Ed is fighting her on everything. He doesn't want to give her anything. Her lawyer tells her that Ed's lawyer doesn't return his phone calls and that Joanna needs to be in New York to fight the case.

***

In the condo dining room corner is a large plant that stands six feet tall. It has mostly green leaves with little white flowers. Walking from the living room through the dining room, Joanna passes the plant and notices there are fewer white flowers. Sitting on the couch one day, Joanna sees Catherine pacing from room to room and as she passes the plant, picks one of the flowers.

"Ca, please don't pick the flowers. It's not our plant."

Catherine looks at Joanna, then at the flower and mimics Joanna, throwing the flower behind the plant. Joanna gets the flower and finds twenty more in the corner. What goes through Catherine's mind when she does this? Does she think they're real? Why else would she pick them?

***

Six months later Catherine's up constantly. It's hard to take her to the ocean any more or anywhere else. Later in March, Catherine went to the sliding glass doors and looking down saw something. She waved to Joanna sitting on the couch, to come. She can't say, 'come here,' but waves her hands and arms beckoning and speaking in another language.

"Rah, Rah, Rah." Softly these words are said.

"Joanna gets up and joins Catherine on the balcony.

"What Ca? What is it? What do you want me to see?"

"Rah, Rah, Rah," she says, pointing down.

Joanna leans over the balcony and doesn't see

anything at first, then in the trellis below she sees a nest with a pair of doves in it.

"Oh, there it is. I see the nest, Ca."

"Rah, Rah."

"Yes, I see them."

Leaning over the balcony they viewed what was below them. Catherine excited over the doves and Joanna excited over her friend spotting nature again.

Every day Catherine and Joanna went to the balcony to see the progress of the two little workers below. They saw after a while, there were eggs in the nest and that's when Joanna got out the binoculars to get a closer look. Catherine was afraid to put them up to her eyes, so Joanna didn't insist. Crazy disease, Joanna thinks. This was a woman who spotted birds with the same binoculars and now she was afraid of them.

Days later calling, "Rah, Rah, Rah," both of them leaning over the balcony.

"Oh Ca, the babies have hatched, and you saw them first. Thanks for showing me, Catherine."

They watched the parents feed their young and time went on until one day Catherine had a sad look on her face when she called, "Rah, Rah."

The babies had fallen out of the nest, and were on the cement surface. As the day went on, they saw the babies being led by the mother, over to a bushy area, where they would be safe.

That was a time of love and understanding of nature that Catherine and Joanna still were able to share, and they thank the doves for that small miracle.

***

In April, Maria has a heart attack and it is a bad one. Through the years, Joanna has spoken to her mom every Sunday and sometimes during the week, but now that she's in the hospital, Joanna speaks with her several times a day. Joanna calls her mom's doctors and they tell her Maria's not doing well and they want her to have bypass surgery. Joanna speaks with her brothers and they also say this should be done.

On the day when her mom went from Long Island to New York Hospital, she told her, "Mom, I love you and though I'm not there in body, you know I'm with you in mind and spirit."

"Yes, I know, and I love you, too."

"I will talk to you in a day or two after the operation," Joanna tells her mom, holding back tears. Joanna wants to be with her, but can't. She has Catherine to look after and Maria understands, without saying it.

"You take good care of yourself." Her mom says. "It's an adventure if I make it through the operation, and it's and adventure if I don't."

That was the last time they spoke, for Maria passed away two days later, on the 24th of a massive stroke. Paul called to give Joanna the news. Crying softly, she made her way to the balcony. Catherine stopped her pacing and followed her outside. With both hands Catherine held Joanna's cheeks, as if to say, "I'm sorry." She looked at Joanna with tears in her eyes. Catherine couldn't say the words, but Joanna knew them.

"It's okay Ca. Mom's with God now." Catherine seems okay and keeps Joanna company awhile on the balcony, until the agitation returns and she's up pacing again.

***

Joanna's friend, Rosie, comes for a visit on her way farther south and offers her condolences. It's good to see her old friend again. It's been awhile. Joanna makes dinner and they sit on the balcony while Catherine eats and paces. Joanna tells Rosie all that's happened in the year. "Oh Joanna, how are you doing?" she asks.

"Not too good. I'm having menopausal problems, if there isn't enough going on already. Other than that, I'm doing the best I can."

"You look pale. Have you seen a doctor?"

"It's hard to go anywhere without Catherine. She takes a lot of looking after now. I don't want her to get lost. She wouldn't be able to find her way back home. She has broken three identification bracelets already and doesn't like wearing them."

"Well, please take care of yourself and get to a doctor. If I could stay, I would."

"I know Rosie. Next time, plan on staying over night and maybe I'll feel better."

***

Rosie leaves and a few days later Joanna finds she is hemorrhaging. She calls the gynecologist and makes an appointment, but thinking at the same time, 'I can't get sick, there's no one to take care of Catherine.'

By luck or prayer, Marc is on his way to Ft. Lauderdale and thinking of living in Florida. Joanna is happy for him and asks, "Can you come now Marc? I have a doctor's appointment and don't know if I will end up in the hospital."

Thank God he says 'yes'. He's renting a car and will come as soon as possible.

Through the Alzheimer's support group Joanna gets the name of a gentleman to come and stay with

Catherine for a couple of hours while Marc takes her to the doctor.

The doctor finds she has polyps and removes them and she returns home the same day, and convinces Marc to stay for a few days before heading south.

Marc and Joanna had talks after dinner and he saw how Catherine had declined. He had made an appointment for a job interview and leaves two days later. Joanna thinks it's because he is feeling bad for his sister and just wants to leave the sight he's seen – Catherine's constant pacing and gibbering to herself in the mirror – something new she's taken up.

***

During that year at the ocean, the first six months were beautiful and it was good to see the sunrise on a new day, even though it wouldn't be a perfect day. It was good to breathe the fresh air and see the fishermen in the morning. To see a rainbow and make a wish for Catherine's illness to be nonexistent, to watch the red moon come up over the ocean, like a ball of fire and to see the storms and know all that God has made. But then, not understand why God wouldn't take away the disease.

The most beautiful sight Joanna saw was after her mom passed away. While looking out the sliding glass doors, on the right side, was a waterspout. In the middle was a large thunderhead with pink lightning flashing through it, and on the left side of the door was a rainbow. She wished she'd taken a picture, because she knew she would never see a sight like that again.

***

By the summer of '94 Catherine paced day and night, until she almost fell from exhaustion. She'd let

Joanna take her hand, "C'mon Ca, lets lie down for awhile and get some rest," and Joanna would lead her to bed, where she would stay for maybe fifteen minutes, then be up again pacing. It was like she had a clock inside her that kept going off, telling her not to relax.

Catherine had forgotten how to sit down. Joanna would bring her over to the couch facing her and push down on her high shoulders. "Sit," she'd say, as commanding an animal, and sometimes she would, especially if there was a bowl of chocolate ice cream sitting in front of her. Joanna would then stroke her head and the back of her neck and give her chocolate ice cream while they watched *I Love Lucy* tapes over and over. Catherine loved funny movies and slapstick. They even tried cartoons, but Catherine didn't care for them and got up to pace. When there was a movie about shooting or any violence, especially yelling or loud noises, she'd get upset and yell at the television.

***

Catherine is wetting the bed at night and the pads Joanna has bought are too small for the bed, so she uses a shower curtain on the mattress. It covers the whole area and works better than a pad. This is information from the support group. Thank God for support groups. Joanna has bought an alarm that hangs on the front door and locks the balcony doors at night, after having thoughts of Catherine climbing over it. She's become fearful even more now.

Catherine's hearing has become sharp and she can hear the slightest noise, whereas before the disease, she didn't. The slightest stir in the middle of the night, the rustle of the sheets, Catherine hears and wakes up, then is off pacing, no matter what hour.

Joanna hires the same man who took care of Catherine when she went to the doctor, to come so Joanna can go to the support group every week. She can't bring Catherine any more as in the beginning. She's finding help among these caregivers like herself, and has made new friends, who cry and laugh with her.

Old friends don't want to hear it. They only want to hear the good stuff. They're not interested in the night Catherine soiled the bed or how she shoved Joanna out of the shower or yelled at the top of her lungs to someone in the mirror she sees.

At first, she liked the new friend in the mirror and grabbed Joanna's arm to show her. But Joanna didn't understand and said, "Catherine that's you, can't you see that?"

After many days of saying this, Joanna found it easier to go along with the new friend idea for it kept Catherine busy. She was happy talking to her new friend in the mirror – she didn't tell her what to do or when to eat.

***

When Catherine wakes in the middle of the night, Joanna leads her to the toilet so there won't be any accidents. But as soon as Joanna leaves the bathroom Catherine is up, walking. Joanna learns she must stay, sit on the bathroom floor and sing to Catherine, so she will stay where she is. A new way of handling the disease, this works, so every two to three hours during the day, she puts Catherine on the toilet and sings to her. She can't figure why Catherine won't sit anywhere for any length of time. Don't the doctors have any answers for this? The support group says it's another stage and others in the group are doing this also.

***

Joanna calls the Catholic Church where they spent every day before golf and Sundays; it seems like ages ago. She needs help and asks the woman on the phone, "Do you have someone who can come and stay with my friend, while I go food shopping, once a week?"

"No, I'm sorry, we don't do that."

"Excuse me? What do you mean, you don't do that?"

"We don't offer that kind of help." The woman repeats.

"The woman I'm caring for donated large sums of money to your church every day and Sunday's, and you're telling me, there's no one who can help her?"

"I'm sorry, we don't have anything like that set up."

"So, you're saying I have to go to the Jewish community, who does this free? I think something's wrong with this picture. Thank you, goodbye."

This hurt Joanna terribly and Catherine would have been doubly upset if she but understood what just happened. After all the years she couldn't even depend on her own religion to offer help to them. It left an awful taste in her mouth.

***

Shopping is hard together because Catherine takes off in the store. Joanna turns to get something off a shelf and Catherine is no longer holding onto the basket. Frantically, Joanna runs straight to the door, hoping Catherine hasn't gone out yet and then she spots her long strides down one of the aisles. She couldn't even have her paged – if you think of it. Catching up with her, Joanna grabs her hand and leads her back to the basket, telling her, "Don't do that again. Stay with me. You scared me half to death," again, just like talking to her children years ago. Then they're in the car and back to the condo.

They've stopped walking the beach because Joanna can't keep up with Catherine's pace. She stares straight ahead while walking and never looks behind or to the sides of herself. She's off on a run to where, Joanna doesn't know. Sometimes Joanna thinks back to when Catherine went for that swim and wouldn't listen. She should have let her keep swimming out to sea that day. Maybe now, Catherine would be at peace.

After speaking with Dr. Ban, who is their friend, as well, they decide to take Catherine off all medication and let the illness take its course, as if it hasn't already.

All hope was gone, now.

OUT OF CONTROL

IT'S JULY 1994, and they've moved back to Garden Parks. Their home has new walls, new carpet, and bathroom tile, all fixed up. But for whom? There was only Catherine and Joanna and they weren't much good for anything right now. Joanna is stressed and depressed, and Catherine has gone into another world, walking all the time away from this one.

Their neighbors, Jay and Bea, welcome them home to the three-bedroom, three-bath condo, and Joanna wonders how she's going to keep this place up. Catherine paces all day, looking for an exit. Once outside, the fear on her face is even greater, because she is not where she thought she was. Nothing looks familiar to her and she wants to go 'Home' – home to the place she knew as a child? Joanna wonders, when Catherine looks at pictures of her parents and smiles and calls their names, as if they were still alive.

By the end of 1994, Catherine's eating habits have disappeared. She uses her hands much of the time and Joanna makes finger foods, so she can feed herself. Joanna didn't want Catherine to lose any independence she had, if Joanna could help it. A bowl is easier, because she can scoop up the food with a spoon, as if it were soup. Someone in the support group gave that piece of information. Funny how a bowl can make life so much easier.

Joanna continues making vegetable juices, containing greens, beets, celery, carrot, and fruits, so Catherine will get the nutrients.

Her sugar craving is astounding. From the fridge or cabinet she searches for anything sweet. Joanna bought a bunch of bananas from the store and when she came out of her bedroom, Catherine had eaten the whole bunch. There were four or five bananas and all Joanna could think was 'She's going to have a bad stomach ache,' but she didn't.

Catherine has become afraid of everything and everyone now. She goes into her room when anyone enters the condo, or she tries to leave. She doesn't listen when Joanna calls her so Joanna always keeps a few cookies. Catherine heads down the sidewalk and Joanna comes in front of her, "Ca look what I have." Catherine's eyes light up as Joanna holds a chocolate chip cookie in front of her. "C'mon Catherine, follow me and you can have the cookie." Joanna feels she is offering a bone to a dog, instead of a cookie to her friend.

Thank God the neighbors are kind. Whenever they see Catherine outside without Joanna, they call on the phone. "She's out again," they say. And Joanna flies after her, or they say, "Catherine, go back inside." And sometimes she listens.

The times she gets out, are when Joanna goes to the bathroom. She leaves the bathroom door open so she can hear Catherine in the house, and if she hears the front door open or the alarm, she is up fast, after her. Just like a two-year old, if she didn't have her in eyesight, she was gone. Picture a six-foot, two-year old, with the strength of a horse. Her strength has gotten greater as the illness goes on. Joanna thinks it's because the brain shuts down, the outer muscles become stronger, and with the constant walking she has become stronger and faster.

***

When Joanna leads her to the toilet, Catherine puts a face on, as if it's a bad place to be. What goes through her mind when this happens? She no longer wipes herself, which seems to be the hardest on Joanna. Sometimes she has accidents and she has to be stripped of her wet clothing. When this started happening, Joanna bought diapers. Catherine came to Joanna in the living room one day with a look of worry.

"What's the matter, Ca?" as if she were going to get and answer? Catherine kept looking towards her bathroom.

"What is it, Ca. Show me."

Joanna followed Catherine to her bedroom then saw water coming from the toilet. Quickly, Joanna shut the main water valve off. Joanna cleaned up the mess and was ready to call a plumber, but saw how wet Catherine was. Her pants and blouse where soaked.

"Ca, let's change your clothes. They're wet."

Surprisingly, Catherine let Joanna take her sneakers and socks off and then her pants. That's when Joanna realized she didn't see the pad she had put on Catherine less than an hour ago. It dawned on her then that Catherine had flushed the pad down the toilet, which the plumber found later.

***

Joanna has taken the scissors, the letter opener and

any other sharp object off Catherine's desk or anywhere in her room. She's taken to marking up the furniture and ripping up anything she finds. She pulls wallpaper from her bathroom walls and Joanna tries a new tactic.

"Catherine don't do that, you're hurting the wall."

The tactic doesn't work and Catherine becomes angry, yelling in another language. Joanna decides to let her do what she wants to do, as long as she doesn't hurt herself.

Joanna believes Catherine is destroying everything that ever meant anything to her, because she's angry and frustrated over the illness and not able to communicate anymore. This is a woman from the College of William and Mary, a brilliant person. *How? Why?* Joanna had no answers.

***

Joanna asked Catherine calmly, one day while she was pacing in her room, and looking in the mirror at her new friend, "Catherine can I please see your necklace? I'd like to clean it for you."

Catherine stops pacing and looks at Joanna with a smile and holds it up, making a sound and motioning with her head, 'yes.'

Joanna reaches behind Catherine's neck and unhooks the necklace, which Catherine lets her do and walks to the kitchen.

"C'mon Ca. I'm going to clean it for you." Catherine follows close by Joanna's side, watching Joanna get the silver cleaner and a cloth out of the cabinet.

Joanna turns on the faucet to keep Catherine focused on the noise of the water running. While Catherine turned her head, Joanna took the little gold

287

rose from the chain. All that was left was Catherine's penicillin med. alert, and her mother's Virgin Mother charm. Joanna had slipped the little gold rose into her pocket and Catherine never noticed. With the chain clean, Catherine kept picking it up to look at the sparkling emblems she wore, looking contented.

It hurt, in one way, that she had forgotten the rose they shared, but Joanna didn't want her to destroy it.

***

On a September morning in 1994, out of a sound sleep, Catherine jumps out of bed yelling, waking Joanna. Swinging at Joanna … and yelling in her own language. Joanna gets out of bed and tries to calm her down.

"Ca, please stop. C'mon let's go get a cookie." Catherine goes for Joanna again with a hairbrush that she's picked up off the dresser and Joanna moves out of her way. Catherine swings at the window blinds and walls, or anything that comes in her path. It's like she's seeing something that isn't there.

Joanna, now out of the bedroom, in the dining room, watches Catherine head for the front door but knows she can't get out, because a lock had been put on, high near the upper frame.

She tries once more to go near Catherine and calm her, but Catherine swings and hits her with the brush. Joanna is distraught now and thinking, if she doesn't call the police, the neighbors will. In her bathroom she cries, looking at herself in the mirror, 'What should I do? Do I call the police and have her put away for thirty-six hours in a padded room?' Roy comes to mind. He lives in the building next door, 'Yes. I'll call Roy. He's big and will be able to handle Catherine.'

Hoping Catherine has not made her way to the kitchen where the knives are, all kinds of thoughts now have entered Joanna's mind, of what Catherine might do. She could kill or hurt her, or kill or hurt her own self. She speed dials Roy's number.

"Roy? It's Joanna." Not waking him, for Roy hasn't been able to sleep since his wife died months ago.

"Catherine's off-the-wall, hitting everything in sight and yelling. Can you please come over?"

"Sure, I'll be right there."

Roy usually stops by on his way home from his walk to the ocean in the morning, just to say hello. He's helped Joanna in talking of their home life and where it's now leading. Joanna knew she could depend on him, but now she had to unlock the front door so he could come in. Catherine was banging on it with the brush, while the other hand was on the knob pulling it. She'd forgotten how to turn the knob.

Joanna had to get to the door, but stay away from the hairbrush.

A loud knock startled Catherine away from the door. Joanna was lucky to get in front of her as she backed into the dining room.

"Okay, I'm coming Roy," she yelled, while punching the alarm numbers to disarm it, then sliding back the bolt up top, to unlock the door. Grateful to see a face that maybe could handle this insanity or the crazy person she was now living with and afraid of.

Coming in, Roy said, "hello Catherine," while Catherine walked farther away into the living room muttering.

"Oh Roy, she's really off this morning. I need to get a pill into her fast and pray the neighbors haven't called the cops yet."

Roy and Joanna tried coaxing Catherine into the kitchen but Catherine gibbers and waves her arms at them.

"She's upset over something. This morning she was acting like someone else was here besides me. I made believe I was shoving them out the door, saying, get out, all of you. She calmed down, but then was back into a rage again." Joanna filled three bowls of cereal while talking to Roy, saying loudly, "let's eat breakfast Roy" so Catherine could hear and maybe come to the table and join them.

Roy and Joanna sat at the kitchen table eating cereal while Catherine slowly made her way through the dining room and into the hallway.

"Is she coming, Roy?" almost in a whisper.

"Yep, she headed this way."

"How about a cup of coffee, Roy?"

"That would be great." They both spoke loud so Catherine could hear and want to be a part of what they were doing. Joanna knew Catherine *had* to be hungry.

Catherine then stood in the doorway to the kitchen behind Roy. Joanna could see her from the counter where she was starting to make coffee. She had already fixed a bowl of cereal for Catherine, putting two tranquilizers in.

"Hi Ca, how about something to eat?" making believe nothing else had happened.

"Come and sit here Catherine and eat with Roy."

"Sush, Sush, Sush, Sush." Catherine repeated, while Joanna held the chair out from the table for her, then pushed down on her shoulders to make her sit.

Joanna then put the bowl of cereal in front of

Catherine with a pealed banana. Neither Roy nor Joanna said anything.

Catherine picked the banana up and started eating it, Joanna hoping she would reach for the plastic spoon and eat some cereal to get the sedatives in her. She didn't know what Catherine was going to do next and wanted to make sure she had sedating medication in her, which the doctor had ordered twice a day.

Catherine started to eat and Roy and Joanna carried on a light conversation about the weather or neighborhood, making believe they weren't noticing Catherine.

In less than five minutes she finished the cereal and banana and was up walking into the hall.

"Thank God. Now she'll be sleepy in fifteen or twenty minutes. Roy, I don't know what I would have done without you. Thank you for coming over." Joanna couldn't stop the tears now, for the tension had finally left and she was not fearful any more.

"I'm glad to help. You know you can call me any time."

"Yes – I know. But I hate to have anyone see her like that. You know how she used to be, when we swam in the pool. She never would hurt a fly, now she's become an animal with the strength of a guerrilla."

Roy got up. "Well, thanks for breakfast," he said in a whisper, and Joanna kissed him with a hug, letting him out the door, and locked them in once more.

Catherine had made it to her bedroom and was lying on the bed sleeping. Joanna took the throw, putting it on her. She had lost all sense of temperature and feeling. She'd cut her finger awhile back, before

Joanna put all sharp objects away, and Joanna saw blood all over Catherine's shirt. "What's this?" Catherine looked and shrugged her shoulders up and down not knowing. Joanna spotted her thumb was bleeding and put a bandage on it. Catherine had lost the sense of pain.

Covering her now, Joanna lay next to her, staring at the ceiling, crying over how the morning had begun, and now the house was quiet. Then fell off to sleep with her dear friend.

TORMENT

THE DAYS and nights continue with the same pattern, Joanna in depression and Catherine in another world.

October 18, 1994 … This morning Catherine has gotten the new rug and her pajamas wet as she stood with her legs apart and peed on the carpet before Joanna could catch her.

"C'mon Ca. It's time for us to take a shower," suggests Joanna.

She's become so afraid of water; Joanna tries to coax Catherine in the shower with her. Another tip learned from the support group.

It's a battle to keep her clean, not smelling of urine or other odors. One woman in the support group takes her husband outside in the summer and washes him off with the hose. What Joanna learns each day with the progression of this disease, brings her back to when they were children. Except then, they were called hose fights.

Both, in the walk in shower, Joanna takes the removable showerhead and sprays herself first.

"See Ca. There's nothing to be afraid of. Oh – it feels sooo, good," as Catherine steps farther back, closer to the wall.

Joanna reaches for Catherine's hand to show her

again, as she did two days ago, that the gentle water spray won't hurt. Catherine's strong and pushes Joanna away. Joanna tries once again to spray Catherine's private area and her legs, keeping it away from her face and knowing she does need a her head washed. Catherine fights her all the way. Joanna knows if she doesn't get her head washed now, she won't today. Quickly, Joanna sprays her head and whole body, and Catherine pushes her up against the glass doors. Joanna gives up in desperation.

"Okay, that's it. You're done," but before Joanna can get the words out, Catherine was out of the shower on a run, through the living room, naked, wet, and growling like a mad animal.

How could this be her dear friend, whom she once knew so well?

Joanna dries herself off, wishing she could stay in the bathroom and not go out to face another day. She wants to fade into the walls and not be here or anywhere. How long can she keep this up? She's lost her friend and nothing means anything to her any more. There are no longer any dreams of the future.

Getting dressed, hoping by now Catherine has calmed down, Joanna grabs two towels, cookies, and heads for Catherine's bedroom. She finds Catherine talking to her friend in the mirror.

She's calmer now and Joanna understands why. She and the water are threats to Catherine. The friend in the mirror isn't.

"Hey Ca, look what I've got for you," showing her the chocolate cookie.

Catherine looks at the cookie, "...um..." and Joanna knows she's interested.

"Follow me Ca. Come and sit here on the bed," as she takes her hand and leads her to the bed to sit on a towel and dry her hair. Catherine munches on a cookie.

"Good girl, Catherine, you took a shower this morning and your hair smells nice and clean."

Joanna gets a shirt on her, no bra on her any more – it's become impossible for that. She gets her underwear on with a large pad, up around her knees, then a pair of shorts, handing her another cookie. Joanna pulls her to a stand-up position, to pull her pants up and Catherine doesn't resist.

After that, Joanna pushes down on her shoulders saying, "sit." So far all is going as planned.

With Catherine concentrating on the cookie she has in her hand, Joanna puts her socks on, lifting one leg at a time. She doesn't know to lift her foot any more, so Joanna coaxes her to lift her foot, by holding one hand under Catherine's knee and lifting it.

Catherine lifts her knee too high and hits Joanna's eyeglasses with such force it knocks her glasses off. Joanna yells in pain and runs to the mirror to see if any damage was done. Her eye is stinging, but her sight is no different. She can open her eye, but is mad at what has happened, as it does every day. She has to fight to keep Catherine clean, fed and kept safe.

Joanna retreats back to where Catherine is still sitting on the edge of the bed eating her cookie. She's not even aware that anything has happened.

Joanna tries to lift her foot one more time, but this time Catherine won't.

"Please Catherine, lift your foot so I can put your sneaker on," no answer or action.

Again Joanna pleads, "please lift your foot, Ca."

Nothing.

"Do-it-yourself!" and Joanna smacks Catherine across the upper arm.

Joanna leaves and heads for her safety area – her bathroom.

"I can't keep this up. Please Dear Lord help us. Please make it all go away," she cries.

Joanna realizes what she's just done and the thought goes through her like a knife. 'I've just hit my dear friend – the person I love – one I admired and gave all of myself to.'

The thought comes to her that she's not doing either of them any good. If she starts hitting Catherine, she could not live with herself anymore.

Crying, she gets the phone book, and dials the nearest nursing home.

"Good morning, Lacy Nursing Home," the woman says on the other end.

"Hello, my name is Joanna Shaker and I have to place someone in your home."

"Hang on please. I'll get someone to help you."

Joanna watches Catherine, who now has come in the living room with her cookies, and seems happy.

"Hello, Mrs. Shaker? Here is Miss Randy. You can talk to her."

"Thank you. Miss Randy, I can't take it any more. I just can't take it. I don't want to hurt her, but this morning was awful."

Joanna was spilling her guts out to someone she didn't even know.

"Try to take some deep breaths and relax, Mrs. Shaker."

"I can't take it anymore. I hit her this morning and

that goes against what I believe. This isn't any good for her," she cries to a stranger.

She's finally letting it all out and feels a connection with the person on the other end of the line. She tells about Catherine and herself and the mess they're in.

'She can help,' is all Joanna can think.

She can get them out of this mess that life has taken on.

"Can you both come by around three this afternoon?" Miss Randy asks.

"Yes, we can. Thank you. We'll be there," and Joanna hangs up the phone.

She watches Catherine looking out the sliding doors at the birds in the back, feeling a weight has just been lifted off her whole body. She feels almost relieved at what she's just done. She has done it for herself and for Catherine. The thought of hurting her is unthinkable.

***

That afternoon they went to the Lacy Nursing home. Catherine took off once there, while Joanna was in the administrator's office. Joanna tried watching her, but Miss Randy told her to let her go.

"Let her walk through the halls," she said.

Catherine went off having fun, talking gibberish to others, while Joanna toured the facility and signed papers to have her placed there, being in a fog most of the time, but knowing she had to do this now, otherwise she wouldn't.

"Bring Catherine in tomorrow around one o'clock, with her clothes and any other personal items."

Joanna gave Catherine a sleeping pill that night as usual, but Joanna was awake most of the night.

***

The next day on their way to the nursing home, Joanna explained, as best she could.

"Ca, you're going on vacation for awhile to help other people." Catherine sat in the passenger seat, quiet and listening.

"You'll like it Ca. They have good food and things for you to do, like helping people that aren't as healthy as you, or any other work they need done."

Catherine was still quiet, but Joanna somehow had a feeling, she knew what was going on. Or maybe it was Joanna's guilt kicking in.

The people at the nursing were ill and did need help. Catherine was always willing to help anyone she could, even with this disease, if she knew how to.

Joanna was taking her to *this* home, because it was less than ten minutes away from their own home. This way she figured she'd be able to see her every day.

***

Once there, Joanna went to Miss Randy's office to sign papers and Catherine went off helping people and talking to them, in the little English that she still remembered and in her new language.

After three hours, Joanna was told it would be better if she left and let them care for Catherine now. "Go home and get some rest," they said, "or do something that's fun."

So Joanna kisses Catherine goodbye, which she doesn't notice because she's busy with other people and pacing. Walking out to the car Joanna feels free, but lonely, missing someone by her side.

'What do I do now?'

'Do something that's fun', they said.

'Where do I go for fun?'

***

Catherine is all Joanna has known, sick or not sick, for all these years. She doesn't want to go home without her there. She calls her friend Fran and tells her what's happened.

"Come here and stay. I won't be home for awhile yet, but you know the key is under the mat."

"Thank you Fran. I'll see you later."

Joanna enjoys her time with Fran and tries to sleep that night, but it's impossible, so goes back home and crawls into bed.

She can't stand being without Catherine and wraps her arms around her pillow, smelling the scent of her hair on the fabric, wishing she were there, sick or not.

"Catherine, how could you leave me here alone to face life?"

"You were the sensible one, the smart one, the one who knew all the answers to everything."

"How could you leave me?"

"Why couldn't I be the one with the disease instead of you? Then I wouldn't have to face losing you?" she cries into the pillow to muffle the sound, thinking of the neighbor on the other side of the wall.

And again, "God, where are You now, when I need You to heal her?"

***

In the morning Joanna eats breakfast, showers and dresses to go to the nursing home. When she gets there, Catherine is in a rage, walking hurriedly through the hallways, trying to find her way out. She is not even aware that Joanna is there. Joanna takes her hand and brings her back to her room to dress her. She's in the same clothes that she wore yesterday and her fingernails are filthy with dirt and feces, which Joanna smells.

Joanna knows this means they're not watching her every move, the way she did. She expected more people than just her, would be watching over Catherine, but they don't love her the way Joanna does. It's just a job to them.

She speaks to one of the aides, "how was Catherine last night?"

"She was up all night walking, but that's normal. It will be better if you don't come often. That confuses her."

Joanna tries to understand and leaves to go home to the empty house, where she doesn't hear Catherine talking gibberish or see her pacing through the apartment. It's quiet and lonely, and she feels lost – like Catherine.

Wednesday is the same and they tell her not to come in on Thursday. Joanna doesn't see Catherine all day but calls to ask how she is. They say Catherine is doing fine and not to worry. Joanna feels a little better knowing she's spoken to someone, and she imagines Catherine in activities, or eating and the professionals handling the disease the way it should be.

On Friday Joanna sees Catherine before lunch. She's pacing, trying to get out the front door, and driving the staff crazy, even though they had sedated her. She has red bruises all over one side of her body and a black eye.

"What happened to her? Did she fall?" Joanna asks the aide.

No answer. She realizes the aide doesn't speak English and obviously doesn't understand her. She then asks the nurse the same questions. Not getting an answer from her either.

Joanna can't stand seeing Catherine like this, stumbling over everything she comes upon. She looks like someone who's drunk and living on the streets.

Bringing Catherine to the bathroom to wash her hands and face and comb her hair, Joanna passes a dirty diaper lying on the floor. She wonders if this accounts for the feces under her fingernails.

"Leave it there, Ca," as she goes to pick it up.

On their way to the dining room Joanna tells one of the aides of the dirty diaper lying on the floor and where it is.

Lunch is served and Catherine gets a bologna sandwich, milk and banana, which she proceeds to devour. After lunch, sitting on the porch, Catherine starts to fall asleep in the chair, as Joanna strokes the back of her head. Joanna leads her back to her room to lie down and take a nap. She doesn't want to lie down, but Joanna feels she hasn't slept in nights and is going to fall again and get hurt. Sitting on the edge of the bed, Joanna strokes her arm to keep her calm and from getting up. She is so tired she doesn't resist and falls asleep.

Joanna watches her friend, exhausted from this new sight she's been around, bruises on her arms, on the side of her face and hands and the black eye, and she prays.

'Dear Lord, what am I supposed to do now? I am so tired myself and she is all I have or want to have.'

***

She is caged and being treated badly by the staff and Joanna feels as if no one understands her, except

Joanna. What have I done? – I'm the one who put her here!

While Catherine is napping, Joanna decides to walk for exercise. While walking down the hall she hears a woman calling, "I need to go to the bathroom."

Joanna thinks, 'how wonderful this woman can speak and tell them her needs,' but no one comes to the woman's rescue.

Joanna goes to the desk, "the woman in 109 needs to go to the bathroom."

"Someone will help her soon," the nurse replies.

One half hour goes by, the woman is crying now and all Joanna can think is, 'I have to get Catherine out of here.'

When Catherine wakes up, Joanna takes her to the bathroom where the dirty diaper still lays. She washes her face and combs her hair and sits her on the toilet. Catherine doesn't fight Joanna this time, as she's still too exhausted.

Joanna again tells the nurse at the desk about the dirty diaper and asks to please call the doctor, she would like to speak to him. The nurse says she will call him and get back to her. Thanking her, Joanna brings Catherine into the activity room to see what the other residents are doing. Many of the residents are sitting in wheelchairs around the nurses' station and then she notices most, if not all, look drugged or sleeping. In the activity room, she turns on the radio for music and starts to dance with Catherine. Catherine is too tired to stand on her feet, even after the nap, or she's hurting and can't say.

Later, at dinner the woman sitting opposite them hasn't been served yet. Catherine has a bowl of chicken soup sitting in front of her and she's picked up the spoon to eat, but is more interested in the woman across from her, without food. Catherine pushes her bowl over to the woman, nodding to her, 'to eat.'

"No, Ca. The lady will get her food in a minute," and Joanna slides the bowl back to Catherine. But nothing comes out of the kitchen.

More and more in the back of Joanna's mind she hates this place.

The woman finally gets her dinner and Catherine finishes eating, so Joanna takes her back to the room to brush her teeth. Joanna wonders why Catherine is easier to handle here than she was at home? Catherine passes the dirty diaper once more and tries to pick it up but Joanna stops her. While she brushes her teeth, Joanna feels the heat from within her building to anger, thinking, 'how can I leave her in this place?'

Her last look at Catherine's face in the mirror is the beautiful human being that she'd come to know. This makes her decision.

"Come on Ca, you're coming home with me. We're getting out of here."

Throwing her clothes in a bag, then taking Catherine's hand, she continues to the nurses' station.

"I'm taking Catherine home."

"For the evening?" the nurse asks.

"No. She's not coming back to this place."

"You can't do that," she says.

"Oh, I think I can. No one has looked after her. Just look at the bruises," and Joanna points to Catherine's arm and eye.

"No one has given me any answers to what has happened to her. We're going home."

***

Joanna takes Catherine's hand and leads her to the car without any trouble, then throws her clothes in the back seat and heads for home. In her mind, she feels calmer that Catherine's with her and she won't get hurt again. Yet as she gets closer to home, in the back of her mind, she knows she can't do this alone any more. As they approach the condo Catherine smiles, and Joanna knows she recognizes where she is.

Inside, Joanna fixes milk and cookies for the both of them and they sit on the sofa, with 'I Love Lucy' tapes, with Joanna's arm around Catherine, like always, so she can't get up to pace. She relaxes and soon is falling asleep. Rousing her, Joanna brings her to the bedroom, undresses her and puts her in bed. She doesn't resist. She's been through hell at the nursing home.

***

As Joanna lay there, stroking Catherine's arm and crying silently to herself, Catherine falls into a deep sleep. She makes jerky body movements, from the medication at the nursing home that's still in her. Joanna then goes into the living room, where she sits recapping what has gone on. She's brought Catherine back home but in her mind she knows she can't keep her here. She is far too much for Joanna to handle.

She calls Jan, the nurse, their old neighbor from Estuary Dunes of 1985.

"Hi Jan? It's Joanna."

"Well hello there. Where have you two been? All we get are Christmas cards from you. Is everything okay?"

"Oh Jan, it's a long story. I just brought Catherine back from Lacy Nursing Home and I can't take care of her any more. She has Alzheimer's."

"Lacy Nursing home. That's the worst! Where is she right now?

"She's in bed sleeping. They drugged her something awful and she has bruises all over. She's like a walking zombie."

"You can't keep her home, Joanna."

"No, I'd love to but I can't. You know she's six feet tall, has lost her speech, and is stronger than an ox. She's become combative and yells all the time in another language that I don't understand. I think the neighbors have had it."

"I understand. You sound awful. It's probably best you do put her in a nursing home. I'm working for Wheitz Nursing Home now, and I feel it's a good one. Let me speak with the administrator and I'll let him know Catherine is a friend and needs help now. Suppose I get back to you on Monday."

"God Jan, I don't know if I can wait till then. I know if I don't do it now I never will."

"Listen, she'll probably sleep most of the night and tomorrow with the drugs in her. Do you have anything at home to sedate her?"

"Yeah, she's been on all kinds of medication, anti-anxiety, anti-depression, sleeping pills. You name it … she's been on it."

"If she gets hard to handle, give her a sleeping pill to keep her down. I'll call you Monday morning."

"Okay, thank you Jan. Thanks for listening."

"I understand. I work with it all day long, so I know what you're going through. You take care now, till Monday … bye."

This may be a good idea to put Catherine in the

home Jan works, and then Jan will be able to keep an eye on her. *The only negative – it's forty-five minutes away.*

Joanna undresses, gets in bed with Catherine on her left side, as usual. Both of them sleep through the night, and the next day Catherine seems better. She sleeps most of the day and Sunday, from the left over medication still in her body from the nursing home.

The doctor she had asked Lacy Nursing Home to contact never called back.

GRIEF

JAN CALLED Monday morning around nine-thirty, as promised, with Joanna waiting and apprehensive.

"Hi Joanna. How'd it go over the weekend?"

"Hello Jan ... pretty good. Catherine slept most of the weekend."

" I'm in the admissions office and I'm going to give you over to Ann. She's head of admissions and she'd like to speak with you."

"Okay, thanks Jan."

"Mrs. Shaker?" a soft voice on the other end asked.

"Yes."

"Jan has filled me in on you and Catherine and what you're both going through. If you agree, I'll ask Lacy Nursing Home to fax Catherine's records over to me and you can bring her in tomorrow morning around nine o'clock. Jan thinks very highly of you both and that's enough for me."

"I truly thank you for doing this on such short notice. I have all the copies of Catherine's records and will bring them with me tomorrow."

"As I said, Jan has told me everything I need to know and I look forward to meeting you and Catherine in person tomorrow."

"I don't know how to thank you Ann," and

307

Joanna hung up.

***

She knew she had to do this for her own health, otherwise, she was going to be dead before Catherine. Then she wouldn't be able to care for any one. After slapping Catherine, she knew she was not acting in Catherine's best interest. She had lost the little patience that she had had and all respect for her own self.

***

Joanna called Izzy, a nurse who came once in a while to care for Catherine, and Kim, a friend from the support group. She asked them if they would go with her and Catherine to the nursing home tomorrow. They both said, "yes," and Joanna felt more at ease.

Joanna wanted to spend the last day with Catherine in her presence as much as possible. Even if she had to follow her around, pacing.

Funny thing, Catherine didn't pace at all.

Joanna tried bringing her outside for a walk around the complex and to the pool, but Catherine balked at anything except chocolate chip cookies and milk. They sat on the couch and watched videotapes and laughed until Catherine fell asleep.

Every moment she could, she looked at Catherine's face and thought how much she loved it, then tears would come, knowing soon it would be gone. Joanna got Catherine into bed that night and asked if she'd like a glass of apple juice. Catherine looked at Joanna and smiled and Joanna had a feeling Catherine knew what was ahead of her. Maybe it was just guilt creeping in. Catherine was so calm and relaxed this past weekend, why couldn't she be like that all the time, and then Joanna wouldn't have to let her go.

Opening a sleeping pill capsule, she sprinkled the powder in a glass of apple juice and stirred it, remembering when the doctor first introduced the pills, Catherine would spit them back at her. Doing it this way, Joanna felt she was deceiving Catherine, but she knew if she didn't give the medication, it would be a night of yelling and throwing things around the house after all the other medications wore off. She was sure the neighbors were tired of hearing what went on downstairs. They were kind and kept telling Joanna she had to do something or she was going to have a stroke herself. They had loved Catherine for the eight years they had lived there, and hated to see this lovely person turn into something she wasn't.

Joanna went to bed that night with a feeling of losing Catherine all over again. She slept little and should have taken a sleeping pill herself, but subconsciously she wanted to be awake for Catherine's last night at her side. She touched her arm at times and listened to her snore. Joanna knew she wasn't going to hear it after tonight in their home.

She lay there remembering Catherine of the past...

Catherine is a loving person, to everyone and every creature she meets. She offers to pay for a woman's groceries, who is in front of them at the check out counter. The woman doesn't have enough money for her groceries, so Catherine reaches in her own pocketbook and hands the clerk the money. The woman nods to Catherine in thanks, but Joanna sees more than that. She sees the love she passes on to Catherine.

They see a young woman covered in filth, when they were going into a small restaurant to have breakfast after a golf game. As they are seated, the young woman comes in and sits across from them. The waitress asks her to leave but Catherine calls the waitress over and tells her to give the young woman anything she wants to eat and to put it on their bill. When they finish eating and get up to leave the young woman is eating eggs and pancakes and nods her thanks to Catherine and Joanna. Again, she sees the love passed on.

Catherine sends money to friends who are in need, for their children's expenses in college. She buys a tool for a young man who's a golf pro and has just opened his own business. She takes young golf pros to one of the best golf courses to play, and pays their fees. They are in awe to have played a course they could never have played without Catherine's gift.

Joanna sees how anyone who comes in contact with Catherine, loves her. She is always thinking about the other person. She takes care of injured birds or animals of any kind. She doesn't even kill the tiny lizard that has come into their home. She picks it up with a paper towel and takes it outside. She tells Joanna, "we are all connected in some way."

She had told Catherine, going into the first nursing home, "You're going to help people here, because they need it." She nodded her head, 'yes.' Sure enough, in the nursing home, she picked up a lap quilt that another resident had dropped on the floor, and she pushed people that were in wheelchairs – even if they didn't want to be pushed.

***

Tuesday morning came and Izzy and Kim were sitting in their cars waiting. Joanna tossed Catherine's suitcase in the back of the car, thinking of the appointment she had in West Palm Beach. She hated the forty-five minute trip, not to mention the reason *for* the trip. She's back having trouble driving alone and the thought of not having Catherine with her any more makes Joanna anxious. Putting her in someone else's care again worries her but she knows it has to be done.

Catherine didn't like getting in the car now, and would grab the upper part of the doorframe. She was strong and hard to move if she didn't want to be moved. She'd stiffen up like an iron rod. Joanna told her they were going for a ride to look at the ocean, which they had done in the past, and for some reason this day she relaxed, getting in the car.

Catherine, Joanna, Kim, and Izzy drove to the nursing home, while Catherine made noises in her own voice, and the others made light talk about the weather or what was new in the news. It helped take Joanna's mind off what was happening. Kim and Izzy had come to know and love Catherine, in their own way, Joanna could see.

Once there, Izzy helped Joanna get Catherine out of the car and they went inside to admissions. Joanna held Catherine's hand and felt her own heart beat fast and irregular, but didn't care, she wished she *would* die.

Ann met them in admissions. "I see you made it down here all right?"

"Yes, the drive wasn't too bad."

"I'm happy to meet you in person Joanna," Ann extended her hand.

"These are our friends, Kim and Izzy. They've been great support for me this morning."

"Nice to meet you both."

"And this is Catherine." Joanna held her hand out

towards Catherine.

"Hello Catherine, it's very nice to meet you." Ann touched Catherine lightly on the shoulder, while Catherine kept quiet. Odd, Joanna thought, she is always so loud at home maybe she *does* know what's happening.

Ann tried to lead Catherine to a seat, but Catherine wanted to stand near Joanna. She tried to ask Catherine questions and then looked at Joanna, "doesn't she speak at all?"

"No, not our language at least," Joanna smiled.

After a few minutes Joanna noticed Catherine was becoming agitated, and asked Izzy to take her outside for a walk.

"Ca, go with Izzy for a walk." Joanna said in a calm voice.

"Sure, c'mon Catherine, let's go and find some pretty flowers," said Izzy.

Now it was down to business with Joanna, Ann and Kim in the room.

"I received the information from Lacy. What else do you have with you, Joanna?"

"Everything from day one. All of her medical records."

Ann looked through the briefcase Joanna had brought with her. "Good she's had a chest x-ray, we won't need to do another. I'd like to make copies of some records here," and she called in her secretary.

"These papers you can take home with you," handing Joanna a packet. "And these have check marks where I need your signature," handing her another set of papers.

Joanna started signing her name and also printing

Catherine's name in places checked off in red. *I feel like I'm signing my life away.* In a sense, she was – signing two lives away.

While Joanna signed the papers, Jan came in at one point and came over and hugged Joanna.

"I'm so sorry," she said. "I just saw Catherine outside with her nurse. She's changed so much I can't believe it."

Joanna held back the tears as best she could. She hadn't seen Jan in maybe four years. This was a person who knew them when they were both healthy and happy, eating the great dinners Jan prepared and playing board games or charades.

Ann took Kim and Joanna to Catherine's room and showed them where she would be. The home was clean, and Joanna knew it was a good one, from being in the support group and listening to other caregivers' experiences. It had a high rating, if that meant anything? But, then, so did Lacy nursing home. What bothered her, was Catherine would be forty-five minutes away from *their* home, but here at least Joanna knew Jan would be watching over her.

Back downstairs Joanna called Catherine and Izzy to come inside the building and they took Catherine up to her room, on the second floor. Joanna held her by the hand and led her, even though she wanted to lead Joanna somewhere else.

Ann advised, "Let her go. She can't get hurt, and can't leave the building. The aides will keep an eye on her."

Ann had made it known the ratio of aides per patient was one to seven, while at Lacy it was one to ten, so Joanna let her go. Someone in the activity room was playing the piano and that's where Catherine headed.

"Joanna, it will be better for Catherine if you leave while she's occupied with something else," Ann advised.

Looking at Kim and Izzy, she reluctantly said, "Then I guess we better leave now."

Joanna thought, 'Just like Lacy Home, they want you out in a hurry. Funny how you feel as though you're not needed at all – you feel like a left over, being kicked out – although I know I'm not. This will be best for Catherine, and this is all I want.'

Joanna gazed at Catherine one last time in the activity room, then left with Kim and Izzy. Ann had told her not to come back for at least two or three months so Catherine would get used to her new home and the daily activities.

On the drive home, little was said and then back at the condo, Izzy and Kim left without coming inside. They hugged Joanna, saying their good-byes.

***

Joanna can't fully describe her feelings that day. It was different from leaving Catherine in the first home, because there, she knew she would see her often. Now, being so far away and with her fear of driving, she knew she would see Catherine very little. She ached for her inside, and hated the fear that would be keeping her from seeing Catherine's face.

At home, she lies in bed and cries again, for this time she knows it's for good. Joanna didn't get out of bed until the next morning, although she slept only a few hours. She kept waking and thinking of Catherine and what she was doing. Was she walking the halls? Was she falling, or was she perhaps, sleeping?

In the morning, she calls the home to see how Catherine had made it through the night. They tell her Catherine is fine but they need more clothing.

"I'll be down in a day or two," she said. "I have to get someone to drive with me." And then went back to bed to stay, for how long, she didn't know.

***

Joanna listens to what they said, "Don't visit Catherine, until she learns who's caring for her. She has to learn a new environment," they say. Joanna wants to tell them that research shows that Alzheimer victims are not able to learn *anything* new, so how can she learn a new environment?

She's lost without Catherine, and with Thanksgiving approaching she thinks of the many Thanksgivings together that were beautiful, full of love, family and friends. She remembers the first Thanksgiving when they arrived in Florida and played golf. She remembers and remembers. She wants to remember, but wishes sometimes she'd forget. There are too many to forget.

***

God must have heard her prayers this year, because He sent an old friend, Annette, who was also going to be alone. She asked Joanna if she would like to go to a movie, and Joanna's response was, "On Thanksgiving?" But she had nothing better to do, except cry all day, the way she had been doing since Catherine left. "Yes, but only if I can cook Thanksgiving dinner for us," she told Annette.

She bought a small turkey breast and made all the

315

trimmings, and after dinner they went to a movie. Joanna will remember Annette for this, for she knew what Joanna was going through and was being kind by joining her for dinner.

She came back home to an empty house.

***

December 1994 … Joanna is still told not to visit Catherine. She did visit once, to bring more clothes and make sure she was being treated well. She felt no one could care for her as well as she did, knowing her every move, of what she wanted and didn't want. Jan assured her over the phone when Joanna would call, "Catherine's fine, try to take care of Joanna."

Joanna learned Catherine was doing the same at this nursing home as she did with her, always up and pacing. They had put a bracelet on her that would set off an alarm if she went out the door, as she did many times. Thank God she's on the second floor and can't get out into the street, like the woman from another facility Joanna had read about in the paper, who was found lost in the woods.

When Christmas comes, Joanna doesn't want to cook for herself and decides to have dinner with Catherine. The drive to the nursing home is hard, but she listens to her relaxation tape of years ago and it helps.

She gets to the large four-story building and walks past the admissions office where she was a little over a month ago. She takes the elevator to Catherine's floor, number two, and her first sight is Catherine pacing in the hallway. After all, what else did she expect to see, Catherine sitting down watching television? Walking up to Catherine, she puts her arm around her shoulder.

"Merry Christmas, Ca," and Catherine looks at

316

Joanna and smiles, saying words Joanna still doesn't understand.

"Are you ready to have Christmas dinner, Ca?"

An aide looks at Joanna and smiles, probably thinking, 'is she nuts for asking this?'

Catherine won't sit at the table to eat and is up constantly, while Joanna continues to bring her back, till finally she gives up and lets her go. There are two hallways she can go down and back and a door that leads outside, where there is a patio with a railing around it. So Joanna takes her by the hand and leads her outside to see the plants on the patio.

She tries singing, "Oh we ain't got a barrel of money," and Catherine laughs.

Then she tries some Christmas songs, "Jingle Bells, jingle bells," but Catherine is up and running inside to the hallways.

Catching up to her, Joanna reaches for her hand, "C'mon Ca, let's go get some ice cream." At this she stares at Joanna, as if she knows what she's saying. Joanna does believe, when it comes to the word ice cream, she *does* understand. After all, she's always loved it, especially chocalotta ice cream.

Walking past the nurse's station, she tells her, "We're going downstairs for ice cream," the aide nods a 'yes' and goes on with what she's doing. At the elevator, Joanna pushes the button, and when the doors open, Catherine is off on a run, but can't go anywhere, as it's just a small square room. They stand together in the elevator while Joanna does the talking and Catherine gibbers. The doors open and her long strides go into action, but Joanna has a good hold on her. She can't keep up with Catherine's long strides, and

317

sometimes is pulled along.

At the ice cream parlor, Joanna meets Valerie behind the counter and asks for chocolate ice cream, telling her Catherine calls it chocalotta ice cream. Valerie thinks it's cute and goes along with the new name she's learned. Then, with Joanna's one hand in Catherine's hand, and the other holding the bowl of ice cream with a spoon, they make their way outdoors to eat.

"So tell me Ca, how are you doing?" as Joanna pulls a chair up for herself, after setting Catherine down and giving her the ice cream.

Catherine eats her ice cream as if it's the last bowl on earth.

"Are they taking good care of you, my friend? Are you sleeping at night? Do they sing to you the way I do?" asking and receiving no answers.

Within minutes, Catherine's finished and getting up to run.

"Wait Ca, I have to throw the bowl away," Joanna holds onto her hand.

As they walk to the garbage can to throw out what's left, Joanna says, "let's go for a walk around the pond." Catherine's happy, Joanna can see the look.

Maybe this *is* the right place for her.

Walking around the pond, Catherine spots the ducks and gibbers to them, looking then to Joanna. When she sees the cars passing on the roadway, Catherine makes a whooshing sound and looks fearful.

"Yes, they're going fast aren't they?"

Her eyes are wide with fear, "It's okay, Ca. It's all right, there's nothing to be afraid of."

They've gotten a workout, walking three times around the pond – at least Joanna knows she has.

Catherine is on drugs now to keep her calm, not like the others when she was stumbling over herself. They're trying different medicines on her to see what works best, but she still has lots of energy and nowhere to go.

Joanna brings Catherine back upstairs to her room and they sit and watch TV for a while. Golf is on and Joanna thinks maybe she'll take an interest, but the interest is short lived and she's back in the hallway, pacing. Joanna tells the nurse she's leaving and to please take good care of her friend. The nurse smiles and says, "We will."

Not saying goodbye, because she doesn't want to disrupt Catherine's pacing or agitate her more, Joanna quietly says, "God Bless you Catherine," and heads for the elevator.

Catherine doesn't look to see where Joanna's going; she's in a world all her own. Joanna steps inside the elevator doors and turns to push the button, and glances at Catherine before the doors close. She's saddened at her friend pacing, like a caged animal, trying to find her way out.

She walks to the car and tears come once more – it hurts, so much. Nothing she's ever gone through in her life before has hurt this badly. She doesn't want to live without Catherine, and doesn't want to live watching her like this.

It takes a while to drive to the movie. She wants to get into another world, like Catherine, to forget where she is and see a funny movie to make her laugh, even though she doesn't want to. She would rather crawl into a hole and not exist.

STRUGGLE

THE FEAR of being alone has struck again and Joanna's feet are stuck in cement. She can't do anything or go anywhere, just like being sixteen again; fast heart rate, dizzy, sweats, everything is the same. Again she wants to go somewhere and hide, but there's no place to hide. Fear is with her wherever she goes. Heading to bed, she pulls the covers over her head, as if that will help. It didn't years ago, so why should it help now? Fear is always there, within her mind, and the feeling of hopelessness and there's nothing she can do about it. People say they care, but it doesn't matter to her, because *she* doesn't matter to herself. Feeling as if she's living outside her own body, watching from a distance – encapsulated in a bubble where nothing gets through to her to make her feel again.

She struggles writing today, not knowing who the real Joanna is. 'Is it the caregiver to my friend? Is it the child of my mother and father or the wife to my ex-husband? Is it the mother of my children? Is it the person full of fear that I know so well? Is it the unforgiving person? Is it the loving person? Is it the child of God? Who the hell is the real me? Or is it all the above?'

Hating these thoughts of insecurity, of not knowing who she is that come so often now, whether in a sleeping-dream, when she wakes disoriented and confused, or in the dream, awake-in-life, like today. Why does she need to keep asking? Why can't she find the answer?

She wants to say to herself when this happens, "Will the real you please stand up."

If God knows the real her, why doesn't He show her more often than not? Why does she go through these self-crucifixions that scar deeply into her, every time they hit.

She's dead inside and has lost her soul – this has to be the answer. "Please, Dear God, answer, comfort me and let me rest in Your love," she pleads.

***

In January 1995, Joanna finally decides to get rid of everything that has anything to do with Catherine. The thought 'How could she leave me?' is constantly there.

Reality is setting in and the depression is so great she can't think. She's spoken to Catherine's lawyer and he says she can stay in the condo until the money runs out, then she'll have to sell it. If they were in a marriage, she would be able to keep the condo and the car, but they're not. It is *just* a beautiful love that goes on forever. Go and figure the laws of life? She's mad, lonely, hurt and feeling displaced.

She has this three-bedroom, three-bath condo she needs to sell, for it's the right thing to do. According to Florida law, Catherine can keep her condo and her car, even though she has this disease, and cannot care for herself. 'Is she ever coming back to this place? I don't think so. Is she ever going to be able to drive again? I don't think so.' Joanna has come to realize that laws were not made for *all* people.

321

Joanna is handling all the household bills, and the trust account along with the bank. It is costing four thousand dollars a month for Catherine's room and care and because the aides have too much work, and can't handle Catherine's six-foot body, the nursing home has asked Joanna to hire private, round the clock aides for Catherine. This is another four thousand a month for the private duty aides, all this totaling eight thousand a month. It takes everything a person owns to pay for this disease, sucking up all their assets and then they are put on Medicaid. Joanna didn't want Catherine on Medicaid, in a County home. That's where people go that don't have anyone who cares about them, or who are indigent. Joanna wants the best care for Catherine that money can buy, so she needs to sell condo.

***

Giving the listing to Fran, a Realtor in the complex, she phones and tells her she will need time to clean the condo and get rid of things.

"That's fine," Fran says, "Can I bring people by to look at it?"

"I don't know. Right now I don't know which end is up."

"Well, suppose I call first and come by when it's suitable for you?" Fran asks again.

"Okay, I guess that'd be all right. Just remember … it's a mess. Taking care of Catherine took all of my time and I haven't had a chance to straighten it up."

"I understand … take your time and I'll let you know when. We should have dinner some time. I'll call you, bye for now."

"Bye, Fran."

***

Strangers come into their home to look and Joanna's embarrassed, angry and furious at what they say about the home Catherine and she had shared. "Oh, it needs this," and "We have to change the colors," and on and on.

It's such a beautiful home, once filled with love, laughter and beautiful memories, why can't they see this? This is the condo Joanna didn't want in the beginning, because of the vague feeling she had. She knows now what that feeling was – Catherine's and her illnesses. But they'd made it into a beautiful home despite that, and now people were saying they wanted to change it. She goes outside when the lookers come, because she doesn't want to hear what they have to say.

***

Joanna thinks, 'Where am I going to go? I have no idea.' She's taking each day as it comes and all the days are bad. She feels like an ant, running around in circles, going nowhere.

Within the month, an older couple decides they want to buy the condo. Sue, their Realtor, asks, "Do you think you could come down in price?

"No, I don't think so." Joanna replies.

"This couple needs a roof over their head and they're hurting for money. Are you sure you can't come down?"

Joanna recognizes the shoes the buyers are wearing. They're the same shoes Catherine ordered from New York at a hundred and fifty dollars a pair and the car they drove up in is a Mercedes, plus they live on the best side of town. Who's hurting here, they or Joanna? She feels angry inside, as Sue keeps pushing her to come down in price.

"You've got to be kidding, Sue. I'm the one without a roof over my head."

Sue argues the point about coming down on the price even more.

Mad she spits out, "For you Sue … the price just jumped, two thousand dollars."

She looks at Joanna, fuming and walks out the door, to go to her customers, who have now crossed over to the pool area to look around.

Joanna thinks, 'I'm not getting a penny of this money, but I refuse to be taken for a jerk.' She feels angry for Catherine and herself.

Sue comes back in ten minutes. "They'll take it," was all she said.

Joanna shakes hands with the couple with no hostility or dislike toward them. "I wish you happiness in your new home and I hope you'll be as happy here as I was."

"Thank you. Where are you moving?" they ask Joanna.

"I don't know yet … I haven't made up my mind. I am going to need time to clean up and get rid of furniture, so if we could make the closing in a couple of months, I would appreciate it."

"That isn't a problem. We still haven't sold our house."

They don't want any of the furniture or drapes, because they are going to build cabinets in the dining room and repaint.

***

The complex has a group of men and women who work there, doing the yard work, cleaning the clubhouse and around the pool's common area and

Joanna asks Sam if he can help her with some of the heavy items. She gives Sam most of furniture that he and his family can enjoy, except the dining table that Joanna and Catherine loved. They had spent weeks trying to find just the right table. Joanna decides to give this to one of Catherine's favorite charitable organizations, who comforts people and their families who are dying.

Leaving everything as is in Catherine's bedroom and the guestroom, she makes the guestroom her home base for now. It has the same small television that she watched with Catherine towards the end of her being home and in the kitchen are the small table and two chairs. She'll keep that and nothing more. Slowly, she gets rid of all the furniture, and rents a small storage unit to keep items that Catherine and she shared, as well as a chair and a lamp from their mothers. She holds onto some pictures, sheets and towels, just in case Joanna ever finds a way to live alone again. She also keeps some of Catherine's clothes for the nursing home, which are leaving as fast as Joanna brings them to her. It seems the aides can't find her cloths the day after she brings them. She knows she's being lied to and they're walking away from the nursing home, but there is no way for her to know for sure. She's even thought of putting a small camera in Catherine's room, just to watch. But, what's the use, if they need the clothes that bad, then let them have them.

She gives items to dear friends that have a part of Catherine in them. A mockingbird that sits on the foyer table, which Catherine used to scratch the top with out of frustration, goes to a woman at the support group, who understands.

Joanna saves Catherine's bedroom for last, knowing it's going to be the hardest. This room has her paperwork, her personal items, like clothing and perfumes she smelled on her, her shoes, photo albums of golf, through the years alone and with them together.

Sitting on the bed she thinks: Where do I begin? I don't want to begin. I want to go back in time, or just become nonexistent.

She starts with one of Catherine's closets. She has two, one for her everyday clothes, and the other for dressy clothes for parties and dinners out. Catherine loved shoes and handbags, and still carries a handbag with her now at the nursing home. Maybe she thinks she's going somewhere? This was a thought the support group tossed around the table. Is it because the restlessness of the illness makes them always prepared to go somewhere – possibly back to their home of long ago?

"God I wish I understood this disease," Joanna says aloud, picking up one of the handbags and throwing it in the garbage.

Filling large garbage bags and leaving them outside for pick up, she works at a panic pace, not thinking. She just wants everything gone, out of her sight.

***

Two friends have phoned to say they will come to help her through this horrible time, both women from the support group. Hearing the doorbell, Joanna goes to answer it.

"Hi Joanna," Marta greets her with a smile. "Leone is right behind me. I saw her making the turn around the corner as I parked."

"Thanks for coming Marta. You don't know how

much this means to me."

Before closing the door, Joanna sees Leone open the patio gate. Leone's father died of Alzheimer's a year ago and Marta's friend also has passed on.

"Hello Leone. I'm glad to see you."

"Sorry I'm late, Joanna. I wanted to be here sooner but I just couldn't get away from the house."

The three leave the hallway and move into the dining room, where there is more room.

"I don't know where to start," Joanna confesses. "I've gone through my room but I can't get Catherine's room done. Every time I start, I find something else to do. I pick up a piece of clothing she wore and I start to remember. I just can't do it alone."

"That's understandable, that's why we're here. You need support in this and help with the heavy items," Leone says.

"Thank you. Marta, I thought you would like the outside tools." Marta had a home of her own.

Joanna opens the door to the hall closet, "Look in here. There are hammers and screwdrivers and a whole bunch of stuff. I want you to take whatever you want, I surely won't need them."

She reaches for a key on a hook in the closet, "Here's the key to the storage room where you will find more you can use. Whatever you don't want, throw in the garbage bin around the corner of the building."

"If you could come with me Leone, I'd like to go through Catherine's closets. I'm sure there are clothes you can use since you're the same height."

"Sure, I want to help as much as I can, Joanna. I remember when mom and I went through this with dad's belongings."

Leone and Joanna walk to Catherine's room where clothes are piled high atop the bed.

"I couldn't do it anymore. I didn't know where to start and just kept throwing clothes on the bed and the pile got larger. Now it's a mess. If you could go through it, see what you want and put the rest on the floor in another pile."

After straightening out the mess on the bed, Leone has put what she wants in bags.

"There's a lot that can go to charity. She has enough clothes here to dress a small country." At least that brings a smile to Joanna's face.

While Marta's in the storage closet packing boxes, Leone comes out of the closet asking, "should I save this?" It's an ankle-length cocktail gown Joanna remembers Catherine wore to parties without Joanna.

"No, throw it over there for garbage."

"It would be a good idea to mark the bags, Joanna. Do you have any masking tape and a marker?"

"Yes, in the upper drawer of the file cabinet in the other closet."

Leone marks three bags, storage, garbage and charity.

At Catherine's desk, Joanna sits – this was where she spent much of her time, writing friends, Joanna's family, congressmen and senators, on snags in the country.' "Write a letter," she'd say when Joanna told her how disgruntled she'd become over their country on certain issues, like divorce. Joanna thought of the many times she'd call her to dinner and Catherine would say, "Okay, just one more line to write."

So many memories to go through – so much of Catherine here in this room – pictures of her mom and dad and Anne and golf albums – so much one person could keep. 'I guess this is what a person's all about; what they collect over their lifetime. Now, she knew none of it.'

Leone steps out of the closet. "Are you all right?" She finds Joanna sitting on the bed teary-eyed and puts her arm across her shoulder. "I know how you feel. It will get easier, take my word for it."

Joanna wonders if she truly knows how she feels? Collecting herself, "I think it's time for a break."

The three break for lunch, and talk about Catherine and what a beautiful person she was – "Still is!" Joanna interjects, "that can't be taken from her, even though everything else has."

"Marta, how's the storage room coming?"

"Good. I took the shovels and tools that I can use around the house, if it's okay with you. There are boxes on the top shelf that say Christmas. What do you want me to do with them?"

Joanna thinks, 'all the beautiful holidays they had shared together and the first Charlie Brown tree. What does she do with all the ornaments now?'

"Throw them out … no … wait. Take the masking tape and write storage on them."

"Will do."

"Thanks Marta."

After lunch, while the girls are still chatting in the kitchen, Joanna sits at Catherine's desk going through her personal papers. She finds the folder marked – Joanna. She has a vivid scene of years ago. "Joanna if you need money it's in this envelope."

How embarrassed Joanna was back then, when Catherine mentioned this. Joanna opens the envelope and there lies the same three hundred dollars. 'I don't want this. I want you back. I want your laughter and our golf games together. I don't want this money!'

She feels anger within at this rotten illness that has taken Catherine from her. Tears start but she holds them back as Leone enters the room.

"Okay, break time is over. What do you want us to do now?" asks Leone.

"Since the clothes are done, would you like to go through the books in the living room and sort them out? Use your own discretion on which ones I'd like to keep and put them in storage boxes. Take what you want and what's left behind, I'll give to a thrift shop."

She's glad to have these two women with her. They take her mind off the subject, and she doesn't think she would have been able to do it alone. She comes across Catherine's little black books, thumbs through the pages, then tosses them to the garbage bag. She watches them hit the bag and thinks, 'Should I keep them? Maybe, I shouldn't throw them out.' Picking them up, she puts them in the bag marked storage. She finds old greeting cards she had given Catherine – cards of congratulations on winning a tournament, and throws them in the garbage.

At five o'clock Leone mentions, "I've got to get home to make dinner for Joe. He'll be home from work soon." Joe and Leone had been together many years, living a happy life.

"Yeah, it's time I got going too," Marta has come back from storage where she's been most of the day.

"I don't know how to thank you girls. You're good friends and I want you to know, I *do* appreciate all you've helped me with."

"If you want us back tomorrow, just call, okay?" says Marta.

They hug Joanna and she watches them close the outside gate and climb into their cars.

Seeing them pull away, she closes the door and returns to Catherine's bedroom. The room is partially done and Joanna believes she can do the rest herself. Boxes and bags are labeled with magic marker as to what to keep and what to throw away and what will go to storage for a later date.

***

One month has gone by and Joanna still doesn't know where she's going. She doesn't want to face the move and thinks of Catherine racing through the hallways at the nursing home, not loved by anyone there. She visits Catherine but not as much as she would like. The fears keep her from taking the long drive. Leone calls at times and asks if she would like to go visit Catherine, and Joanna is happy.

The Realtors have gotten together and have agreed on a closing date. It's like pulling teeth, for Joanna to leave this place she had almost prophesied. Deciding to use the money her mom had left her, the thought of going back to Sea Trail lifts her heart.

She calls Bob and asks, "Is 305 for rent?"

"Yes, it is. In fact the owner is thinking of selling it. Is Catherine still with you?"

"No … I had to put her in a nursing home. Bob, ask the owner if she'd like to rent it to me for a year."

"So you want to come back to the ocean again? I couldn't live anywhere else, Joanna. It's so peaceful and calm here. I'm glad you're going to be my

331

neighbor again. I'll call you back, later."

"Thanks Bob. I appreciate all you've done for Catherine and me."

Bob calls back with a 'yes.' Joanna feels much better and almost happy now that she has a place to go to.

***

The closing takes less than an hour and the couple who is buying it doesn't show up. It's just the Realtors and Joanna meeting.

"I have to go back and get my suitcases," she says. "Is it all right if I leave the keys on the kitchen counter?"

"Sure, that would be fine. Do what you need to do," says Fran who has been a friend through all of this.

Fran gives her a large sum of money, which Joanna takes to the bank and deposits into the trust account. She speaks with the person handling the trust, and tells her, "If anything happens to me, I want you to handle everything. Just make sure you pay the nursing home."

At home, she collects her belongings, only two suitcases of clothes, since 305 is fully equipped. She writes a note to the new owners, "I hope you'll be as happy as I was here." Then looks around the empty rooms and closets, making sure everything's out.

At the front door, she turns for one last look and a flash of love and happiness comes over her, with a vision of Catherine's face and laughter.

Then closes the door behind her...

REST

MAY 1995 … once again Joanna drives up to Sea Trail but this time she's alone.

She meets the woman at the guard gate, as she did in '84 and '93 when her other half was with her.

Loraine is just as pleasant, "Well, hi stranger. I heard you were coming back."

"Hello Loraine. Yeah, I figured I needed a rest."

"How is Catherine?"

"I had to put her in a nursing home."

Loraine knows what's happened. Word travels fast when you live in condos, even if it's around the corner.

"When I saw the two of you last year, I figured it would happen sooner or later. I knew she was going to be hard to handle. Remember me telling you about my mother?"

Joanna had forgotten Loraine's mom had Alzheimer's.

"The cars are stacking up behind you. I'll talk to you later. Good luck now and take care of yourself."

"Thanks," and Joanna drove off.

Funny, how she always felt God was here at the ocean because of all the happiness and laughter she shared with Catherine. This was where it all began.

She parks the car in the underground garage and takes the elevator with the glass mirrors. Ten years have passed since that night of reflections. Who would think two lives could change so much over such a short period of time?

Letting herself in, she drops her bags and heads straight for the balcony to smell the clean fresh air and see the ocean. 'It's much easier to breathe here – your lungs are filled with no impurities,' are her thoughts. She sits a minute and looks downstairs to see if the doves are building a nest again, but there's nothing. People are in the pool and the ocean's a little rough as a Nor' Easter has blown in. There are white caps almost as far as the eye can see, and yet there are windsurfers getting their exercise and fun for the day.

Time to get some work done, as she unpacks and goes through the linen closet taking sheets and towels to wash. She has no idea who's been here since Catherine and she left. Removing towels from the closet, she finds a rolled up sock, with a blue dot on the toe. Catherine's – hers had a blue dot. Joanna's was purple, so they could tell them apart. "Catherine's hidden it here for me to find," she's convinced of that. Catherine knew Joanna hated being alone and now she wasn't. Catherine is here with her. "Thanks Ca."

She tapes the saying behind the medicine cabinet door: "don't look forward, the everlasting Father looks after you…." and reads it once more wondering, 'how can you not look forward?'

She does as much as she can around the condo, then attempts food shopping for the week. It's good to be back home.

***

It's been years since she's done anything except care for Catherine and she now finds she's able to relax and spend time alone, comfortably. She visits the young woman in the office downstairs when she gets her mail. The maintenance man and Loraine at the guard gate call to see if she needs anything. She feels as though they are family. Recently, when Bob moved out she felt a loss knowing he wasn't next door, but he still comes by to check on the condo for the owner. She has a safe feeling here.

One day follows another and her weeks are simple. She goes to the Alzheimer's support group meeting once a week, looking forward to visiting with her old friends of four years now. Using the Internet, she searches for information on the disease to bring to the group, to help them and her. There is a bond among this group that others couldn't relate. Since everyone is going through the same situation in different ways and different times. The group lives each other's fears and happiness as they talk about their week's events. Luckily, the support group meets around the corner from her home, so she doesn't have to drive far.

Joanna tries to visit Catherine once a week even though leaving the security of her home on long drives makes her experience panic and fear once more. She knows she can call on a neighbor or Leone, or someone from the support group, to go with her.

***

Joanna got a call from Marc saying that John has passed away and sadness fills her heart once more. It's almost a year since her mom has left. Joanna's guess is, John couldn't go on without Maria, and her next thought is, 'Will I be able to go on without Catherine?'

John will be remembered for the happiness he brought to her family and friends. When he walked in to a room and sat at the piano, everyone was happy, and his saying of 'Sunshine to You' will never be forgotten – God Bless John.

***

Late one afternoon Joanna feels Catherine calling her, in her mind. Trying not to think of it, she does some paperwork, and pushes it farther back in her mind. The call gets stronger. She's had these callings before but has been able to direct her thoughts to something else. This time the call keeps appearing. It was a bad day already and the thought of driving forty-five minutes she tries desperately to throw out of her mind – but can't.

It's as if Catherine is in the bedroom with her, yelling, "I need you. Come."

In a haze she puts on her clothes, she *has* to go. She told Catherine she would never abandon her. The fear is there, but not strong enough to stop her before she's out the door and on her way. Catherine is in trouble is all she can think. "I'm coming Ca." She says leaving the garage.

During the forty-five minute trip, she plays loud music, trying to keep calm. The fear of driving alone comes, but Catherine's calling overshadows it.

Once there, she's better and the fear is not as overpowering. There are people in the hallway, as she makes her way to Catherine's room on the left side at the end of the hall. Passing the nurse's station, she says hello to the nurse behind the desk and continues down the hall. The door is closed to Catherine's room. Why?' It's usually open, unless they're dressing her or she's sleeping, but even then, it's left slightly ajar. She hears the television, which isn't uncommon, for her aide leaves it on while Catherine is napping.

Opening the door quietly thinking Catherine is in bed, she sees Catherine's private aide lying on the bed watching TV and an aide from the floor sitting in a chair. Both are laughing and don't see Joanna. Standing there in amazement, she hears and sees Catherine to the left of her in the bathroom, banging on the mirror in madness. Catherine is angry, and seeing this, Joanna becomes furious.

"What the hell do you think you're doing?" she yells at the aide on the bed.

"You see this woman," pointing to Catherine in the bathroom. "She's paying you to watch *her*, not the TV!" The other aide runs past Joanna and out the door.

"Dammit, I'm paying you to make sure she doesn't get hurt. Do you even care what happens to her. DO you?"

The aide is speechless and Catherine has stopped banging on the mirror and is looking directly at Joanna. The aide has gotten up from the bed now, walking towards Joanna and Catherine.

"Get out of here. You're fired." Her hand out stretched toward the door.

"You can't do that," the aide says.

"Oh, yes I can …Get out!"

Catherine's wide eyed now, and knows Joanna's angry. She's nodding her head almost saying, "You're right. I'm glad you came."

Just then Donna, the director of nurses, comes in with Catherine's aide.

"Mrs. Shaker, can we please go to my office?"

"No," pointing to the aide. " I don't want this woman to lay a hand on Catherine. As far as I'm concerned she's gone."

"Calm down Mrs. Shaker. Come with me where we can discuss this."

Calmly Joanna answers, "I don't need to discuss it. Did the aide tell you what happened? Did she tell you no one was watching Catherine and that she and a floor aide were watching television, instead?"

At this, Donna turns to the aide for a response and none is given.

"Donna, I'm sorry but this is very upsetting, for me and Catherine. I am going to bring it to the administrator's attention. It shouldn't have happened. This woman," nodding toward Catherine, "is paying a lot of money to be kept safe. If she didn't need it, she wouldn't be here."

"I'm sorry. I didn't know the whole story," and Donna tells the aide to leave. "It will be reported. You have my word."

"Thank you Donna. Now I'd like to spend some time with my friend."

After Joanna combs Catherine's hair, "Look how pretty you look." She tells the Catherine in the mirror. They make their way to the ice cream parlor and then outside. At the end of Joanna's visit, she stops by the office where the aides are hired, telling them she no longer wants that particular aide with Catherine.

Joanna gets angry with people who can't do their job. Is television more of an interest to them than their patients? Why do these workers stay in health care?

The drive home is better and she doesn't feel the urgency as she did on the drive to the nursing home.

She no longer heard the 'calling.'

***

Weeks go by and again, her feet feel stuck in mud and she needs to push herself to go outside – otherwise, it will be just as it was when she was younger and homebound. She makes herself get in the car to drive around the neighborhood, just to be outside. She hears sounds and sees things, but nothing registers in her mind – the fear is there – like she's under water hearing muffled sounds. She stops at the store and tries to carry on a conversation with the clerk, to bring herself back into life. She then drives through the car wash listening to the machine making brushing sounds and watches the monster strips cover her windows, as if it were seaweed under the ocean. This makes her feel better and brings her back into the real world. She wonders if she can ever feel any way but this?

Why does this feeling come over her every time she's alone? Knowing Catherine isn't coming back and they'll never have the happy life they once had together? Will she ever rid herself of this feeling? So long it has been going on, forty years now, but she did get rid of it after learning self-hypnosis.

The one thing that is saving her is the sun every morning coming up over the ocean and hearing and seeing people below her balcony, swimming, or having parties, poolside. This keeps her from feeling totally alone.

Her thoughts are of going to the fourteenth floor and diving off. This would make everything go away and would stop the crying at night and during the day. This would be the cure to it all but she's here well into the fourth month now, and hasn't done it yet.

***

The panic attacks are back night and day, and an attack of VT, with 911 dialed in the middle of the night. They say it's anxiety, because an irregular heartbeat caused panic and they offer her tranquilizers. She is reliving when she was a teenager and her married life. She thought this was gone, but it has come back, full force. She's either going to make it now or she's not. It's really that simple. As far as her divorce proceedings, Ed's fighting her every inch of the way and she doesn't care what happens any more. The lawyer tells her, she needs to be in New York and face the judge, but Joanna knows she can't go anywhere, except stay in her own little world she's living in. Everything is coming down on her – fears – Catherine – no divorce and soon no money. She can't live like this any more.

Joanna's thought is to take the elevator – she's been thinking along these lines for months. "Go ahead, you're feeling strong today. All you need is to get on the elevator. … "

Dressed in her blue shorts, yellow golf shirt and Catherine's v-neck sweater, she leaves the condo. The weather is beautiful as she walks along the catwalk to the elevator doors. She has only one thought in front of her, her mind not cluttered with other thoughts. She pushes the elevator button, and watches the numbers as they come up from G – the ground floor where the garage is – then three, and the doors open. Getting inside, she notices the mirrors, but sees only a blur of a person in blue shorts and a white v-neck. Her fingers brush over the buttons till she pushes fourteen. No thoughts, as she watches the numbers light up – six, ten

– Debbi's floor – then a blur and the doors open at fourteen.

Still not thinking, she moves forward, almost as Catherine had done in golf, to the next hole – on a mission. She makes a right turn, once out of the elevator, and heads towards the ocean side, seeing the red lighthouse far in the distance below. Everything's so small – just as she feels – tiny and nothingness. Looking down at the people in the pool, she thinks they look like ants. She's been here once before when Hope and Catherine wanted to take pictures years ago, but she must stop thinking of the past and go forward now.

The wind is blowing strong and, looking out to sea, there's a mist near the horizon. The sun is in the afternoon sky and showing shadows over the sand and pool. All she needs to do is climb over the four-foot rail …Does she have the guts?

"NO! – Stop thinking or you won't."

Her mouth is dry and her heart pounds faster, but this time her heart pounding is not on her mind. Putting her hands on the cold, hard railing, she leans over, making her head swirl.

Looking out to the green-blue ocean where she always felt God was. She's waited too long and now thoughts are speeding into her mind. She feels – He *is* there – He really *is*. You can't do this – it wouldn't fulfill His plan for you to follow your path, even if it is a rotten one. He can make everything right again – just have faith. Where are these thoughts coming from? Surely not from her. She was going to kill this body, just minutes ago.

Her heart has settled down and she takes a new look at the ocean. Yes, *it is* beautiful, but there is far more there, than the eye sees. She saw the beauty and heard the Voice this time. It surely wasn't her voice she heard, for she had only known negative thoughts. She has a second chance to change her way of thinking. She wants to live.

***

The lawyer calls on a Friday afternoon, telling Joanna she needs to be in court Monday morning for the divorce hearing. Otherwise the judge is throwing the case out of court.

She hangs up the phone thinking, 'Son of a bitch, all those years of being with him while he got his degrees and she stayed home changing diapers and cooking. He opens his business and does well and this is how he repays her?'

He knows what she went through living with him – he knows the panic attacks and fears. He's doing this purposely to keep *his* house, *his* car, and everything else that he said was his. All Joanna ever was to him was the chief cook and bottle washer, while he went out for his three-hour martini lunches with 'clients.' Did he think she was that stupid? Why did he have this hatred for her – because she had left him? But they had agreed. He knew it wasn't a good marriage from the beginning, just as she did.

Did he want her living on the streets, pushing a grocery cart with her belongings in it? Most of the time she treated him with kindness even when he drank. Every night she had the dinners cooked and on the table when he came home. She washed his clothes and pressed them. In the beginning, he asked her about going into business and she told him, "Yes, do it now, otherwise you never will. I have faith in you, Ed. You can make it work," And this was the way he repaid her now?

She went to bed that night but was unable to sleep, feeling nothing but hatred for the man she had married. Then she finally gave in, gave it to God and fell into a deep sleep. She woke at some point in the middle of the night, went to the computer, and typing a letter to the judge wrote, "You nor Ed can take anything away from me, because what I have no one can take. It is a gift from God. I have *Me*." If they wanted to leave her without money it was fine, because God was the only one who could take anything from her. She knew God wasn't going to take from her, because He had, if anything, given her, her life back, by putting Catherine in her path.

The next day she sent the letter, overnight, return receipt requested. On Monday, late afternoon, the lawyer called saying the judge read her letter in court, which he seldom did. As a result, the decision went slightly in her favor. She would still get the alimony every month, plus a yearly distribution over time. She was happy to hear this, but she knew, deep down, he couldn't have taken anything from her and that was what mattered.

PATIENCE

IT'S ALMOST a year since Joanna has moved here and seven months after her fourteenth floor endeavor. She's in the pool now, exercising, riding her bike and walking the ocean, looking for shells and wave-worn glass. It's nice to be among the living.

She meets Debbi by the pool to go over her thoughts, good and bad. She's become a friend and counselor, with weekly visits and Joanna remembers the first day she met her at the tar station in '93 with Catherine. Debbi has stood by her through fears and Alzheimer's but Joanna is not a good patient and sometimes falls back in to her old habits.

Joanna's writing about Catherine, thinking she might work more on a book about this life of hers. But, every time she starts, she becomes upset and depressed and puts it away.

***

This day, in July of '96, Joanna's gotten up the courage to visit Catherine and finds her in bed with a urinary track infection, running a slight temperature. The nursing home called to let her know, as they do when anything goes wrong.

The drive south is different from in the past;

Joanna's calmer listening to her relaxation tape when a light bulb goes off. I thank God for the pain you have gone through, so I can feel the pain along with you. The fear on your face I can understand. I give thanks for the awareness that you are not alone, therefore, I am not alone, here, now or after. This is what love is – to feel what the another is feeling. Love never dies, so *we* never die. This is the purpose of life. I finally know why I'm here – There but for the grace of God go I. It's a comfort to feel and think this way – a joining of the minds.'

Parking the car, then walking to the front entrance, she has a quick step in her walk. As she passes the front desk to get her pass and sign in, she greets people differently than before. She's surer of herself now. Past the ice cream parlor and to the elevators, she passes a maintenance worker cleaning the floor, who smiles at her. Once in the elevator, she pushes two, wondering what she's going to see in Catherine's face today. She rounds the corner of the nurses' desk and someone new she's never seen is on duty. 'They change workers like they change toilet paper,' she thinks to herself.

Once in Catherine's room, she sees her body almost flat to the mattress with only a head showing. The aide is sitting with the television low.

"How she doing, Mavis?"

"Oh, she's a little under the weather today. They've given her antibiotics, so she sleeps most of the time."

"If you want to get lost for awhile and relax, I'll be here to feed her lunch."

"Thank you, Mrs. Shaker. I'll be back later."

"No problem Mavis, enjoy your time off."

345

Joanna remembers when she first put Catherine here and she and Mavis didn't get along. Mavis took it and now she's helped Catherine just by being close to her. This was all Joanna ever wanted from any of the workers – to be near her so she wouldn't get hurt and see she's fed and diapers changed. This was all Joanna ever wanted from them.

With Catherine sleeping on her back, Joanna pulls a chair up close to her head and reaches under the sheet to hold her hand. She looks so peaceful and quiet. 'Is this the same person who ran through the hall and threw Joanna out of the shower? Why couldn't you be like this at home, then I wouldn't have had to put you here. Other patients are quiet and easygoing, but not you. You were the strong one – always.'

As Joanna looks deeper into Catherine's face she says, "I want nothing more than for you to be well, but that doesn't seem to be happening. I'm praying now that you pass from this life soon. This is heartbreaking, and I can't stand to see you like this. I can't see the purity in you today, Catherine. Why? I feel as though we're not connected."

She turns away from Catherine and to the television, so tears won't come, but they do anyway. Will she ever get used to this new Catherine? If she can't see the purity in Catherine today, that means it's not in *her* either.

Oh Catherine, how I wish you could hear my cries.

Leaning once more over Catherine's bed, she tries to understand her feelings and thoughts and tries to see the love in Catherine. She cries the whole time, trying to put her energy into Catherine. "I am so sorry for you, Catherine. You, of all people, didn't deserve this. No one does. Why does this happen to good people?" No answer.

"Oh, Catherine. I love you and hate to see you like this. The aide told me you're up walking the floors all night. I wonder if you are looking for me at times. That idea makes me sad, and I hope you're just getting your exercise that you always loved. You were always moving, even when you slept, your body twitched."

***

The aide came back and woke Catherine up for lunch, but she didn't open her eyes. Joanna tried tickling her to wake her, and she started to laugh, but wouldn't open her eyes. Does this mean the disease has made her forget how to open them? They finally got her out of bed, because she can't do it herself any more, took her to the toilet and found she had already wet herself. The aide said it would be good if she sat for awhile on the toilet before lunch, so Joanna knelt on the floor and sang to her. Catherine's not able to look up any more and Joanna wanted to be recognized. She thought maybe because of her haircut, Catherine didn't recognize her.

After, Joanna fed Catherine in her room and left when Catherine fell asleep. She cried all the way back to the ocean and found comfort in bed herself.

***

Her lease is up at the ocean. She loves it so much she doesn't want to leave this beautiful place she's called home. She feels she has grown and has learned about herself with the help of Debbi. She decides to take the condo for another six months, until her savings run out. This is her mom's gift to her and she knows her mother would have approved.

***

Joanna has gotten a call from the nursing home, telling her Catherine had fallen, which she hadn't done in the three years there.

"Is she all right?"

"Yes. She had x-rays taken and nothing's broken," the nurse says.

"Well, that's a good thing. I'll be there in a few days." Joanna hates saying this, but she can't see any other way right now to get there. Maybe she'll call Leone later.

"Give her a kiss for me, please." Says Joanna.

"I will. See you in a few days," and the nurse hangs up.

Joanna is upset over this news, hates herself for not jumping in the car to go to her friend. 'How can this fear be greater than her love for Catherine?' Mad with herself, she then transfers it out loud. "How could she have fallen? She has round the clock aides. Maybe they're not watching her and are watching TV again?" She spent the entire day mad at herself and the aides.

***

The next day she's able to drive herself but had asked Leone to be on call just in case she can't get back home. She expected to see Catherine roaming the hallway when she got off the elevator, but she wasn't. Entering Catherine's room she found her sitting watching television with an aide – a new one.

"Hi. Why are you both sitting down?" then to Catherine. "Hi Ca, how you doing?" Joanna then bent down to kiss Catherine, and introduced herself to the aide. She noticed the name on her tag said Cathy.

"Good to meet you Cathy. How come she's not up

348

running around?"

"I think something's wrong with her."

"What do you mean?"

"I've been with her since seven this morning and every time she goes to get up she sits back down, moaning. I told the nurse at the desk I thought something was wrong, and she thinks Catherine's bruised from the fall yesterday."

"Oh, maybe." Bending down to Catherine's level, Joanna kneels on the floor looking up at Catherine. "Hi Ca. Why aren't you up walking?" even though she knows she's not going to get an answer.

Joanna sees a disturbing look on Catherine's face. Her attention is on something else besides walking.

"Something's not right here."

"Yes, I agree," the aide answers, appearing nervous.

"Let's see if we can find out what the problem is." Joanna moves Catherine's arm where she has a red mark on it. "That seems okay."

Then Joanna felt her feet and got no response. She felt up her leg looking for bruises. There was nothing, except some redness. She then put one hand behind Catherine's knee and the other hand under her foot and tried to lift her leg.

"Eeee," Catherine yelled, in her own language and Joanna knew something was wrong.

For Catherine to sit for any length of time she had to be hurt or sick.

"Cathy, I'm going to the nurse's station. I'll be right back. Please stay with her."

"I will."

Telling the nurse there was something wrong with Catherine, the nurse gets out Catherine's records.

"She was x-rayed yesterday after the fall and nothing showed." Joanna hearing the same words as the phone call the day before.

Joanna told her how she lifted Catherine's foot and she yelled out. Now, they both walked down to Catherine's room. Seeing Catherine not able to lift her foot, the nurse agreed Catherine was hurting but it was probably from the fall and too soon to show any black and blue marks.

"I would like another x-ray done," Joanna tells her.

"It can be done tomorrow morning. I'm sure they've closed for the evening."

"No. I want it done right now," Joanna persisted.

It was 3:30 p.m., shift change, but Joanna wasn't going any where until she found out what the problem was.

"If you get me a wheelchair, I'll take her down to radiology myself." Joanna insisted.

After a few words exchanged about time change and no one being there, the nurse called downstairs and the radiologist answered.

"Okay, she'll be right down," Joanna heard the nurse say.

Catherine made noises but didn't resist, like an animal that knows they're hurt and needs help, while the nurse and her aide and Joanna got her into a wheelchair. Joanna went down to radiology and the doctor met them at the door.

"I x-rayed her yesterday. Nothing showed," were his words.

"Could you please x-ray both hips, knees and ankles this time." They had x-rayed one leg yesterday, Joanna had noticed on the reports upstairs.

The doctor and Joanna helped Catherine onto the hard, cold, steel table and Catherine's cries vibrated through Joanna's head. She was feeling the pain right along with Catherine. Catherine made faces with her eyes closed and Joanna *knew* she was badly hurt. Her cries of pain broke Joanna. She tried stroking her hair saying, "I promise after this is over we'll go get chocalotta ice cream, even if we have to rob the kitchen."

A few seconds later, the doctor came out from his little closet, with the x-ray. "Her left hip is broken."

They had x-rayed the wrong leg yesterday!

"Oh damn," and Joanna slumped over.

"How could this happen?" as she banged her own head against the wall.

"What do we do now? Where do we go from here?" These were the questions she asked herself, aloud.

In the support group she facilitated, everyone said not to do anything when a hip breaks. Let them go into a wheelchair and give medication for the pain.

She was tormented inside trying to make the right decision.

Then she asked him, "What would you do if this were your own mother?"

The radiologist answered, "Because she's young and active, I would fix it. They will probably do a hip replacement."

After much indecisiveness, he had made the decision for her, and within an hour Catherine was on her way to the hospital emergency room. Joanna stayed behind to collect her records and then got stuck in commuter traffic, playing the relaxation tape all the way.

***

Twenty minutes after Catherine had arrived at the hospital, Joanna gave all the information to the clerk outside emergency, along with her health care surrogate and power of attorney papers that she kept in her pocketbook always. She walked in to find her friend tied down to the bed and yelling, "Rata Rata Rata Rata."

This made her ill and she wanted to throw up, but she asked the nurse nicely, "Would you please untie her?"

"She can't get out of bed," the nurse replied.

"She won't – I promise. But if you keep her tied down she's going to keep yelling. I promise she won't get out of bed" and Joanna helped the nurse untie her wrists, then they were left alone.

Joanna stroked Catherine's arm to calm her and the nurse came in with a sedative.

They waited a couple of hours, which seemed like an eternity to Joanna, till Catherine was assigned a room. Catherine slept on the way to the elevator and then was put in bed.

Joanna went to the nurse's station and asked if copies could be made of the important legal papers she had with her, the living will, healthcare advocate, and power of attorney. While the nurse used the copy machine, she assured Joanna they would take good care of her friend, and Joanna felt better, having heard a kind word said.

Catherine slept with Joanna watching her. The nurse came in saying nothing was going to be done tonight. Joanna made the sign of the cross on Catherine's forehead, kissed her on the cheek and left the room, stopping at the nurses' station to make sure they had her home phone number, just in case there was a change in the middle of the night. Now her drive home was over forty-five minutes and dark, but she didn't think of herself. She thought of Catherine only.

She got home around 10:30 p.m. and called the nursing agency to tell them what had happened and to please send an aide to the hospital. She then had a bowl of cereal and went to bed. Lying there most of the night, thinking of the day and praying Catherine would be free of pain and sleeping.

***

The next day, Joanna called the hospital and spoke with Catherine's aide from the agency.

"How is she doing today?"

"Sleeping since I got here at seven."

She was an aide who was familiar with Catherine, and Joanna was happy, if there was anything to be happy about. However, she found that Catherine had been up during the night with heart irregularities, and they were going to wait until this calmed down before operating.

"I'll be there in about an hour. I just wanted to make sure someone was with her. Thank you. I'll see you shortly," and Joanna hung up.

***

Joanna got to the hospital to see Catherine around 10:00 a.m. and first stopped at the nurse's station, to ask how Catherine was.

Not being the same nurse as yesterday, she asked, "are you family?"

"No, she's my friend."

In a cold voice, Joanna heard, "Well, we can only

give information out to family members."

Joanna was angry, for obviously, the nurse had not seen the legal papers she had left the day before.

"I'm her healthcare surrogate, and if you look at her records you'll find all the necessary papers," and walked away. She wasn't going to waste her time with a closed-minded person and went straight to Catherine's room.

Joanna was stressed by what her friend was going through, being in a new place where she couldn't walk the hallways, was seeing new faces and God knows what else. She spoke with the doctor over the phone in Catherine's room and he said he probably wouldn't operate until the heart stabilized, which might take a few days.

***

Five days later Catherine was operated on. Joanna went to church that morning and then waited in Catherine's room for her to come back from surgery. She called the agency and told them not to send an aide until late evening, that she would be there all day.

Four hours later she heard a voice she recognized, "Rata, Rata, Rata, Rata," over and over. Joanna smiled and thought, 'Here she comes. Good for her, she made it.'

They brought Catherine in, awake. She had been given a spinal for the operation and was still a little groggy. Two men transferred her from the gurney to the hospital bed and during this time, she spoke in that language that was unknown to Joanna's ears or their ears.

"You better be careful with her. She's 'speaking in tongues' and has an in with you know, *Who*."

The attendants laughed with Joanna and one of them said, "Yeah, I thought it sounded familiar."

They were careful with her. Thank God.

NEW FRIENDS

WITH CATHERINE back at the nursing home, in the months following surgery she's not allowed to walk. She's kept in a wheelchair and has therapy every day, that consists of her standing in a wooden box up to her waist, unable to move.

Joanna asks, "Why can't she just walk? She *wants* to."

"She has to learn to stand before she can walk," the therapist says, "just like children learn to stand before they walk. If she walks now, she'll get hurt and be back in surgery."

Joanna watches Catherine stand in the wooden box, feeling sorry for her, as she falls asleep after an hour of standing.

As the weeks go on, frequent phone calls come in from the nursing home: "Catherine fell out of the wheelchair, but she's all right. Just a few bruises."

At first Joanna listened to the calls and was happy Catherine was trying to get up and walk, but when she drove down to see her and saw the bruises on her knees and arms, she felt differently – once more in pain for her friend.

Finally, one day she spoke up, "Does she need to

break the *other* hip before you do anything about it? Can't you attach something to the front of the chair, to keep her from falling out?"

"It's against regulations. We cannot restrain a patient," was the answer she received.

Joanna finds out this *is* a law and others she speaks with in the health care field say the same. After many falls, a device called a *lap buddy* is attached to the chair that can be removed easily – a piece of hard foam, which also acts as a tray. Catherine is happy now as she not only has something to keep her from falling out but something to hold on to and bang on, to get out her frustrations.

The therapy goes on as long as Medicare will pay for it. For what reason, Joanna wonders? Catherine isn't going to walk again, for the simple reason – she's forgotten how. Just like they spoke of in the support group, now it had happened to Catherine.

Hard for Joanna to understand and believe that this woman she first saw years ago, with the long stride, was not only captive in her mind, but also now captive in a wheelchair. The little bit of independence she had was taken from her. 'How much more can this woman take? How much more does she have to go through in life, for God to say, "that's enough?" Joanna wants to yell, curse and rip everything apart for Catherine, almost like *she* did in the beginning of the disease. Joanna knows it won't help, and tries to go on with her own life.

***

She takes the pages she has written out of the drawer and tries to write once again. She writes of the hip break and of her anger, becomes depressed and returns it to the drawer

***

Her lease of a year and a half is up and she has to say good-bye to the ocean. Her friend Fran, the Realtor, says she can rent the other bedroom in her condo. It's in the same complex she lived in with Catherine. Does she really want to go back there? She doesn't have a choice, without money except for the six hundred a month in alimony. She will pay Fran four hundred, buy food with the rest, and maybe a movie once in awhile. She still has Catherine's car, so she can get around if she needs to and doesn't go anywhere except to visit Catherine.

She puts her clothes in a suitcase, cleans the bathroom and takes the message, 'Don't look forward.' Packing other items of shoes and clothes to bring to storage. Will she ever see any of these things again? Her life's baggage is getting less and less to carry around.

With the suitcase waiting by the door, she goes to the balcony for one last look. The ocean is calm and there are no white caps, as the day she moved in. "Goodbye," she says with a tear and a smile.

***

Her bedroom at Fran's is small, with a daybed, table and chair – quite different from what she'd been used to. In fact, it's similar to the bedroom she grew up in. It's light, because of the morning sun, Fran has put a new spread on the bed for her and she can use the guest bathroom. Joanna doesn't think of trivial things any more, like four bedrooms or three baths, she only tries to go forward.

Fran is a lovely person, who was once in the ministry and Joanna learns even more about God. She's still facilitating the support group and helping people as much as she can, but above all, her driving has gotten better. Fran has asked if Joanna would do some work for her on the computer during the day while she is showing houses. This way Joanna can earn a little extra money. They have conversations at the dining table on God and how He influences their lives without them realizing it. They talk of the people He puts in their path and how He smoothes the potholes or bumps in the road ahead. *They* make the choices to walk around them or not. Yes, Joanna is learning.

***

At the support group in the spring, a woman came to ask questions. She told the group she wants to open an Adult Day Care Center in the area. Joanna tells her she'd be willing to help in any way she can, and Joanna is offered a full-time job to help open and run it. Joanna says good-bye to her friends at the support group and continues her path.

Days are spent in preparation for the opening while Joanna works on a monthly calendar consisting of different activities. She thinks of Catherine in the beginning of the disease and what they did while they were home together. They played cards and crossword puzzles when Catherine was able, but Catherine went down hill fast – maybe the job will be different. The owner says, 'yes' it will be different. She plans to have elderly people whose families work, who would like something to do during the day and those who are in the beginning stages of Alzheimer's.

They open with five visitors every day. One of their visitors is in a wheelchair and she says she wants to take Joanna home, and Joanna knows she's met a friend. Another visitor doesn't know what day it is and reminds her of Catherine, "What day is it, What day is it?" over and over, she hears, but without the combativeness. A gentleman visitor is quiet and calm and just wants to read the paper or watch TV and enjoy being around people. Loved ones from the support group come and visit, and Joanna finds she likes this type work very much.

She's become proficient at the computer, typing up the activities they offer. She has planned activities for each day, serves food and everyone eats together as a family. They do puzzles, word games, chair exercises, sing-alongs and have talks on healthy eating habits. God has led her down her path once more.

It's a 7:30 a.m. to 5:00 p.m. job and only a mile and a half from where she lives. She's tired at the end of the day but has a good feeling that she's accomplished something on her own, being a servant of God. 'After all, this is why we're here, isn't it? To look after our brothers and sisters so they won't be alone.' She practices the same thought she had with Catherine.

***

A year goes by and she has to move again, not knowing where. Fran's mother is ill and she needs to sell the condo and move in with her. Joanna's fears are still around, but not as often as they once were. She's visiting Catherine on weekends and going to the movies.

***

An old friend Ruth, invites Joanna to Virginia. "Come and have Christmas with us. It'll be good for you," she says. She'd like to go, but she hasn't been away since she went to Long Island in 1992 with

360

Catherine, that was six years ago. She's afraid to fly and pushes herself to take the train, because this way she won't be alone. Marta takes her to the train station and tells her, "You can stay at my place when you come back, go and have a great time. You haven't had a Christmas in a long time."

As the train pulls away from the station, she waves good-bye to Marta, feeling apprehensive, then settles down in her seat, and looks out the window thinking. She has no real home of her own, then thoughts of train trips she took as a child with Maira, upstate to visit relatives. She and her mom would eat sandwiches on the train watching the passing scenery. They were lovely memories of her mother. They had become very close as Joanna got older, 'too bad we don't know our parents when we're old.' Her thoughts are of Catherine at the nursing home and hopes all will go well there, while she's gone. She's given the nursing home the number of the cell phone and Ruth's home phone. What could she do anyway if something went wrong? She remembers the words in her bathroom cabinet, now with her in the case under her seat, 'the same everlasting Father will care for you today and tomorrow', and places Catherine and herself in His hands, without worry.

Joanna meets people traveling for Christmas, loaded down with presents. As the train travels north, it gets colder in the car. She hasn't felt this in a long time and hopes there will be snow for Christmas. On the long trip she has small anxiety attacks but is able to control them, listening to her relaxation tapes and reading.

After eighteen hours Ruth is waiting for her at the

station and they drive to her apartment. The next day Ruth goes off to work saying, "Enjoy yourself. You have the whole place to yourself. Do whatever you want."

At first Joanna is nervous being alone but finds some happiness playing with Ruth's cat, then goes out for a walk. It's been a long time since she's seen hills and it *has* started to snow. Snow for Christmas, and then a small miracle comes in her sight – a red cardinal sets down not far, chirping and eating under the trees. "Oh Geech, you've followed me north."

She enjoys a Christmas tree again and Ruth and her mother treat her as family. After a week of cold weather, she heads back to Florida and work.

The train trip is long but she has much time to think and write. Yes, she's writing, making notes of memories and experiences for there isn't a drawer on the train to hide it.

***

Back in Florida, Marta picks her up at the station and Joanna tells her, "I'll only stay with you on one condition that I can pay you something weekly."

"Don't worry about it," Marta says.

"I'm not worried. I just would like to give something to the household, if I'm going to stay with you."

"All right" and Marta agrees.

Joanna won and feels better about the arrangement. She finds it amazing that she's calm, knowing she's living on a wing and a prayer, but mostly prayer. She's left it all up to Him and it's a load off *her* mind. She has faith He will lead her in the right direction.

***

Sitting at the diner for dinner after work, looking through the classifieds, she finds a room for rent, back in the old neighborhood not far from the Sea Trail. She calls about the room and sets up an appointment to see it.

A young woman with long dark hair greets her at the door. "Hi Joanna?"

"Yes, hello," Joanna has a feeling she knows this woman, but can't think from where.

"I'm Christina and happy to meet you," inviting Joanna in and shows her the room. "Would you like something to drink, soda, wine, coffee?"

"A glass of water will be fine, thank you," still thinking, 'where do I know her from?'

For two hours they sat in deep conversation about their ancestry and Joanna found that Christina is Greek. Her father brought his family to the United States from Greece when she was a young girl. They chatted on and on, as if they had been friends for years and were being reunited.

Joanna looked at her watch and saw it was after 11:00 p.m. "I better get going. I have to get up early for work in the morning."

"I've enjoyed talking with you, Joanna."

"Me also Christina. I feel as if I've known you for a long time."

"I feel the same way," as they walked to the door, with Joanna almost forgetting about the room she was renting.

"When do you think I can move in? I forgot to ask," laughing.

"I guess we forgot about that detail. How about tomorrow?" Taking a key off her key chain and handing it to Joanna. "Come anytime you want. I'll probably be at work most of the day."

"Thanks, that would be great. Christina have a good night and I'll see you tomorrow."

"Night, Joanna."

Joanna walked to her car, knowing she was connected to this new person she had just met. A feeling of warmth came over her and she was able to sleep that night soundly.

***

The next day after work, with her suitcase and some clothes from storage, she moved in with Christina. The first thing she did was scotchtape her message behind the medicine cabinet door.

The days go fast, working, then coming home, working on the computer, seeing friends and visiting Catherine on the weekends. Joanna's fears are leaving and the panic is just about gone. She still sees Debbi for counseling every few months, but it's more like seeing an old friend now and she's living almost like a normal person.

Christina and Joanna have fun cooking and deciding who's going to cook and what. They sit at the dining table discussing their backgrounds and say how similar they were with Christina's dad from Greece and Joanna's father from Italy. Joanna finds they are alike in the important areas, like living life and the willingness to help others.

A year goes by and Christina's boyfriend comes from Greece and they decide to buy a house and raise a family. Joanna says good-bye – they'll miss the deep conversations after dinner, about life. Joanna wishes them the best and gives them her love.

***

So once again, God leads her down the path to a neighbor down the block, an older woman, who is having a difficult time making ends meet and needs a roommate. Again she finds it amazing how her faith has grown.

Her new roommate, Kathleen, is fourteen years older than she, and they also have great conversations. Kathleen's daughter and grandchildren live next door and it gives Joanna a chance to see a vision of what her own children and grandchildren might be doing now.

They don't have any contact, because they've chosen not to see, write or call Joanna. She sends birthday and Christmas cards with no response, so she honors their wishes and lets them live their own lives. She tries not to linger on this thought because it makes her feel down, and God knows she doesn't want to feel down any more.

WISDOM

AS TIME went on Joanna moved on into a position at an Assisted Living Facility with thirty-five residents. She took the job as activity director and is working from 8:00 a.m. to 5:00 p.m., every day and sometimes on weekends. The money isn't great, but she loves what she's doing and has health benefits. She's developed a program similar to the day care center and it's going well, working in the activity area, like a kid again, playing games.

When she comes home at night, she sits with Kathleen and they talk about their day's work. Kathleen is caring for an Alzheimer's victim and Joanna can relate to that, as she has Alzheimer victim's at the ALF. Others are there because they have no one at home to bathe them or make their meals.

***

She enjoys making the monthly calendar, keeping it simple, yet fun, with lots of activity. She wants the residents up from their beds, moving their bodies and minds, while she's there. Mondays they are off to church, in the morning then back for chair exercises for forty-five minutes. Afterward, everyone sits on couches or chairs and she hands out juice, and then reads them their daily horoscopes. She reads to one woman,

"You're going to meet someone tall, dark and handsome." Like kids in fifth grade, they laugh and tease one another, and Joanna laughs along with them.

Next, they sit at a large round table and anyone who wants to play stays for table games, such as Poker, Domino's, and Gin rummy, while others play Bridge and teach Joanna. Then it's time for clean up and lunch. At times, no one wants to leave the activity room because they're having so much fun, and Joanna tells them, "I'll meet you back here this afternoon at 1:30 for more fun and games. Enjoy your lunch and please come back."

Some say, "aren't you going to eat?" and "when will I know it's one thirty?"

Joanna answers, "yes, I'm eating now too, and I'll knock on your door to remind you."

Then she goes over the morning's activities of who was there and how they participated. Some, all or none, she writes keeping a daily log of their activities. When done with paperwork, she eats with her co-workers, enjoying a different kind of conversation.

After lunch, she knocks on all the doors saying, "We're having a chat in the activity room. C'mon … down."

There are those who want to lie in bed, especially the new residents and Joanna knows they're afraid and feel out of place. After a week or two, they become depressed because they're in assisted living and can't do for themselves anymore. But Joanna keeps after them and wants them out of their rooms and beds, and in the activity room. She wants them to be with other residents to hear what they have to say, to know they're not alone, and may have something in common.

Joanna and the residents chat about everything and every one has his or her own story to tell. She lets a few stay in their rooms because she knows they want to be alone and it's hard for them to join the group. Making time during the week she spends quality time with those in their rooms, to talk or listen to their stories. They feel alone and left behind and she can understand where they're coming from, because she was once there, herself.

Later in the afternoon on Mondays, she takes them for ice-cream shakes and there is usually a lineup. They sign their names to a piece of paper at the desk but she knows the van only holds six people. There are those who run to the desk and sign up faster than others, so she has to choose who will go and who won't. Feelings are hurt when she says, "you went last week, we have to give someone else a chance."

"She's your favorite," some say and she has to explain afterwards, to get back on their 'good side.'

***

Tuesday mornings Joanna hops in the van to take them on a shopping trip for personal items or just to window shop. She reminds George, who is ninety-two and healthy, "stay with the group, George." He's a good-looking Irishman, who knows the women love him, especially when he dances or sings. Joanna knows George usually doesn't listen, but she reminds him anyway.

One day after shopping ready to leave for the facility, George couldn't be found anywhere. Deciding to drive around with everyone in the van and look for him, someone spots him walking from the doughnut shop. Joanna tells the group, "When we pass George, everyone wave good-bye to him." Everyone laughs.

As the van pulls nearer George, everyone waves good-bye and smiles. He gestures with his palms to the heavens, as if to say, "Hey, where are you all going?" Joanna backs the van up letting George in and reads him the riot act, "don't you go and get lost like that. You scared me, and everyone else here. Next time you won't be allowed on the trip, George. I'm serious."

The others rib him all the way home and everyone has a good laugh, including George. He has a great sense of humor and loves the attention.

On the way home from the store, George asked Joanna to stop at the bank because he had a check to cash.

"Do you have an account here?" Joanna asked.

"No."

"You need to have an account George, otherwise they won't cash it. Why don't you give it to the facility and they'll cash it for you."

"Take my word for it, they'll cash the check. I'll bet you a nickel," as he insisted in a sing-song way to Joanna.

"Okay, you got a bet."

She stops the van at the bank and says to the group, "Don't anyone drive away without me."

Taking George under the arm, they walk into the bank. As George and Joanna went through the back doors toward the tellers' windows, three women tellers yell, "George where have you been? It's so good to see you."

"You son of a gun, they all know you here." Joanna said, as George turned and grinned at her.

She then left him to do whatever business he

needed and sat in the van with the group singing, waiting for George.

When he came out Joanna went around to open the door for him and he couldn't but help say, "see, I told you I could cash the check without an account."

"Here's your nickel," she said laughing. "It's only because you're so good looking and everyone loves you."

Later that same afternoon, after all the activities, it was time for the men's outing. They had wanted to go to the ice-cream parlor, instead of the bar they had gone to the month before. When they go to the bar, the men and Joanna have nonalcoholic beer and snacks or cokes, but the guys liked going just the same. It made them feel independent, and Joanna felt proud to be with these gentlemen. At the ice-cream parlor, George and the others ordered ice-cream sundaes or sodas, and the five men and Joanna sat, eating their ice-cream and talking of old times when they were kids.

It was a great day with her friends.

The next day, when Joanna came in to work, she found George had passed away during the night. It was a shock to suddenly lose her friend but she was thankful she had gained much wisdom from him. His daughter came to get his belongings and Joanna met her in George's room. She told Joanna how he loved her and loved to kid her.

The only words Joanna could say were, "your father made my days much easier. He gave many people happiness."

It made Joanna feel good that George had told his

daughter about the fun they had during the day. He was such a fun person – enjoyed life and it spread to the other residents and staff. He did help Joanna very much at her fun place of work. Later there was a memorial for George in the activity room and residents spoke of the things they liked about him. He was what life was all about, happiness and laughter. George would be missed by all.

***

Another resident, Emma, at the ALF, jumped into the pond on the facility grounds one day. Joanna had only been working there a month and every time she had been into Emma's room to tell her there was an activity going on, Emma would shake her head 'No.'

Emma was usually reading a book and spoke broken English, due to her heavy German accent. After the pond incident, Joanna took it on herself to spend a few minutes each day with Emma in her room, whether she wanted it or not. Many times she told Joanna to get out, and she left, but said she'd be back tomorrow. After a few visits every day, Emma began to look forward to Joanna coming. She told Joanna one day she didn't want to live any more because she couldn't hear or see well and needed a walker.

"What's the good of living if I can't do anything at ninety-eight years old?" she'd say to Joanna.

Joanna responded. "You can't go anywhere. You have to stay around and teach *me* your knowledge. You've lived longer than me and you know more."

Emma looked at Joanna and shook her finger at her, smiling. Joanna had made another friend.

The other residents were not kind to Emma, because of her hardness, but Emma and Joanna became friends. She came to exercise and bingo and Joanna took her shopping sometimes, just the two of them. Emma came out of her shell, and at one hundred, she was transferred to the nursing home, when she could no longer walk. On Joanna's way to and from lunch and when leaving for home, she'd stop by to see Emma in the adjoining building.

"Hello Emma, how you doing?" and Joanna would listen, to gain more wisdom.

Emma passed away at age one hundred and three.
***

One day at arts and crafts, Joanna puts a white sheet of paper and magic markers on the table in front of her friends who came to activities. She'd brought two tapes of music with her this morning, one classical – soft violins playing, and the other fast – pop music. Joanna's friends sat in their seats with questions on their faces.

"Today we're not going to paint birdhouses or make beaded flowers. We're going to see what we are about inside, our emotions. I'm going to play music and want you to pick the marker up and draw to the timing of the music."

Before she could get all the words out, she heard, "Oh I don't want to do that. Oh I can't do that," and "I can't draw."

"This is not about being better than anyone else or taking a test. It's about having fun. I want you to try it," and she started the music.

Their marks went from dots and dashes, to soft flowing lines with the timing of the music. When it was all over, they talked about their works of art, and how much fun it was after all.

Joanna felt it was an interesting activity, saw how happy they were and told them "next week we're putting our art work up for sale."

***

Joanna signs up entertainers who play the piano and they sing the old songs of the thirties including one song that Joanna knows well, "Oh we ain't got a barrel of money," and her buddy Catherine is with them in spirit and thought.

Joanna sees Catherine in all the faces she looks into who need her help and compassion. She's learned when fear attacks, the way to rid it is to face it and challenge it, and then it leaves. It doesn't have a hold on her and she can carry on with her life, of visiting her friend Catherine in the nursing home and her work.

The days at work are fun for her and sometimes it feels the day is only an hour long. She's gotten close to several residents, even though her employers tell her not to. They say it will hurt her in the end, since they are in the last days of their lives. She feels she's here to make life easier for others and in doing so, it makes her life easier and happier.

Joanna found out more about herself working with the elderly than she'd ever expected. She found you have to love what you do, because that's when you give your all.

Her fears are gone now, maybe because she's given to others. She feels one with them when they sit around in a circle and have reminisce hour. Her old friends have taught her much about herself and the start of it came with Catherine.

ACCEPTANCE

AFTER a few years, Joanna quits her job because she knows she can't do this type work any more. It's too demanding on her health and her heart is acting up again, and she feels tired most days.

There are problems with co-workers who don't put forth enough effort, or don't care about the residents, while other workers give everything they have. She hears disgruntled residents at the council meetings held every month, where she's the only worker there taking notes to give to her boss.

She hears remarks such as, "someone couldn't change me because they were too busy." And the resident goes for hours with the same soiled pad.

They tell of the stealing that goes on at night when the residents are asleep, because the worker has a drug addiction and needs money for the habit.

Joanna's colleagues are underpaid, overworked and they are tired, just as she. This plainly is true in most health care for the elderly, as she listens to other activity directors and people working in the health care *industry*. It needs to be fixed – and not with just a band aide. It has to be addressed fully, to benefit the adult population and the care they get. She can't watch the so-called abuse any more and it has become trying on her body.

She reports to her boss, " I can't work for a place that doesn't put their residents first."

Her boss has meetings every month on this subject, and everyone leaves the meeting with a renewed determination to give themselves more fully, but it all becomes a vicious cycle, over and over again, because of long hours and little pay. The abuse is there and never goes away.

***

So after Joanna left her job, she decides to move into her own rental apartment in 2001.

There are no more raised ugly heads of fear.

She has a little savings from her alimony and divorce settlement and finds a small, one-bath, one-bedroom apartment in a fifty-five and over community.

She first tapes her message to the medicine cabinet and reads it carefully, again, "He will look after you today, tomorrow and always." She must believe this.

For the first few months, she fixes the condo to her liking, getting items out of storage for the first time since 1995. She hasn't seen them in years since Catherine and she lived together. It's comforting to see them again and to know Catherine *is* with her. She decorates sparsely and buys inexpensive or used furniture.

While looking one day in a thrift store, she spots a couch that looks familiar.

"My God, it's *our* couch," she whispers to herself.

It's covered in pink and green material with soiled brown marks. She finds it hard not to cry, thinking of the times they watched television sitting on it, or of the parties when friends and family sat on it. It has many good memories connected to it.

A second thought, "I wonder if it still has the urine stain from Catherine?" and she turns the cushion over. "Yep, it's there. Poor Catherine, she didn't know what was happening to her back then."

Joanna feels a piece of their life is sitting here in public, open for everyone to see. She wants to burn it, so it doesn't exist, then decides to walk on through the store looking at other items. She turns and looks back, says another good-bye, and leaves the store.

***

She goes to bed each night, knowing there is no one else with her in the condo, not like when she had roommates, but this doesn't bother her. She has a new feeling about Joanna and it's a good one – a feeling of worth.

For many years she's given herself to dementia of one kind or another, Alzheimer's, stroke, or any other form. Even now, where she lives, she's gotten calls from caregivers who live here. They say, "can you come and stay with my wife while I go to the store?" and Joanna remembers when she asked for help, and goes to stay.

She finds this is a community where everyone helps one another. On another call this morning from a neighbor, she's told, "my wife walked out of the house and I've called the police." The neighbors get together, form a search party and find her in the next complex across the street. There are stories like this and more. It's like a large assisted living facility without the name or corporation behind it. It's a group of condos where residents get together to play golf, go to the pool, exercise, play games, bingo, bridge, have parties at the clubhouse, much to keep a person active.

The other day she saw a golfer walking to the green pushing a walker that had three wheels, just like she saw when she worked and in Catherine's nursing home. He was bent over with a Dowagers Hump and possibly in his nineties. In the middle of his walker there was a bag, where he carried a couple of golf clubs. She watched him hit the ball and push his walker – hit the ball and push his walker. Her thought, 'what determination this golfer has' and wanted to yell, "put it in the hole, good for you, keep going forward."

She's happy living here, even though she doesn't join in the activities. She has other things on her mind. Everyone is in their seventies, eighties and nineties and Joanna is in her early sixties. But she knows she has a future here, if she wants it.

* * *

Joanna's found a new church that accepts her for who she is – a child of God and no more. On the first day she met Pastor Jim, she shook his hand and told him of Catherine, with a feeling she belonged. She tells Pastor Jim of the items Catherine gave her long ago, the God Bless you sticker that she still has behind the car's visor, and other items. Briefly, she tells him of Catherine and how she would have liked him. He has been a help to Joanna, listening after her visits to Catherine, in pain. He listens with heart and soul and makes her feel she's not going through life alone. He prays with Joanna so she may find the way and that Catherine may not be in pain. She tells him, "Jim, I think Catherine is no different from Jesus, who suffered and cried out," *'My God, My God, why have you forsaken me? Take this cup from me.'*

377

***

While unpacking boxes from storage, she came across Catherine's little black daily entry books – the books where she kept all the dates of her activities and appointments. They go back to 1981 and Joanna now has taken the time to read them.

Deciding, after finding Catherine's little black books, the first thing she needs to do is to write her book, in its entirety, instead of putting it back in a drawer. The pages are full of what Catherine did each day and plans for the next day ... birthday cards to send and phone calls to make. She writes of the outside temperature and how her back hurts after a golf game.

She leads Joanna into the next day with every word ... Joanna touches the words ... they're faded now and the pages soft, with rolled up edges from age. Joanna feels Catherine here with her – within the pages.

Her heart goes out to Catherine as she reads more about her before they met. She stumbles across names they had in common up north. Some of the words have no meaning to her, and then, she comes across words she first wrote of Joanna. Catherine writes of the times they had together at the West Meadow beach and on the golf courses, doctor appointments, visits from friends and family and Joanna's operation and heart palpitations.

She can see something besides Catherine's words and activities. She notices the difference in the handwriting. The first years are clear and scrolled to the right in large soft strokes. Then came the illness and short, pointed, choppy strokes. Catherine's feelings, which were calm the first few books, then after 1991, the anxious Catherine. She recalls the times when

Catherine had trouble remembering, and sees it in her writing. She tried so hard to remember with little clues to the pages to help her write, like J for Joanna and C for Catherine.

Joanna comes across Catherine's birth date of February 14 and a circled – B – for birthday. She has dates of 1992 and 1926, to figure out that her age was 66. She writes of the beach club and names of people they were meeting for her birthday lunch. She writes 'lovely time + fun.' Some clues are hard to read, as only Catherine knew what they meant. There are golf dates on every page, TV times of golf tournaments, hair appointments with Jack, who did her hair for years.

On January 27 she writes, "went to a movie."

Feb. 1991 she writes: "7:30 a.m. Dr. Mike, research center."

Saturday, August 22, 1992, she writes, "hurricane Andrew 110 mph off Florida, boarding up. Joanna and I to friends' home."

August 31, 1992 "auto train to Long Island."

Wednesday, September 9, 1992, "we see the house again and eat in Stony Brook."

And so, the books go on and on. Joanna reads the writing and remembers the past....

DEAR FRIEND

THROUGH THE YEARS Joanna pushes Catherine's wheelchair forward, passing the nurses, aides and other residents. She hears behind her, "there they go down for ice-cream. She comes every week. How sad." Joanna smiles at them, letting them know nothing has changed – the love is still there.

Downstairs at the ice-cream parlor, Valerie, behind the counter smiles, "how are you two today?" she says, in broken English. Joanna has been getting ice-cream from her for eight years now.

"We're both fine thank you, and you?"

"I'm fine, chocolate, right?" Valerie remembers.

"Yes, one chocalotta for my friend, please," and Valerie laughs with Joanna.

This has been a joke through the years with the three of them. Valerie hands Joanna a bowl of chocalotta ice-cream for her friend and they head outside for their quality time together – their connecting time – their together-as-one time.

With the bowl and spoon in one hand, she pushes Catherine with the other, Joanna heads for the large shade tree, so the light won't bother Catherine's eyes. Inside each day, her eyes don't know sunlight any more. Her right eye is shut for no medical reason and her face on that side is drawn tight, making deep crevices in her cheek.

They are facing the pond now and Joanna fixes the brakes on the wheelchair, 'as if she's going to go anywhere?' she thinks. Placing the bowl on a planter's ledge, she drags a chair for herself from the side of the building. Seated and settled, she watches for a smile from Catherine ... not yet ... maybe later.

She's been asleep since they've left upstairs. Hoping to wake her, Joanna starts her song.

"Oh, we ain't got a barrel of money, maybe we're ragged and funny, but we travel along, singing a song, side by side." No connection yet.

While singing, she remembers the times they both sang the same song from Florida to New York to visit family and friends almost every year. It always made the trip seem shorter, and they didn't sound half bad together.

A while back when she sang, Catherine gave her a smile and a wink, although now she sits and stares off into space. Joanna prays she's not losing total contact with her, for that little contact comforts her and makes her *feel* again. Oh, how a little look from Catherine would lighten her heart today. Sometimes Joanna thinks she hears, "I am a prisoner in this body and I long to play the game of golf again."

"Kaditchka, open your eyes. You have such beautiful eyes. Let me see the both of them," Joanna says, as she strokes the right side of Catherine's face. It takes a while, but soon both are wide open and she's alert.

Joanna remembers when she first gave Catherine the name, "Kaditchka", many years ago when she told

Joanna her grandmother came from Germany. Why she picked this name, Joanna doesn't know, just a fun thing to do, back then. While working in the condo, she'd call, "Kaditchka, what do you want to eat?" just to see Catherine laugh. Now she uses it to see if it will bring back a memory of Joanna.

She puts a small amount of ice-cream on the tip of the spoon and touches Catherine's lips. She wrinkles up her nose and lips as if it's lemon instead of ice-cream. Joanna finally gets some into her mouth, she realizes what it is and wants more. Catherine eats fast and is happy once again. Joanna tries to make it last for *her own* sake. She loves to see Catherine with her eyes open and aware of a simple thing like ice-cream. She knows once it's gone Catherine will be off to sleep and *somewhere* else.

She finishes the ice-cream and Joanna strokes her hair, tells her of friends who say hello and of golf tournaments on television. Catherine's not interested and is closing her eyes once again.

Joanna lets her sleep, so she can cut her fingernails. They've gotten long and the aides have trouble cutting them, because Catherine grips her own hands together and won't let go. Joanna guesses it's from gripping a golf club for so many years. Then Catherine grips Joanna's hand, and she feels this is another contact that they have. She's asleep, making faces and movements with her head – sudden jerks. Joanna talks and sings to her as she clips, feeling there are only the two of them. No one else exists. 'We are in our space' is her thought.

Joanna sits back and studies Catherine, sleeping.

Catherine's hands are wrinkled now and have spots the color of red-blue and purple, probably from holding onto her own hands so tightly. Joanna wonders, if she thinks it's someone else's hand she holds. They are no longer brown from the sun.

She's shorter and bent to one side in the wheelchair and cannot pull herself up to a sitting position. Her face also has a red-purple look to it, but not all the time. Her lips are dry and wrinkled, with no life in them and white, as if there isn't any blood circulating to them. She dribbles and has no teeth left, from years of grinding them down. Her feet and ankles are swollen, because of fluid build up and lack of movement. Her legs are bent and stiff, and when Joanna tires to straighten them, to put a shoe on, she's sure Catherine is in pain by the expression on her face, but cannot say. She has scales on her white skin now, no longer that beautiful bronze tan. She no longer smells of baby oil, but reeks of urine and other odors. Joanna tells them she needs to be changed, and they say, "Yes, okay," and they go on with something or someone else and forget. Just like when Joanna worked and it doesn't get done till later – she hopes.

Her hair is in disarray and the beautician has bleached it blond. Joanna has asked them not to but they don't listen. Maybe because she's not a family member or maybe because they want to do it their own way. Joanna lets it go after many times of getting angry. Catherine has scales on her scalp because the aides use a gel on it, which she's also asked them not to do over the eight years. But no one listens. She's written letters and spoken to supervisors, but the gel goes on, and she's given up on that, too.

The curves on her body are points now, because of the great weight loss. Her ribs show under the blouse she wears and her neck is stiff, with great hard cords, from trying to hold up her head. She holds her head up at times but most of the time it rests to one side.

Her shoulders are bent forward. She leans to one side in the chair, and her hips look large because she has on double diapers. To change her, they put her on a hoist to get from the chair to the bed. Joanna doesn't stay to watch this, because she sees the pain on Catherine's face and can't bear it.

Joanna looks at her watch and sees it's 2:30 p.m., time to bring her back upstairs for a nap, but first, four hands are joined as one, and she prays the Lord's Prayer.

NIGHTMARES

IN 2002 Joanna and her friend, Mary, visit Catherine today *after* lunch instead of Joanna's normal time. She's tried over the years to visit on different days and at different times, for a reason – to not let the staff know when she's coming. Today it's 3:15 p.m. and Catherine's on the bathroom in the hoist. Joanna wasn't aware that they still put her on the toilet.

The belts under her arms, holding her up, are cutting into her skin, and she asks the aide, Nora, a new aide, "Would you please take her off the toilet?"

"Not now, I'm too busy," Nora replies.

"I think she should be taken off. Her arms are turning blue from the belts." Joanna repeats again.

"No, it's good for her to sit on the toilet after lunch." Said in a defiant way.

Catherine seemed slightly agitated, so Joanna knelt on the floor, talking to her while Mary stood in the hall outside the room.

After twenty minutes, Joanna told Mary, "Her arms are turning blue-purple. It's crazy to keep her there like this. I'm going to the nurse's desk."

"Okay, I'll stay here with her."

Joanna walked to the desk and again there's

someone new. She read her name-tag, Jean.

"Excuse me Jean, I'm a friend of Catherine in room 219 and she's been on the toilet a long time. Her arms and hands are turning purple." Joanna now pleading for her friend.

She also said it was good for Catherine to sit on the toilet to try to move her bowels, so Joanna went back to Catherine's room. She looked through the closet to see if there was any clothing she needed, so she could tell the Social Worker and then she noticed a purse on the dresser.

"What the heck is this doing here?" speaking to Mary.

"Who does it belong to?"

"Well, it sure as heck doesn't belong to Catherine and I know it isn't her roommate's. She's like Catherine, not able to speak or walk."

The large purse was open and inside on top was a plastic bag full of bottles holding prescription medication. Joanna had seen this once before in another nursing home, in the bottom of Catherine's closet on the floor, when she was with another friend who worked in health care, and they had reported it to the nurses' desk.

Today Joanna went directly downstairs with the plastic bag and brought it to the administrator's assistant. Joanna had known Maureen since Catherine had entered the home in 1994, and she liked her. Maureen had helped her in the past with problems of the staff and she wanted this to be brought to her attention. Her secretary said she wasn't busy and to go right in. Maureen's door was open.

"Hi Maureen."

"Hi Joanna, how are you?"

"Not good at the moment. I found this on top of Catherine's dresser in a large purse." Showing her the plastic bag of medication. "I know it's not Catherine's. What do you think it's doing there?"

Maureen looked at the plastic bag and its contents and seemed disturbed, wrote something down on a pad and made a phone call.

"With so many Alzheimer people walking around in and out of rooms on that floor, I didn't think it was a good idea to leave it there."

"No. It should not have been there. I'm sorry Joanna. I'll take care of this, thank you."

Mary and Joanna went back upstairs to see Catherine still on the toilet. Joanna checked her watch and now it was 3:50 p.m.

"She's been sitting there for more than a half hour, God knows how long before we came." Joanna said to Mary.

"This is terrible," Mary replied. By this time, Catherine's right arm was purple.

Joanna walked down the hall and waited for Nora to come out of one of the other patient's room. "Nora, I want Catherine off the toilet, now."

"You have no right to speak to me like that, and besides, I have other people to take of."

"Catherine's arm and hand are purple," Joanna persisted.

Nora continued to tell Joanna that it was okay and that it would come back to normal color when she put her arm down.

"I know you have a hard job here, Nora. I worked in health care for awhile and know it's hard work, but this is ridiculous. Will you please take my friend off the toilet!"

Nora looked at Joanna then asked her to wait outside the room, while she took Catherine off the toilet.

"Well at least I finally got my point across," Joanna said to Mary standing in the hallway.

"I can't believe they would leave someone in Catherine's condition that long on a toilet. It doesn't make any sense to me, but it never did." Joanna is thinking about all of health care now.

"You know, Mary, it probably has something to do with shift change at three-thirty."

A few minutes later they saw a woman come out of the director of nurses' office, and go into Catherine's room. The woman closed the door and later came out holding the purse.

As she passed, Joanna couldn't resist but say, "I don't think it's safe to have that around, do you?"

She shook her head, 'No', and Joanna could tell she was annoyed. Maureen had gotten her message through, and Joanna had gotten hers across also.

A male aide entered the room Joanna thought, to help Nora take Catherine off the toilet hoist.

Several minutes passed. "What are they doing in there?" Joanna said.

She finally opened the door and the aide was slowly combing Catherine's hair as the two aides spoke in another language, *not Catherine's*.

"I'll do that, Nora. Thank you very much. I'd like to take Catherine outside." At that, the male aide left, followed by Nora.

***

Mary and Joanna took Catherine downstairs.

"I'm always afraid the aides will take out their revenge on Catherine when something like this happens. It's happened so many times in past years, and I worry about her."

"I can understand, and I pray not, Joanna, but you need to do what's right for Catherine."

Mary went to the kitchen for ice-cream and the three sat under the shade tree until Catherine ate and fell off to sleep. Joanna noticed Catherine had a small amount of blood running out of her left nostril and reported it to the floor nurse.

When Joanna has a visit like this, it seems that nothing has ever changed in all the years of Catherine being here. The aides have too much to do and not enough time to do it in.

And the nursing home nightmares go on … .
***

Sunday in the nursing home, Joanna entered the dining room while an aide was feeding Catherine. She told the aide, "I'll feed Catherine, if you want to help others."

Catherine seems agitated or angry at something. Usually it's because something is bothering her – she either has wet diapers, is hungry or just unable to communicate.

Joanna feeds her the ground-up yellow and green food that's on her plate. It's supposed to be a casserole of some kind, and applesauce, which she always loved. Joanna alternates giving her a teaspoon of the 'yellow-green stuff' and a teaspoon of applesauce. She also has thickened fluids, apple juice and water to drink. Joanna is sure she doesn't get enough liquid, because her lips are always dry and cracked. It was the same where Joanna worked, where most of the residents became dehydrated.

The dining room is noisy and filled with agitation among the patients. Something or someone is bothering them. One woman in the corner, decides to get up and start walking out.

An aide yells to her, "sit down in your chair, Evelyn. You know you can't go out alone".

Evelyn says, "I'm not alone, I'm with her," pointing to another woman coming in the doorway. Evelyn starts repeating "You're never alone – you're never alone – you're never alone." Over and over she repeats this as Catherine used to repeat and Joanna feels it is being said for her benefit.

Catherine finishes her meal and they go to her room where Joanna combs her hair and then takes her downstairs for ice-cream. Joanna finds there is no one staffing the ice-cream parlor.

"Well, we're not going to let that stop us, are we Ca?", wheeling her to the kitchen and for a cup of chocolate pudding.

She has always loved chocolate – ice-cream, pudding, anything. Now she is happy, her face changed and smiling. Joanna in her mind could hear her say "thank you," with her eyes both now open.

After eating, Joanna brings her outside to get some air in her lungs and to have quality time. Joanna sits with her friend as a flutterby comes over to join them. Catherine doesn't see it, because her head is slumped down, but Joanna knows for the both of them; a beautiful spirit has come to say hello and bless them. Soon, Catherine is asleep, as her head drops even further and her body twitches, just as it has since the beginning of the disease.

Wheeling her upstairs, Joanna tells her, "I love you and God bless you," then makes the sign of the cross on her forehead.

Passing by the nurse's station, she tells the nurse, "Catherine smells of urine and needs changing. Thank you. I'm heading home now. Have a good day."

Joanna never looks back. She doesn't want her last look of Catherine to be sitting alone in a wheelchair. She hasn't looked back in all the eight years.

***

It's the day before Thanksgiving and Joanna feels nothing – no sadness, no happiness, no feelings at all. It's like living in a vacuum. She tries to put the idea of another holiday out of her mind. She does better when she doesn't think of holidays. She's noticed through the years she copes better with the idea of no one around. There's too much emphasis placed on holidays. Every day should be a holiday as it was when Catherine was home and they lived life to its fullest, with always a feeling of goodness, were her thoughts.

She dreads the holidays because of the fibs she has to tell, when people ask what she's doing for Thanksgiving or Christmas. She lies and tells them, "oh, a friend has invited me," or "I'm going to my brother's for dinner."

Most of the time she visits Catherine in the nursing home and then goes to a movie, to be among people she doesn't know, to watch *them* have fun with family and friends.

***

Another Christmas has come, different from ones of

long ago. At lunch, Catherine is slumped over to one side in her wheelchair as usual with her eyes closed and a look of pain on her face.

One of the aides brought Catherine's food tray in and said hello. Joanna undid the saran wrap, which covered the hot pureed meal. Also there was beef soup and for desert pureed peaches, with thickened water and juice to drink, as usual.

Catherine slept while Joanna arranged the food, putting a little beef broth over the pureed meat and vegetables, so it's easier for Catherine to eat.

Joanna asks, "How about some peaches for a start," rubbing her cheek softly to wake her.

She won't open her eyes, but Joanna knows she's awake, just something you learn after being around someone for so long. She puts the tip of the spoon of peaches to her lips and she opens her mouth. It brings back memories of feeding her own children, when they were six months old or younger. Joanna studies Catherine's face and sees only a painful look on it. Sometimes it's like this and then she's better after a few minutes.

Joanna starts singing their song, 'Barrel of Money' but gets no response. When this happens, she feels all is lost and wonders why Catherine has to go through this Hell.

'What is the purpose of it? For me to see how the one I love has deteriorated and someday soon will never more be? Years of this makes no sense.'

All through the meal, over forty-five minutes, she opened her eyes once for less than five minutes to look at the aide across from them, who was feeding another patient. Joanna tries talking to her – no response.

At the end of the meal, "Ca, now it's time to go downstairs and get chocalotta ice-cream," and Catherine smiles, or was Joanna seeing something that wasn't there?

Wheeling Catherine out of the dining room, she tells the nurse, "I'm going to cut her nails in her room, then we're going down for ice-cream."

"Okay, have fun, see you later," the nurse replies.

After clipping her nails, Joanna gets a jacket from the closet and drapes it over her friend, it's chilly today.

The ice-cream parlor wasn't open yet, so they go outside where other residents are sitting in the sun. A private birthday party is going on in the corner of the building, where some of the residents are having fun singing. Catherine still didn't open her eyes and looked asleep. Joanna noticed for the first time that her hands were white and she wasn't griping them together as she usually does.

Joanna's thoughts are, 'this is what a dead person's hands look and feel like. No life in them, no blood circulating, the pink look is gone.' She hates the thought, but it's there.

They sit in the sun for half an hour with Joanna thinking, 'this will be good for Catherine's chest congestion and the cold she has.' She sleeps all the while, Joanna listening to the sounds around them, like the birds and a flutterby coming to say hello.

She brings Catherine upstairs to her floor and finds a cup of chocalotta ice-cream in the dayroom. Setting Catherine in front of the birdcage and thinking if she opens her eyes she will see the birds on the floor of the cage. Joanna puts a teaspoon of ice-cream to her lips and she opens her mouth to take her favorite food. She eats everything in the cup. While throwing the empty cup away, Joanna asks the nurse, Jean, how Catherine is doing.

Jean shook her head side to side, "she's failing," words Joanna's heard since the hip break.

"We have colds or a virus, everyone is coughing."

"Please take good care of my friend, Jean."

"I will," she replies.

Joanna kisses her on the cheek, "I love you and God bless you," and makes the sign of the cross on her forehead. She never opened her eyes.

***

She has her eyes closed most of the time now, except at ice-cream time, when she opens them for a moment.

Valerie is at her post as usual, "I'm sorry we have no chocolate today," before Joanna asks for it. This is one of the few times in nine years they won't be having chocalotta ice-cream.

"We have vanilla cheesecake," Valerie says.

"What do you think of vanilla cheesecake today for a change, Ca.?" as if Catherine's going to answer. Funny, Joanna thinks, 'she's probably annoyed there isn't any of her favorite chocalotta.'

Catherine looks at Joanna only once today, as Joanna gets up to throw away a napkin which she has used to wipe her mouth. As she is coming back, it startles Catherine and with both eyes open, she looks straight at Joanna in surprise and smiles, then once again her eyes close.

Someone once said it's because she is getting ready to cross over to the other side and then will have no recognition of what is here in this life – including

Joanna.

It isn't a good day for her, for it seems she's ill all the time with urinary infections, or colds, or viruses. The small illnesses are coming more often now.

Afterward Joanna wheels her to the main cafeteria, where Joanna gets something to eat for herself. She fills her plate with a few pieces of lettuce, some beets and some pink dressing, which she's seen for nine years and still doesn't know the name of it. Joanna places Catherine near the window opposite her, so she can see the waterfall outside in the garden. Catherine looks at it, briefly, but never looks across the table at Joanna. She tries to move forward with her upper body. Joanna watches and thinks, 'she could fall out of the chair', then realizes she's not going anywhere and just moving her shoulders.

People pass and smile at them, probably thinking they're sisters, which they are, in a sense. Joanna eats fast, just to get away from the area where there are couples sitting enjoying one another. It's not like on Catherine's floor, where everyone is in another world speaking another language. Here in the cafeteria, people are just elderly and can't take care of themselves, but have most of their wits about them. They will soon go in to play bingo, or go to the music room and listen to someone playing the piano. Joanna sometimes brings Catherine to these activities, but she becomes agitated and Joanna knows she doesn't want to be there, so they leave for the outside and their quiet time.

She gets her fingernails clipped – they've gotten long in just the two weeks since Joanna was there. It's easy to do this when she falls asleep, but she's awake and it's impossible. She grabs Joanna's hand or fingers so she can't move, and she's afraid of hurting her in the process.

It's hot and humid outside and it's only May, but it seems as though summer is coming sooner this year.

For some reason Joanna doesn't want to be here today and feels depressed. She feels old and spent, with nothing to look forward to. Her life is here with Catherine and she has no other life.

The drive home is long and without feeling – like a death has come over her once again.

Before home, she stops at the ice-cream shop to get a chocolate ice-cream soda. As she sits and drinks her soda, going over the day's events, she can't dislocate herself from the nursing home surroundings.

This is a feeling that takes hours, or sometimes days, to get out of her system.

***

Joanna was late getting to Catherine this Sunday. She'd stayed at church after service for coffee and cake with the parishioners, and now it was 12:45 p.m. as she walked in the front door of the nursing home lobby.

Signing in at the desk, then rounding the corner near the ice-cream parlor, she saw in front of her long buffet tables draped in white cloths with different kinds of food. It spread part way down the hall and she noticed new faces, working. She then took the elevator to the second floor.

When she reached Catherine's dining room, she couldn't find her, then looked in the dayroom. Still … no Catherine. Her thoughts, 'Please don't let her be in bed ill.' She hadn't received a call that anything was wrong.

Catherine's door was open and she was lying on her back looking one with the mattress. Joanna's thoughts again were 'what's the matter with her?' Joanna tried to wake her but Catherine was in another place, better than the one Joanna was now in. She felt her forehead and it wasn't warm. She checked her pulse and it was steady. 'Why was she in bed?'

She then made her way back to the dining room to ask one of the aides if Catherine had eaten lunch. Everyone looked unfamiliar. 'What was going on?'

Every one of the workers looked new and she couldn't figure what was happening. The tables were decorated with flowers and white cloths. Then she remembered, it was a Holiday ...not her own ... that's why she'd seen food of all kinds and decorations downstairs in the entryway and throughout the center. Only on Catherine's floor there was nothing going on. A few family members were visiting their loved ones, dressed up in suits and ties and dresses. Everything looked clean, with new tablecloths on the dining room tables, and fresh flowers in the center. What struck Joanna differently was the fact that on Catherine's floor, all the regular aides were missing.

"Can I help you?" a woman dressed in a dark suit came to her and asked.

"Yes, I'm Mrs. Shaker, Catherine Benbrock's partner. Catherine is still in bed, is she ill?"

The young woman looked surprised or caught off guard, for lack of a better word. "Oh, I'll find out," and excused herself.

She never came back but Terra, a regular aide Joanna has known all through the years, came to Joanna and Joanna asked, "What's wrong with Catherine? Why isn't she up?"

"Everyone's downstairs working this morning. We didn't get a chance to get Catherine showered and dressed."

Joanna's next thought is 'Did she eat breakfast?' but doesn't ask. She was let down once again and didn't want to make a scene. She'd been through many scenes through the years and it wasn't going to change anything now, except the upset within her own self. She knew this was the health care industry and just another nursing home horror.

"Could you please fix a lunch tray for Catherine and I'll feed her in her room."

Terra tried her best to apologize, but Joanna told her she understood and knows what happens when the homes try to impress families on holidays. The ones who don't matter or can't speak up get pushed aside, or left in bed. Then they proceeded to Catherine's room.

Another aide came in and Joanna waited in the hall while they changed Catherine's stench and propped her up to eat. A lunch tray was brought in, Joanna thanked them and they left. On the tray was pureed food, which Catherine liked, 'or was it that she hadn't received breakfast and was hungry?' She ate all of her meal and Joanna sang, as usual.

A new nurse came in and gave Catherine her pain medication, two kinds now, and Catherine was asleep within five minutes. Joanna's thought is, 'when I'm not here does Catherine get fed?' But she knows she does, because when she calls and hasn't seen her for a few weeks to see how she's doing, they say, "She's fine," and she asks about her weight.

Joanna was happy with her visit today. Catherine

gave her eye contact, even though it started out bad. She stayed for two and a half-hours, with Catherine never out of bed. There was no sense in trying to get her up and it would have been hard to find an aide who wasn't busy with someone else. After lunch, Catherine was asleep and Joanna was happy to see her in her own world, calm. No ice-cream today – the first in years.

She *did* feel sorry for Catherine's roommate, who was left in the hallway for two and a half hours while Joanna was in Catherine's room. She, like Catherine, is not able to hold up her head, and keeps her eyes closed, but you know she's awake because you hear her grinding her teeth the same way Catherine did.

Leaving Catherine's room she turned for a last look at Catherine and watched her try to lift her upper body, while sleeping. Joanna wished her love within her own mind and left.

Leaving tears come once more, as she drives to the ice-cream shop and has her usual ice-cream soda. She sits and remembers the love they had for each other and how they drank sodas long ago. Joanna knows the love for Catherine is still within her.

Not to be alone, she takes herself to the movies, as every Sunday.

***

Months have passed and Joanna sees Catherine today and brings her into the dayroom to feed her. The wheelchair is still upright instead of tilted back, like it's supposed to be after she'd seen the doctor about Catherine's head falling to one side. Tilted, they said, 'would keep pressure off her spine', but it's not tilted today, so what else is new?

Once settled in the dayroom, The *Sound of Music* is

playing on TV and they are singing Edle Weiss. Catherine and Joanna had sung it years ago, so she tries singing it to wake her, but it doesn't work. She remembers John playing it on the piano with all of them singing and also at work with the residents. It only brings tears of memories to her.

Catherine's head is leaning against the pad of the chair and slanted down as if it isn't attached to her neck, but flopping like a ball attached to a string. Joanna tries to wake her by lifting her head and rubbing her cheek and arm. It takes a long time to arouse her, which may mean they are giving her heavier doses of pain medications. She's also taking antibiotics for a bladder infection, since the urine sample showed a 'strange organism.' They haven't told her what's wrong or how they're treating the problem – seems she always has to find out herself. She'll ask when she sees Catherine's doctor tomorrow.

Catherine finally wakes up as Joanna sings and puts a little desert to her lips. Her lips open slightly and Joanna is able to get the tip of the spoon in her mouth, and she wants more. She still comes alive when sweets are offered, and finally opens her eyes. Then Joanna feeds her the pureed turkey, potato, and stuffing, alternating sweet, so she'll keep eating. She drifts in and out of sleep and after an hour has eaten a quarter of her food, but Joanna makes sure Catherine drinks all the water and cranberry juice.

During the time she *was* awake, she looked directly at Joanna, with a stare of anger. Sitting back in her chair, Joanna looks deeply into her eyes and hears in her own mind, "Joanna, why do you want to keep me alive? For you, or for me?"

'What am I doing? I feed Catherine and say 'good girl' when she finishes a spoonful but for what reason? She's not going to get better, unless God steps in and changes things. So why do I want her to finish all of her meal?'

Realizing this *is* for her. Joanna stops trying to feed her and keep her awake and lets her head rest against the pad. Saying to herself, 'You can't even find a comfortable place to rest your head. Maybe tomorrow when I see the doctor I'll mention this to him and maybe I'll ask if you can be put on a larger dose of medication. This way you can be totally asleep and have the look of pain gone from your face.'

Maybe tomorrow I will ask....

DIZZINESS

SUMMER OF 2003

It's 11:30 at night and Joanna feels dizzy when she gets up to get a glass of milk. Fear has crept in once more, except this time she is not in another household with a roommate or someone else sleeping in another bedroom. She is alone, by herself. She feels alone in body and in spirit. She checks her blood pressure with the pressure cuff she bought years ago when the doctor said, "keep track of your blood pressure and heart rate."

It's up – higher than she's ever seen it before, 180/160. She knows from working in health care this could be serious, but she can't think straight and doesn't know what is going on within her body, almost like years ago. She takes a tranquilizer and waits fifteen or twenty minutes, but feels even more trembling in her body. She feels as if her head is going to explode.

Finally she realizes this may not be a false alarm like a panic attack, and knows it's not her usual problem. Her heart is beating fast, but not out of rhythm.

She reaches for the phone and calls her friend, Mary, on the other side of town. Mary answers with a sleepy, "Hello?"

"Hi – Mary?"

" Joanna? What's the matter?"

"I think something's wrong."

"Yeah – What?"

" Well … uh … my blood pressure's up and I'm very dizzy. I'm afraid to call 911 if it's just a panic attack."

"You don't sound right to me. I'm calling 911 for you."

"No, please don't. Can't you just come over? I'm sure I'll be all right if someone's here."

"No! You need help … hang up. I'm calling them right now."

Joanna took a deep breath and thought this *is* a good idea, but what about health insurance? She didn't have it and how was she going to pay for this?

"Okay, if you think so," saying without hesitation this time.

As she lies there after hanging the phone up, she tries relaxation exercises, but nothing is helping. The room keeps spinning. The thought of unlocking the door for the paramedics went through her mind. She foresees them breaking the kitchen widow to get in. It's late and she doesn't want to disturb the neighbors.

Slowly, swinging her legs over the bed to a slumped sitting position, she feels her head spin even more, as on a carnival ride. Closing her eyes and feeling along the bedroom wall into the hallway, she unlocks the door and walks cautiously back to her bedroom with her eyes still closed.

The phone rings and a young woman's voice asks, "Mrs. Shaker?"

"Yes."

"This is the fire department. Your friend called and

said you're not feeling well? What's the matter?"

"I'm dizzy and can't stand without falling into walls. I'm not good at all."

"Stay in bed, the medic's are on their way. Is your address, 140 North Elder Road?"

"Yes, and I've unlocked door for them."

"Good, do you want me to stay on the line with you, until they arrive?"

"No, I hear them now at the door, thank you."

Hearing the door open and the medic calling out, "Hello, Mrs. Shaker?"

"Yes, come in. I'm in the back bedroom."

Entering her bedroom is a young woman with long blond hair and a young man with a large muscular build. They introduce themselves, but their names are quickly forgotten. Both are dressed in dark blue shirts with short sleeves and dark blue pants with a red and white emblem on their sleeve and chest pocket.

"How are you doing?" one asks.

"Not too good."

Joanna tries to lift her head to greet them, but then quickly slides back down on the pillow.

"Oh – very dizzy." The room won't stop spinning.

"Stay where you are. I want to check your blood pressure and pulse," says the young woman, while the young man puts a clothespin-type gadget on her finger.

" I'm checking your oxygen level," he says.

Both ask questions of past history. She reads off numbers of 174/140 and says, "Do you have a history of high blood pressure?"

"No, but I take an anti-arrhythmic drug, for Ventricular Tachycardia."

"I notice a rhythm disturbance and think you should

go to the hospital."

"But I … don't have health insurance."

At that, the young man turns and starts to walk out the bedroom door.

Scared, Joanna asks, "are you really leaving?"

Laughing, he looks back at her, "Mrs. Shaker, my Mother doesn't have health insurance either. The hospital will take you, don't worry."

By now Mary has come in. Joanna thanks her for coming and asks if she will go to the hospital with her.

"Yes, I'll meet you there."

Being taken downstairs in a canvas chair, she keeps her eyes shut. Joanna notices it helps keep her dizziness down to a minimum.

"Mary, would you please lock the door and turn the lights off."

"Okay, I'll see you at the emergency room. Don't worry, you're going to be all right."

Joanna tries holding back tears and hates the idea of saying good-bye to Mary. She's letting her imagination run wild and thinks she may not see her again. Kind of like days of old.

"Okay – I'll see you there, bye," she says in a weak, shaky voice.

Switched to a gurney, while the young woman checks Joanna's vitals again in the ambulance, "Your blood pressure is still high. I'm putting and IV drip in," and sticks her with a needle.

On the ride to hospital she feels even dizzier watching out the back window as the trees and lights pass by. The young woman keeps checking Joanna's vitals, saying, "Think about your breathing, try to control it and slow it down."

Joanna's trying hard to do her relaxation exercises but cannot keep focused.

The medic has called ahead to alert the hospital of a sixty-one year old female being brought in with dizziness, high B/P, and throwing PVC's. Joanna remembers the same words years ago.

Once there the emergency room doctor asks many questions mainly of her heart condition, while the nurse hooks her up to a heart monitor and oxygen. She's told the doctor the same as she told the paramedics. "VT, I don't have high blood pressure but do throw PVC's – premature ventricle contractions – once in awhile."

He realized she had been this route before and knew what she was talking about.

When Mary arrived, he asked her questions about Joanna's family.

"Her only family here, is her brother, Marc, and I think he is in Italy on vacation."

"Yes, my brother is in Italy at the moment." She thought of the other so-called family member living at the nursing home.

While speaking with the doctor, blood work was taken and in a few minutes the results where in the doctors' hands.

"Your blood work shows signs of small clots somewhere in the body." he said.

Joanna hearing this thinks of her mother dying of a massive stroke, and working in health care, knew clots traveled to the heart, lungs and brain. She was afraid, yet felt confident she was in God's hands and would handle whatever it was.

"Do you think it's a stroke?" she asked.

"We won't know till some tests are taken." He calls

to have her taken for a Brain Scan and Lung Scan. Looking for clots *she* was sure of.

***

3 a.m. the reports are back from the scans and there were no clots in the brain or lungs.

Mary was still there, tired after a day's work.

"Mary, go home and get some rest. I'm sure I'll be fine."

"I'll call you tomorrow after work," and kisses Joanna on the cheek. Joanna is glad to have this good friend.

"Mary – Thank you for being there for me, I appreciate it very much."

***

Joanna was told they were going to keep her overnight and she was assigned a room. Telling them she didn't have health insurance was an embarrassment beyond her control but it didn't seem to matter to them. So, she stopped worrying about it, also. By 6 a.m. she was taken to a room upstairs where she had been a few times in the past.

Her blood pressure was dropping because of the medication in the IV drip. She felt she was in good hands and slept a few hours, waking off and on.

The next day her doctor came and recommended seeing an ear, nose and throat doctor, plus a neurologist. She mentioned again she didn't have health insurance, but again it didn't matter. She was the only one who thought of the cost being in the thousands and how was she ever going to pay for it? Also in the back of her mind were the words she had heard downstairs in emergency, '*small clots*'. Where were they?

***

For three days she took test after test – scans, MRI's, ultra sounds – and again she repeated, "I don't have health insurance," and again no one was interested.

If it weren't for her friend, Pastor Jim, she would have totally lost it. "God will provide", were his words, as they prayed together. He visited for three days and she laughed with him, not worrying about the money.

Ready to go home on the third day but still dizzy and no diagnosis, except the small clots, which where never found. So where were they? 'T I A's' Joanna thought, 'these are common as you age.' Joanna saw them all the time when she worked. Maybe that's what it was. She had new medication for the dizziness and she knew she had to get home and finish the book she started after finding Catherine's little black books.

***

Marta picked Joanna up and brought her home, after a stop at the grocery store. She stayed a while with Joanna, then Joanna said she was tired and wanted to rest. She hadn't gotten any sleep in the hospital with them coming in all hours of the night, drawing blood and taking blood pressure.

Bushing her teeth that night, she saw the saying in her medicine cabinet and tried to believe it even more. It was good to be home in her own bed tonight. Other than tiredness and slight dizziness, she felt pretty good. She watched a half hour of news, then TV and the light was turned out. Saying her prayers of thanks to have a place to come home to, she fell into a deep sleep.

***

Joanna spent the next few months at home, except

to venture out to the grocery store and to doctor visits. Where was she going to get the money to pay for her mini-vacation in the hospital? The bills came in and she sent a letter to each saying she was sorry, but didn't have insurance and would be able to pay only five or ten dollars a month.

This would probably go on for the rest of her life. She was happy to find, as time went by, some doctors had cut their bills in half, but the total was still in the thousands. Only one had sent the bill on to a collection agency.

***

She was still dizzy and finally was diagnosed with Meniere's Disease. The medication was working and she was feeling a little better. She could keep writing and finish the book soon, which was all that counted.

PRECISIOUS GIFT

CHICK, CHICK, CHICK … "What the heck is that?" Joanna woke, still sitting on the porch in the rickety old web chair, and realized she'd fallen asleep.

In the tree at eye level outside the screened balcony is a tiny gray bird, making sounds. Two of them now, causing leaves to fall to the ground, slowly bringing her back to the present, with a grin.

I've never seen this type bird and she runs for the bird book, coming back quietly so not to frighten the creatures away. Searching through the pages, she comes across birds that are similar but not exact. Finding no match she thinks, boy, I wish Ca was here, she'd find it. But she's not, and Joanna shelves the book.

It's getting dark and I need to find something for dinner, even if it's cereal. No, maybe I'll have those hot dogs in the freezer and a chocolate ice-cream soda, to celebrate the new siting with no name.

Church tomorrow – then a visit to Catherine. I haven't been to either place in awhile because of the dizziness, but hopefully I won't be dizzy. I have a few phone calls to make tonight, and then I'm going to bed early to watch television and rest. I have to stop falling asleep with that blasted thing on and waking me at two in the morning. Not tonight, I'm turning it off early right after the news.

***

The day started dizzy, weaving my way to the bathroom, as I've done for several months. Taking a shower the curtain moves as I bend down to pick up the bar of soap which had fallen. I could feel my heart pound in my head and ears while bending over. I thought, I better make it out of here before the paramedics find me this time naked in the shower. That wouldn't be such a pretty sight.

After a glass of orange juice, an equilibrium pill, my diuretic and heart medication, within the hour I began to feel better. I should know not to take a shower before eating something. You'd think I would have learned something by now.

Driving to church, she thought of serving communion today. They had put her on the calendar for once a month to usher or serve. She thought back to being a child in church, kneeling with her parents watching the priest give communion, and wished back then she was a man so she could become a priest and she, too, could give this wonderful gift of life to others.

In church today, I'll be doing just that and I can't let God down because I'm dizzy.

The service began and I asked my friend sitting behind me. "Jer, if I'm too dizzy would you please take my place and serve?"

"Sure, no problem Jo."

He called me Jo, which made me feel ten years old again.

Sitting listening to the preacher talk of the gifts we

411

have to give to others, he mentioned, "those of you who have singing voices, sing and praise God; those of you who are good with words, preach His word."

I thought, what gift do *I* have to give? To me the only gift I ever had was to give love and compassion to others, remembering my job and Catherine.

In the middle of the service, communion time came, to take the chalice – a large cup, with a small cup built in the middle of it holding grape juice, representing the wine. Spread along the larger cup, were small wafers of bread, which the minister had consecrated into the Body and Blood of Christ. Holding the chalice in my hands, I realized the wonderful gift *I* held. It was the same the priest had offered me over fifty-five years ago when I made my first Holy Communion. I, now, had it to give. It had come back to me, as the people in the congregation came to receive the wafers and drink. I offered them the most precious gift of all – the bread of Life.

***

My feelings going to visit Catherine afterwards, were not feelings of dreading to see her body slumped over in a wheelchair. I had a different feeling. This time they were more intense and backed up by God. We have only a body to serve Him with and that's it. He has put us here to be happy and enjoy life with our fellow human beings and not to be lonely.

Arriving at the nursing home, Catherine was in the dining room waiting to eat. Her head down and upper body over to one side of the wheelchair, as usual. The aide was feeding Catherine's roommate.

"Hi Mike, how are you?"

"Hi, I haven't seen you in awhile," he answered.

"No, I haven't been here. I've been sick with terrible vertigo attacks."

"Oh, I'm sorry."

"Thanks, Mike. How's my girl today?"

Turning to Catherine and kissing her on the cheek, "Hello Kaditchka, how are you?"

Turning her head towards me with both eyes wide open, she smiles almost in a laugh.

"Hey, look at that. She recognizes you." says Mike.

I'm stunned. I haven't seen this since I can't remember when. So alert, as if she *does* know who I am, but then I feel she does know me even if it looks on the outside that she doesn't.

"Mike, I think I'd like to feed her in the dayroom, if it's okay."

"No problem, let me get you a tray and I'll bring it to you."

"Thanks, Mike, I'd appreciate that."

Maneuvering Catherine's large wheelchair around other chairs was a task in itself. I was glad I had worked in the area once before and could handle it. I've seen other caregivers come in and not know how to move another person's chair without disrupting them. I had come to move them slowly and softly so the person in the chair didn't know they were being moved. Once in the dayroom, I put the chair by the large window so the sun could shine on Catherine's body.

"Ca, you need that bronze tan you used to have," and again she looks at me, as if knowing what I'm saying.

She's on a program for the terminally ill now and has other aides and the nursing home aides looking after her and I find she's getting more attention this way. The nurse had called during the week, as usual, to tell me her vitals, saying she was down to 118 pounds. I thought, I am forty pounds more than she is.

I hope she eats today, just a little something. Starting with thickened cranberry juice, she opens her mouth and I say, "good girl." I hate when I say that, but it comes out naturally without thinking. Then I feed her the pureed turkey, potatoes, and green beans, plus pureed vanilla cake.

With the first spoonful of turkey, I start singing 'Oh we ain't got a barrel of money.' She is staring at me and smiling while chewing, which she hadn't been doing. She had been storing the food in her mouth like a chipmunk and not swallowing, common when the swallow muscle doesn't work well.

On a roll, I kept shoveling it in and singing, but then ran out of songs.

"Ca, what would you like to hear?" She looks at me and tries to talk. I'm stunned and feel hope again.

"C'mon Ca, tell me what you want to hear. I know … how about something we used to sing in church," and I start, "Let there be peace on earth and let it begin with me." She looks at me and smiles, making sounds as if she were singing along with me and a happiness has been brought to me.

***

An hour later, we're on our way for chocalotta ice-cream. Passing by the nurse's station, I whisper to one of them, "we're going downstairs, to run around the block and get some ice-cream and if Catherine lets me, I'll cut her nails."

Putting her arm around my shoulder, she tells me, "You're good to come and see her."

Then we are off to the elevator. I'm happy and jumping for joy today, my friend has smiled at me and tried to talk and sing with me. What more could anyone ask of life? I'm ecstatic. I want everyone I pass to know it, as I smile at the other caregivers when they pass me in the hallways.

At the ice-cream parlor we see our old friend Valerie, with the treats.

"No chocolate today. I only have Bing Cherry and Pistashio."

"Oh boy, I'll have to take the nuts or cherries out, otherwise she'll choke," I say.

"I'll scoop around the side of the container so you won't have as many. That should help."

"Thanks Valerie, that'd be great. Give us the cheery then."

Catherine's eyes are still wide open, watching and listening, as I look back to see her sitting facing us from the side, taking it all in.

Seated back down on the left of Catherine, and feeding her. Valerie says to me, "boy, she sure is alert today. I haven't seen you both in weeks. Where have you been?"

I tell Valerie of my illness and we talk about her children she's going to visit, as I feed Catherine the cherry ice-cream. When Catherine's finished I say, "Good-bye, we'll see you next week, God willing."

"I'll be here until the end of the month, and then I leave to go to my son's home."

"Okay, see you then. Thanks again Valerie."

It's too chilly and windy to go outside to our quiet place and it's started drizzling, plus I know I still need to cut her fingernails. They are so long and haven't been done since I was here last. Upstairs on Catherine's floor, we settle for the outside, enclosed balcony. Sitting so I can face her and taking the scissors she once gave me, I start to clip. This agitates her a little, because I'm pulling her hands apart from each other. She still clasps her hands together as if she's holding someone else's hand, gets mad at me when I try to pull them apart and growls almost as she did, when we lived at home.

"I know you're mad at me, but your fingernails need clipping. Please let me have your hand."

Joanna tries to unclasp Catherine's hands and finally she relaxes them for her to clip.

I'm in awe at how this visit is going today. "Ca, thanks for being awake for me today. I love you. Let's say the Lord's Prayer," and four hands are once again joined. "Our Father who art in heaven .... "

When finished, I make the sign of the cross on Catherine's forehead and she smiles. Bringing her back inside, for she's started drifting off to sleep, I park her in front of the birdcage where it's quiet and all she can hear is the chirping of the birds in conversation.

Telling the nurse I've clipped her nails and she's eaten her lunch, including the ice-cream, I say, "Good-bye, have a good week."

And she responds, "You also."

Walking to the car, my step has a spring in it of happiness and I feel everything's right with the world. I repeat the words, "Thank you Catherine for a beautiful visit today and thank you Father for the gift of Catherine. This is what it's all about, isn't it, Father? We don't need anything but to show the gift of Your Love, and that's what You gave me on this day. You showed me Your Love through Catherine. Thank you."

Driving home the feeling of serenity and all is right with the world stayed with me. I had given the gift of new life in church this morning and Catherine had given me her gift of love this afternoon.

***

Four months later on July 19, 2004 a morning call came from the nursing home saying they were sorry that Catherine had passed away in the early morning hours.

At first I was numb, then words flowed from my mouth, "She's finally free."

The nurse said a few words and I thanked her for being there for Catherine.

Hanging up the phone, I could feel happiness and sorrow within. I spent the next few days happy knowing she was free, then crying with sadness of not seeing her face again.

***

Not too many days later I got a call from the funeral home saying Catherine's ashes were ready to be picked up. Fear and sorrow enveloped me as I picked up her ashes, even though I knew I had planned years ago to scatter them in the ocean. I thought to give her to the ocean at sunrise the next day, but something told me not to wait.

At seven that evening, I walked along the wooden planks to the sandy beach in front of Sea Trail Condo. The sky was the color of gun-medal gray, meeting the ocean at the horizon. As I approached the water, I noticed a spot of pale pink on the edge of the horizon. With the round container under my arm and a beach chair from the car trunk in hand, I walked forward.

Then sitting, I removed my socks and sneakers.

The outgoing tide was rough and I thought how beautiful it still was after all these years since she first brought me here.

I sat staring at the ocean and the pink spot, saying a short farewell prayer and opened the container. Inside was a plastic bag full of ashes. Carefully taking the bag out of the container and loosening the twist tie around it, I headed into the water. It was warm as I waded up to my calves.

Opening the bag I saw the ashes were beige in color, not what I had expected. I guess I thought they would be the color of ashes from a fire, but these were like sand.

Bending over, I spread Catherine to the left of me, into the water, thinking 'this isn't really her. Why are you so sad? She's with God already.'

As soon as they hit the water they sparkled, then like darting fish they were gone.

Looking out I thought back to the day when she swam far out and I had gotten scared, calling her back. Not this time.

"Go Ca, you're finally free."

Tears ran down my cheeks, thinking of the reality. Then I walked back to the beach chair watching the ocean and sky, thinking she *was* free among nature now. Off to the right a rainbow started to form as I watched in amazement, and in a few minutes it joined the pink, along the horizon.

Another gift to me – she's letting me know she's joined with God. Then another rainbow appeared above the first – two rainbows now, in front of me. This truly was a precious gift from God.

Happiness within me wanted to burst out. I wanted to laugh and cry at the same time. I wanted to shout and tell everyone of this gift.

In a few minutes it started to drizzle and I picked up the empty container, the chair, my sneakers and socks and headed for the car. Walking back along the wooden walkway, I turned looking over my shoulder to see if the rainbows were still there. Then, on my last look, they began to fade and I knew Catherine had fulfilled her life.

So, when *do* you part? Never – if you have loved another, you're never parted.

****

AN AFTERTHOUGHT

Writing this book was a quest of mine for many years, but I thought anyone who attempted to write a book needed a college degree. When I started writing in the latter years of life, I found a person could write in their inner voice. On the pages this cover binds, I wrote what was deep within my heart and soul. Some of you may have read it for enjoyment, but I hope most you read it and will think twice about your own life. Some may say "she should have gone to college," but I think all of us have a story hidden deep inside and you don't need a college education to write – just do it. Above all, please don't make any judgments unless you yourself be judged.

Always remember fear stops our growth, warps our thinking and makes us neurotic. Only love can heal us. Through the time I had with Catherine and my work, I found the love that is in one of us is in all of us. We need to take responsibility for our thoughts, in order to take responsibility for our lives.

Once I stopped thinking of the sickness within our bodies and thought only of the love within each of us, it changed my life.

Catherine was one of the chosen few, as I call all Alzheimer victims, because of the language they speak and the simplicity of their lives. There is no worry over worldly things and they respond only to love.

What was real between Catherine and me was the love. It wasn't her sickness or my fear. I was finally able to let the sickness go and let Catherine be where she needed to be. By doing that, I was able to conquer my fear and be where I needed to be.

Catherine was not a crutch, but a beacon, pointing the way in my life. She showed me how to love life while living it, both with her and without her – she will always remain with me.

Thank you Catherine, for your little black books that led me to write this story and thank you God for the gift of Catherine and Alzheimer disease.

Printed in the United States
R1898100004B/R18981PG40549LVSX00004B/